The Great Organizers

ERNEST DALE, Ph.D.

President, Ernest Dale Associates, New York City

McGRAW-HILL BOOK COMPANY, INC.

New York   Toronto   London

THE GREAT ORGANIZERS

First McGraw-Hill Paperback Edition, 1971

07-015173-3

2345678 VBVB 765432

Preface

A good part of our life, both business and social, is influenced by the organizations of which we are members and the way in which they are structured. We may be stretched or compressed, as in a bed of Procrustes, in our organization boxes, which are rarely perfect fits.

Beyond that, governmental organization increasingly affects individual and business lives for good or ill. The strength of the country, both economically and militarily, is influenced by the way in which organization problems are met, and these problems are growing in importance. Among them are the relationship of the Armed Forces to one another, the need for unity of command in the satellite program, and the relationships of the growing number of powerful government agencies to one another.

Finally, there are the most important organization problems of all: How shall we organize for the preservation of peace among the nations, for the expansion of the frontiers of human thought, the discovery of other worlds?

Organization is a means or a tool for achieving ends that can be gained only when a number of people can work together. It is only one of several such tools, but it can be an important aid in alleviating a wide range of human difficulties by reducing the complexities and misunderstandings that arise when human beings are thrown into close association in pursuit of a goal. The study of organization also has intrinsic values, for the history of it is a fascinating story of human development and human ingenuity. And it presents some degree of intellectual challenge that may appeal to the student and teacher.

There is now a considerable body of thinking on organization which has wide currency among students and teachers and great impact on large aspects of life. But the concepts so far developed seem inadequate to the needs, and our present methods of organizing groups face some severe challenges. On the one hand, there is the charge of inefficiency—popularized in the book *Parkinson's Law*—and on the other, the moral challenge represented by such books as *The Organization Man*, by W. H. Whyte, Jr., which charge that large organizations force a straitjacket of conformity on the individual. The instant success of these books and the fact that their titles have become popular bywords indicate that a great many people find in them a parallel to actual experience.

All these developments point to the need for a stocktaking of our current knowledge about organization, what it has achieved in the past, and its problems and possibilities in the future.

The first chapter of this book is devoted to a reexamination of some of the foundations of organization theory and the suggestion that a more modest approach to the study of the subject may be in order than has been customary in the past. It is suggested that those who attempt to formulate theory take in less territory and form less sweeping concepts. Different types of organizations have different aims and different tasks to perform, and it is not to be expected that one set of theories will apply to all. Thus a fruitful approach may be a comparative one; that is, one good course for the organizer may be to examine the work of those who have achieved the best results—"best," that is, in the light of the ends in view—and adapt it to his own needs if the situations are comparable.

In other words, examining the methods and plans used by men who have proved themselves great organizers in actual situations may be of help to those who are confronted with a need to reorganize existing institutions.

Accordingly, the body of this book is devoted to accounts of the work of several great organizers—cases in which organization itself produced definite and measurable results. These examples may hold lessons, if not for those entrusted with all types of organization, at least for those who are confronted with the need to structure a large or growing business.

Three of these four cases deal with similar situations: companies faced with the need to replace "genius management"—often represented by the founder—by some sort of systematic organization. This is a problem that is likely to confront all companies once they reach a certain size.

It was the problem that confronted the Du Pont Company around the turn of the century. Systematic organization and planning introduced at that time not only saved it from disaster but were largely instrumental in its further growth.

The methods used by the du Pont family were successfully applied two decades later to General Motors at a time when it was practically bankrupt under William C. Durant. Durant had invented the idea of General Motors, but it was the du Ponts, Alfred P. Sloan, Jr., Donaldson Brown, John Lee Pratt, and their associates who made it work. Members of this group have always held that the organization philosophy and structure they evolved was a major, if not *the* major, contribution to the recovery and success of GM, and certainly the reorganization they introduced was followed by unexampled growth and prosperity for that corporation.

Another example of a reorganization that was followed by substantially improved results is the case of the Westinghouse Electric Corporation under A. W. Robertson in 1935 to 1939. Here, too, the problem was to shift from genius rule to systematic organization. But unlike Du Pont and General Motors, where the basic problem of reorganization was the welding together of a number of separate entities, Westinghouse had to split asunder a large, highly centralized, top-heavy aggregate.

The last figure in the book, Ernest Tener Weir, unlike the men who completed the reorganizations at Du Pont, General Motors, and Westinghouse, was actually the founder of the business. The most successful and most unpopular steel man of his time, he conceived a lifetime plan of organization that made it possible for the company to grow from small beginnings to major size without drastic reorganization.

It is perhaps significant that three of these four great organizers were part-owner–managers, or "partial proprietors." Thus there was a direct linkage between their personal interest and the interests of their companies. In the Westinghouse case, where there was no such direct linkage, the beneficial effects of the reorganization did not outlast its originator.

Observation of these facts led to the final chapter of this book, which attempts to examine the contributions of partial proprietors to company success through their "rebuttal power," or the checks they impose on the potential abuse of absolute power by internal management. Since such partial proprietors are now disappearing, some means of providing a substitute are suggested.

These studies in organization are based to some extent on analysis and interpretation of existing organization theory. To a larger extent they are based on studies of actual events and on interviews with those who may qualify as great organizers: Pierre S. du Pont, Irénée du Pont, Walter S. Carpenter, Jr., of Du Pont; Donaldson Brown, Alfred P. Sloan, Jr., John Lee Pratt, James D. Mooney of General Motors; A. W. Robertson, Ralph Kelley, and Frank D. Newbury of Westinghouse; and Ernest Tener Weir. Information on Lammot du Pont's work was obtained in part from his widow, Mrs. Margaret F. du Pont.

Many of the codirectors and associates of the men mentioned above were interviewed also, and original documents, memoranda, reports, and studies were used. Some completely new documents were discovered, parts of which are published in a book for the first time here. These include excerpts from the papers of the High Explosives Superintendents' meetings at Repauno Chemical Company and Du Pont around the turn of the century and the original organization plans used by the du Ponts in 1918–1919.

The men who were interviewed made their contributions in the years before and up to World War II. Thus sufficient time has elapsed to evaluate results. The first blush of success—so often and so wrongly publicized too early—has long been a matter of record. And the passions surrounding the issues of that time have been largely spent. Those involved in them have retired and are old enough to have the benefit of perspective, yet young enough still to remember what happened and free enough from current responsibilities and public-relations considerations to talk frankly and leisurely.

My greatest single debt, among this group of "tall Americans," is to John Lee Pratt. While I was engaged on the General Motors organization studies, he first drew my attention to the pioneering contributions of H. M. Barksdale and J. A. Haskell and to the fact that they were among the real originators of systematic organization in the management of explosives research, production, and marketing, in what were to be the forerunners of the Du Pont Company as we know it today. John Pratt always gave me generously of his time. When he attended the monthly General Motors meetings, he introduced me to many of his associates and supported the search for the old organization documents. He will always be remembered as "the man behind the men" who were genuinely cooperative in their work, free in discussing the best solutions, incisive and direct in their decisions—the catalyst and driving force in the development of large-scale organization and a persistent influence in the follow-up. John Pratt will be remembered as one of the genuinely able chiefs of staff of a large organization.

I also wish to acknowledge my gratitude to that remarkable group of organizers, most of them now in their seventies and eighties and still with a physical and mental vigor which is almost essential for a successful executive of a large corporation, who assisted me in my studies. Particular appreciation goes to Donaldson Brown for much firsthand information from his pioneering and original contributions to systematic management and for his unfailing encouragement and continuous help. He is remembered as one of the most important developers of new management skills and one of the most successful practitioners.

Work on this book has been carried on at intervals over the last ten years and reflects the author's own participation in numerous reorganizations of large and small companies and membership on more than half a dozen national and international boards of directors. It has been constantly supported by Dean C. Stewart Sheppard of the Graduate School of Business and Public Administration of Cornell University and before him by Edward H. Litchfield, now Chancellor of the University of Pittsburgh, and by a grant from Cornell to defray the statistical and clerical expenses of the last chapter. The author also had the benefit of criticism and suggestions from the editors of the *Administrative Science Quarterly* of Cornell University, Professors Robert V. Presthus and James D. Thompson (now head of the Administrative Science Center of the University of Pittsburgh). By their kind permission Chapters 2 and 3 are printed here in revised form after publication in the *Quarterly* in June, 1956, and 1957. The author also gratefully acknowledges suggestions from the faculties of the University of California (Los Angeles and Berkeley), especially those from Professor George Steiner, editor of the *California Management Review*. Chapter 1 (first delivered as a lecture to the California University Faculty Seminar and then to the Council on Organization Development in New York City) and Chapter 4 were published by the *Review* in 1959 under the titles "Some Foundations of Organization Theory," in vol. 2, no. 1, 1959, and "Ernest Tener Weir: Iconoclast of Management," in vol. 1, no. 3, 1959. These are copyrighted by the Regents of the University of California, and revised versions of the articles are published here with their permission.

Chapter 6 was presented to the Organization Development Council in the fall of 1959 and published in *The Harvard Business Review* of March–April, 1960, and is published here in an extended form with their permission.

The author also acknowledges assistance from the Social Science Research Council in underwriting statistical, traveling, and clerical expenses in the writing of Chapters 2 to 5.

In Chapters 4 and 5 the author received aid on a number of the charts from R. S. Weinberg, at that time with the MIT group in Washington, D.C., and now manager of market research of IBM. His imagination and skillful application of mathematics and statistics to business problems have been extremely helpful, as will have been

gathered by those who have read some of the technical contributions
from these studies which he has published separately, especially the
concept of the multiple break-even chart, which was his path-breaking contribution to the Westinghouse studies of this book—one of
the few pioneering efforts at quantifying the problems of top management. The author also expresses his deep appreciation to James
Q. du Pont, "unofficial historian" of the Du Pont Company, for
his help on Chapters 2 and 3; to Alice Smith for her outstanding
editorial contributions to the book as a whole; to the late Eunice
Raimon (one of the ablest editors in her short life) for her fine
editorial work on Chapters 2 and 3; to my Cornell colleagues Robert
L. Raimon and Henry Landsberger for many suggestions; to Charles
Meloy for assistance with the research; and to Della Jaffee for re-
typing many drafts of each chapter.

In conclusion, it should be made clear that only the author is
responsible for the facts, their accuracy, and their interpretation.
Obviously, also, neither the organizers studied in this book nor the
author feel that the last word has been said on this complicated, vital,
and constantly changing subject. The men described were among
the first to recognize the need for changes in their own organizations
as economic, political, and especially technological circumstances
changed. But they held vigorously to the organizational tools of
comparative analysis and to genuine freedom in discussing organizational change. It is hoped that these qualitative contributions may
aid in a future in which the quantification of change and the influence of technological and moral considerations are likely to play
a much more important role.

Ernest Dale

Contents

1

Some Foundations
of Organization Theory[1]

> We have become more and more aware that con-
> centration on the practical issues may lead to big
> theoretical advances. Class distinctions, in fact,
> have been much weakened, and there is no longer
> any stigma attaching to an idea or to a technique
> that was born and bred in a workshop rather than
> in a university.
>
> LORD ADRIAN, "The Risks of Progress,"
> *The Listener*, November 26, 1959.

We need to cultivate the restraint of Galileo, who
left the world of angels and spirits until the time
should come when it would be explored, and con-
tented himself with such principles as he could
extract with confidence from experience, though

[1] In preparing this chapter I have drawn on work of many writers on and
practitioners in organization, but since some of the ideas are widely held and
widely used in practice, I have not quoted exhaustively. I have also drawn on
the methodological thinking of John Neville Keynes in economics, of Gunnar
Heckscher in political science, and Elliott Jacques in psychology.

the resolution committed him to such trivialities
as the timing of balls rolling down grooves. It is
that self-control—the voluntary restriction to the
task of extending knowledge outwards from the
observed to the unobserved instead of imposing
imagined universal principles inwards on the world
of observation—that is the essential hallmark of
the man of science, distinguishing him most funda-
mentally from the non-scientific philosopher.

H. DINGLE, *Monthly Notices of the*
Royal Astronomical Society, London, 1953

All philosophers find
Some favorite system to their mind.
In every point to make it fit
Will force all nature to submit.

T. L. PEACOCK, *Headlong Hall*

"Organization," as used by organization specialists, may be defined
as a method of breaking down broad and overwhelming tasks into
manageable and pinpointed responsibilities and at the same time
ensuring coordination of the work. Using the term in a broader
sense (to include aspects of management), Alfred Marshall, the
great economist, raised organization to a place among the three
traditional factors in production—land, labor, and capital. And
even in the more restricted sense in which the word is used here,
organization may deserve that status, for no widespread use of land,
labor, and capital is possible without some form of organization.

Organization charts and job descriptions provide a map of the
major features of an organization structure. Ideally, they ensure
that everyone knows the extent of his organizational box and his
powers and that lines of accountability are clear. Thus, relationships among groups and individuals are made plain; everyone knows
who his boss is, what hat he is to wear on what occasion, and on
whose team he is playing for what status and what goals.

But charts and job descriptions cannot provide much help, except in so far as they are an aid to memory and visualization, with the real problems of organization: What is the best way to divide the work in the light of the objectives? Who should be whose boss? How much responsibility and/or authority should be allocated to each position? What form of organization will ensure that each individual can utilize his powers to the full? How can coordination be achieved?

It is with questions like these that organization theory must be concerned if it is to be of help to those who deal with concrete problems.

Unfortunately, the rapidly growing number of schools of organization thought is tending to obscure the commonsense approaches.[2] Gradually such a school acquires a staff, students, research, conferences, a library, large and growing funds. Even during the lifetime of the founder, a vast verbal structure may be built up. Some even create a special language, intelligible only to the initiated. Thus it happens that in the field of organization research there arises an "organization cathedral," complete with an organization bible, commandments, rites, liturgy, inquisitors, crusades, holy wars, martyrs, and saints. Woe to those who stray beyond the dogma, who question infallibility. If they do not wish to be burned at the organization stake, they must fit themselves to the Procrustean bed of inviolate organization truth.

[2] For example, a recent advertisement in *Advanced Management* asks:
"How can I build a better organization? Atorgenics Has the Model and You Can Apply It."
"Atorgenics has the model of ideal organization because it has found and systematized the governing elements common to all organizations of human effort.
"During its 14-year history, Atorgenics has been applied with success by many people.
"Organization and management in Atorgenics brings smooth functioning to displace both human and structural conflict.
"Find this out for yourself. Follow the step-by-step explanations appearing in the periodical *Atorgenics Aspects.*
"*Take the first step toward a better organization.*
"Order *Atorgenics Aspects* at $4.50 per year, subject to refund on request.— THE ACADEMY OF ORGANIZATIONAL SCIENCE"

But in many cases only a lot of bric-a-brac, rather than a cathedral, is visible; it no more constitutes a workable theory than a collection of bricks is a house. And when the prophet has departed, sterility and senility continue to linger in the ruins. The school of organization continues its existence in accordance with Parkinson's law.

The specific "theory" of organization lives on in the minds and actions of the pupils who become full- or part-time organization experts, either in corporations or as advisers to them. And now the organization dogma is enforced and practiced with little regard to its original shortcomings or to changes in circumstances. Those living within such organization straitjackets, organization rules and standard practices remind one of the description given by the Oxford professor Richard Crossman of his visits to a state farm and *kolkhoz* in White Russia and a state farm and people's commune in China, each with a dairy herd. He reports:

In all of them I asked the same questions about the labour force and received exactly the same answers. Although the size of dairy herd and agricultural conditions varied greatly, there was always one whole-time worker to twelve cows when they were milked by hand and one to sixteen when they were milked by machines. Chinese and Russian cowmen gave almost identical answers to my questions. When I said that in the Western world a cowman will handle up to fifty beasts without difficulty and without assistance except on his off day, I was met with that look of absolute blank incredulity which dawns on all Communist faces when they are met with a fact which does not fit their intellectual patterns. It is a look which combines a loyal conviction that you are a capitalist liar with the disloyal suspicion that there may be something in what you say.[3]

If we compare this attitude with that of some of our organization men, we cannot but recognize some similarity.

Their rapid rise and the multiplication of organization schools and dogmas and their widespread impact appear to call for a sifting of the good from the bad.

The purpose of this chapter is to suggest consideration of certain

[3] "Inside 'The Other Camp.'" *The Listener*, November 6, 1958, pp. 715–716.

methods of studying business organization and to set up some criteria that may aid in assessing the value of the growing body of work on the subject. If some of these methods and criteria are acceptable, some neglected writers may deserve consideration. And, more important, the ideas and achievements of some of the men of action, men who have set up unusually effective business organizations, should be studied.

THE UNIVERSALIST APPROACH

In large part, the search for theory has been a search for principles and concepts that can be universally applied to organizations everywhere. Thus a well-known textbook on organization states:

> It is now possible to develop a theory of management applicable to all executives in all occupations...the principle implies that *managerial* knowledge and experience are transferable from department to department and from enterprise to enterprise. Merchandising executives may be shifted to manufacturing; the military commander to peaceful pursuits; foremen from flour milling to warehousing; and production managers to sales. To the extent...that their tasks are managerial rather than technical, and with proper motivation, executives will employ their skill as well in one occupation as in the other.[4]

Most of the "management principles" in use today were derived from the work of Henri Fayol (1841–1925). These include:

1. There must be specialization.
2. Responsibility is a corollary of authority.
3. There should be unity of direction—one head and one plan for each activity.
4. There should be "unity of command"—each person in the organization should have only one boss.

Amplifications of or additions to these principles have, however, been contributed by many other writers, including Lyndall F. Urwick, V. A. Graicunas, Alvin Brown, and many others. Grai-

---

[4] Harold Koontz and Cyril O'Donnell, *Principles of Management: An Analysis of Managerial Functions,* 2d ed., McGraw-Hill Book Company, Inc., New York, 1959, pp. 42–43.

cunas, a Lithuanian management consultant, has appended the more definite principle of the "span of control," that is, that no one person should supervise the activities of more than five, or at the most six, other individuals whose work is interrelated. It has also been largely accepted that a "short chain of command," or as few layers of supervision between the top man and the rank and file as possible, are desirable.

While the last two principles are to some extent contradictory (probably the only way the span of control can be reduced is to insert more levels of supervision), this is not an insuperable objection since the organizer may seek a compromise in the light of circumstances.

However, if organization theory is to be useful, it must meet harder tests than that of complete internal consistency. The principles may perhaps be seen in better perspective if viewed in the light of Milton Friedman's excellent definition of a good theory: "A theory is 'simpler' the less initial knowledge is needed to make a prediction within a given field of phenomena; it is the more 'fruitful' the more precise the resulting prediction, the wider the area within which the theory yields predictions, and the more additional lines for further research it suggests. . . . The only relevant test of the validity of a hypothesis is comparison of predictions with experience." [5]

The difficulty of experimentation and measurement in cases where multiple variables exist does not appear to be a sufficient excuse for the "soft" sciences to avoid the development of hypotheses that can be used to make predictions. At the edge of knowledge, the "hard" sciences face not dissimilar methodological difficulties. Yet unconventional researchers may obtain recognition in the hard sciences by successfully testing the predictability of their theories and reducing the areas of ignorance, while some of the writers on organization seem unaware of the problem and confine themselves to explaining changes with the benefit of hindsight or

[5] "The Methodology of Positive Economics," in *Essays in Positive Economics*, University of Chicago Press, Chicago, 1953, vol. 3, pp. 10ff. (Copyright, 1953, by the University of Chicago.)

indulge in subjective speculation for which there is no test of validity at all. Too many social scientists tend to seek recognition by achieving harmony with their peer groups rather than through the demonstrated workability of their results. The theories of the political scientists or students of international relations are characterized by an almost complete lack of predictability and provide practically no guides for practicing statesmen—a fact that may partially account for the unsatisfactory state of the world today. Should not the thinkers on organization attempt to do better?

Thus the "principles" of organization—if they are to deserve the name—should yield fairly accurate predictions. They should work. For example, limiting the chief of a series of complicated interrelated functions to five or fewer subordinates should give the most efficient results. But in such a definite form the principle obviously does not predict correctly; numerous exceptions could be cited.

Actually, the universalist position on the short span of control is probably derived from the British general Sir Ian Hamilton, who wrote in his memoirs: [6] "The average human brain finds its effective scope in handling three to six other brains."

As the commander at Gallipoli in World War I, Sir Ian himself was an outstanding victim of his own universalist dogmatism. There was an abysmal lack of proper staff-command liaison at the time of the actual landing on April 25, 1915.

Hamilton chose to immure himself in the conning tower of the Queen Elizabeth and thereby he cut himself off both from his staff and from direct command of what was happening on shore. . . . All tactical authority was handed over to his two corps commanders. . . . Since these two officers also remained at sea through the vital hours of the day, they, too, were without accurate information. . . . No senior commander had any clear picture of the battle . . . troops at Y beach were equal in numbers to the whole of the Turkish forces in the tip of the peninsula that morning; they could have marched forward at will and encircled the entire enemy position. By midday they might have cleared the way to Achi Baba

[6] *The Soul and Body of an Army,* Edward Arnold & Co., London, 1921, p. 229.

and turned a massacre into a brilliant victory...their operation had been planned in circumstances of the utmost confusion. Two colonels had been landed with the force, and each thought he was in command.[7]

In contrast to this was the attitude of a more successful commander, Dwight Eisenhower, whom the author interviewed on this subject in preparation for a book on organization [8] some years ago. The General, who was at that time president of Columbia University, reported that the trustees had appointed a management consulting firm to review the university's organization structure and make recommendations for change. On learning that the then president, Nicholas Murray Butler, had a span of control of 132, the consulting firm, among other things, recommended that the new president, whoever he might be, should have a span of control of only three. When this recommendation was presented to him, Eisenhower demurred. He felt that the very essence of his contribution would be his ability to handle a large number of subordinates, inspiring them and welding them together.

In World War I, when Eisenhower was in charge of supply of a regiment, he had insisted on a larger span of control than his competitors, and in this way he had been able to inspire more subordinates, stay close enough to actual events to identify particularly good and bad performance, untangle more "puzzlements" than his rivals. As a result, his performance was superior and he and his subordinates got more medals than their opposite numbers in other regiments.

Similarly, in World War II, Eisenhower felt that a long span of control had enabled him to exert much more of his integrating influence, successfully, than he could have otherwise. He concluded that the span of control should depend both on personal factors and on the organizational aids—for example, the general staff—that are provided. Hence the consultant's report, which cost

[7] Alan Moorehead, *Gallipoli*, Harper & Brothers, New York, 1956, pp. 129 and 145–146.

[8] Ernest Dale, *Planning and Developing the Company Organization Structure*, American Management Association, New York, 1952.

$80,000, was "the most expensive and least read book the university ever acquired."

While Eisenhower's judgment does not necessarily apply to the whole consulting report, it does raise the question whether the universal principles do not suffer from being either untrue or so obvious and so broad that they provide little or no help to the practicing organizer. For the "span of control" principle is about the only one that is definite enough to provide any sort of guide.

For example, the principle of "specialization" is undoubtedly true, but it does not tell us whether, under given circumstances, more or less specialization will produce better results.

Again, few would quarrel with the principle that each activity should have unity of direction or with the view that each person should have only one boss. (One of those few was, of course, Frederick Taylor, who suggested that each employee take orders from several functional foremen, an idea that is not taken seriously today.) But the problem of the organizer is to identify the activities that should be grouped together under single direction or single command, and the principles provide no specifics.

Finally, it is quite obvious that authority and responsibility should, ideally, be equal, but the principle affords little help in measuring one against the other. For example, if a foreman is responsible for obtaining a certain amount of production, it might be argued that he should have unlimited authority to hire and fire the men under him. Yet very few companies find it feasible to allow him that much authority today.

Much time has been and could be spent in arguing the fine points of the "principles," but this would not be much more helpful than arguing, like the medieval theologians, about how many angels can dance on the point of a needle.

Sometimes a principle is merely a hypothesis or a hunch or rather a gleam in the eye of a writer. Then he endows it with universal truth without bothering to verify it. Or the writer may have observed a particular set of circumstances at a particular point of time—in a hospital, say, or among a group of like-minded

fellows—and rushed to apply his observation universally, taking
no account of the influence of such factors as technology, market,
and personality. He omits them because he is unaware of them or
cannot handle them. So he attempts to apply a principle developed
from the observation of one situation to others that are not at all
comparable with it.

We all know of the universals of management which all managers
engage in to a greater or a less extent—POSDCORB—planning,
organizing, staffing, directing, coordinating, reporting, and budgeting. But we may say that Sewell Avery of Montgomery Ward,
Frederick Donner of GM, Charles Luckman as head of Lever a
few years ago, Sir Jehangir Ghandi of Tata Steel in India, Mikoyan
of Russian foreign trading, the small-town merchant with a few
employees, and the cardinal in charge of administration in the
Roman Catholic Church all posdcorb—but what a world of difference in the way they do it, both in aim and method! Only
an empirical study could uncover the differences and similarities.

A statement broad enough to cover all these cases—and the many
more that must be considered if *all* types of organizations are to
be covered—is necessarily so general that it is meaningless. For
example, a paper on "How to Choose a Leadership Pattern" con-
cludes lengthy discussion as follows: "The successful leader ... is
one who maintains a high batting average in accurately assessing
the forces that determine what his most appropriate behavior at
any given time should be and in actually being able to behave accordingly." [9] The leader will be baffled about what these forces
are, how he can assess them accurately, and what appropriate behavior is. And if he is not successful, it can always be said that he
has not assessed the forces accurately or has not behaved accordingly.

Another study, which took six men six years, and several million
dollars, to complete and is reported in three volumes of close to
2,000 pages, came up with such lessons for management as:

[9] Robert Tannenbaum and Warren H. Schmidt, "How to Choose a Leadership Pattern," *Harvard Business Review*, March–April, 1958, pp. 95–101.

Management policies and the quality of leadership have a lot to do with individual performance. Indoctrination and training of supervisory personnel, skillful use of assignments and reassignments, equitable treatment of employees, proper motivation, and sound personnel planning all can contribute to the effective utilization of manpower.[10]

Since so little practical value has been developed from the universalist approach, we may do better if we attempt to find, not generalizations that will apply to all types of organizations, but guides to what may be reasonably expected to work in reasonably comparable situations. If it is then agreed that organization theory to be "good theory" should be able to predict, what is there available?

THE COMPARATIVE METHOD

Some of the best answers may be derived from the comparative method of studying organization, an approach which is concerned with the recognition and description of fundamental similarity among different organization structures. The collection and analysis of similarities may yield general conclusions that can be applied to other similar or comparable situations as a means of predicting developments.

The value of the comparative method is that it attempts to delimit the area to which generalizations may apply and the circumstances under which they hold true. Rather than attempt a Copernican or Einsteinian approach that is all-embracing and explains all organization in a few brief statements, the comparative method at its best is used to formulate generalizations on more limited organization problems, such as the impact of decentralization on administrative expense, the effect of "Caesar management," or one-man control, on the development of management potential, or the impact of an "egalitarian," or committee, structure on top-management effectiveness.

[10] *Business Week*, May 9, 1959. The magazine comments: "These recommendations have been made before. The novelty of the study is the massive size of the research project on which the recommendations are based."

The generalizations may be deductive (i.e., proceeding from hypothesis to test in actual situations) or inductive (proceeding from observations of specific events to generalizations), or a combination of the two methods may be employed. The limited generalizations developed by either method are tested. In this way it may be possible to arrive at guides that will make predictions possible, if only in very limited areas, provided the differences between the organizations are taken into account and the necessary adaptations made.

If comparative studies of organization are to be useful, however, they must meet certain requirements. Among the more important of these requirements, often easy to overlook, are the following.

1. *A conceptual framework.* The researcher must select the variables to be observed in different situations, and these variables may be of many different kinds. Organizations can be studied, for example, in terms of functions: What functions must be performed and what authority and responsibility are necessary for the performance? Or we might consider classifications of other types, such as the process of executive work suggested by Chester I. Barnard: (1) the place where the work is done, (2) the time at which work is done, (3) the persons with whom work is done, (4) the things upon which work is done, and (5) the method or process by which work is done. For example, Professor Sune Carlson conducted such an analysis of the working conditions and methods of twelve chief executives of different companies, taking quantitative measurements and correlating results in terms of work efficiency.[11]

Comparisons might be made between different types of chief executives, through use of a typology, such as Erich Fromm's division of individuals into several types: receptive, hoarding, exploitative, marketing, and productive.[12] Study of chief executives on this basis might enable one, perhaps, to draw some inferences about the types of organization structure they head. For example, an exploitative chief executive might tend to mold the organization into an instrument designed to afford him maximum

---

[11] *Executive Behavior*, Strombergs, Stockholm, 1951.
[12] *Man for Himself*, Rinehart & Company, Inc., New York, 1947, pp. 50–117.

personal power; the hoarding type to produce a structure characterized by rigid orderliness. Finally, one might test a hypothesis or a series of hypotheses. For example, the hypothesis that the span of control becomes increasingly short as one goes up the managerial hierarchy might be tested in comparable situations.[13]

2. *Comparability.* The description and analysis of the similarities of different systems must also take into account the differences among them, for the latter may be so great as to make comparison meaningless.

Comparison will be of no value unless there is a fundamental similarity between the two objects to be compared. This is illustrated by the famous story of the union organizer who demanded that the company give a pay increase to pregnant women workers because other comparable companies were doing so. Negotiations were about to be broken off because of the intransigence of both parties until someone analyzed the labor force and found that it included only five women, all of whom were over 60. Hence we must carefully define the elements of difference and their approximate influence on results.

3. *Objectives.* There is no way of evaluating the results of comparative work except in terms of the purpose or objectives of the organizations studied. That objective may be profit maximization, power, morale, or the happiness of the members of the organization or a combination of these. It can probably be shown that those who know what they want to organize *for* are more successful than those who do not.

Sometimes, however, those who are explicitly successful in achieving what they set out to do are attacked by others who fail to state the basis of their attack.

Some organization "engineers" are apt to assume that good-looking organization charts are ends in themselves, that their job is done when the organization boxes look symmetrical or fit into a pyramid or look "flat," and so forth; that deviation from their "symmetry" is heresy. Again, some organization studies from the "human relations" point of view (impact of organization on people)

[13] Dale, *op. cit.,* pp. 56–60.

have been irresponsibly critical of formal organization theory and structure because of the inhibition, unhappiness, and frustration which they have observed in individuals working within the structure.

If the objective of the organization is the so-called "satisfying" of the individual in the organization, this should be made clear. And the standards should not be subjective, but as objective as possible.

But this type of approach may be of little or no help to organizations that have standards of evaluation different from those of the investigator. Many organized activities have to equate income and outgo, at least roughly so, over a period of time. The organization structure required for that end may not make all its members fully "happy." And—to take a case which is not as extreme as it may sound to some—should the goals of the organized activities *not* be met in order to keep the informal organization or some of its people "happy"? If that is the basic assumption or standard of the human-relations critics of formal organizations, they should clearly state so. Or they should state that they are more interested in the welfare of some employees (e.g., workers) than in that of others (e.g., management) and set out clearly what their standards are and the consequences of following these standards. They would also have to show that individual members of the organization would continue to be happy (or satisfied or adapted) if the formal organization should collapse and its goals be abandoned. Or the reverse would have to be demonstrated, namely, that the "happiness" of the members leads to better accomplishment of the organization goals.

The antipathy of some individuals to formal organizations may be inherent in their make-up. They may be essentially anarchistic, tending to be unhappy in any organized society. Even if there were no organization, there are some who would still be unhappy because of their own internal conflicts.

Some, at least, of the frustrations of individuals in formal organizations are due not to structure but to their own problems. Individuals may, for example, expect the boss to be a father substitute; they may be proving to themselves that they can be what their fathers expected them to be, even that they are bound to be failures. Employees' historical relationships to their parents may thus play a destructive role in their organizational relationships. An employee's belief in his parents' apparent accomplishments, security, and opportunity for creative work—carried over from youth—may militate against his superiors, and so may his constant battle to attain these imagined heights. Again, there may be a tendency to project upon the business organization the despotism and sadism that the employee in his childhood associated with the giver of orders and a paranoid feeling of persecution and helplessness before an omnipotent power.

The "human relations" analysis of organizations and individuals undoubtedly reveals much that is pertinent to the individual's feeling about and behavior in formal organizations. But the frequent failure to state the bases or standards of evaluation and criticism is not helpful to theory or to organizations themselves. The attempts to "adjust" the individual to the formal organization, or vice versa, may be neither desirable nor possible. In part at least, the critics overlook the stimulus of conflict and frustration.

It would be better to examine the realities of the work situation, the "stubborn needs" of the organization and one's inner self rather than take either the organization man's usual neurotic step and conceal or ignore these realities or the human-relations flight into unconscious identification with others. Pooling the unwanted and painful parts of our unconscious lives is a vast escape hatch, not a real solution.

4. *Validity*. The comparisons made and the conclusions drawn must be valid; that is, they should be applicable on the assumptions made and under the conditions postulated. There is nothing wrong if these are restrictive or if initial results are inconclusive because the data are inadequate, provided this is clearly stated. For as descriptions and analyses are refined and carried further, as data increase and improve, the implications or tendencies may become widely applicable or necessary revisions may become apparent.

USES OF THE COMPARATIVE APPROACH

These are among the prerequisites for useful comparison of organization structures. They provide a framework for testing theory and tentative generalizations that may explain why organizations behave the way they do, perhaps predict or delimit the way in which they will behave. In this way one may learn the lessons of experience without the large cost of undergoing it. And the comparative method is of practical value in describing what a particular organization does.

The comparative approach can be applied to studies of institutions, functions, and ideologies. As applied to human institutions, for example, there is the intra-company and the intra-industry study in which different phases of the organization of the same company or in similar companies can be analyzed historically or simultaneously. There is the inter-industry approach—much more difficult—in which different companies in different industries are compared. Most difficult of all is the comparison of activities in even more different fields, where there is an even wider diversity of objective—business, military, government, church, and so forth.

Another type of comparison of value and importance is between the organization of different functions of the same or different undertakings: forecasting, planning, staffing, coordinating, controlling, communicating, and so forth.

Finally, there is the comparison between the organization ideologies or systems of thought of different countries and different thinkers.

SOME COMPARATIVE ORGANIZERS

We find examples of the use of the comparative method wherever men have analyzed the ways in which the challenge of organizing cooperative effort may be met. To discuss them all would be a monumental task. The following, therefore, is merely a brief outline of some of the more important, which will illustrate the use of the comparative method.

One of the first systematic expositions of the comparative method in the study of organizations and the development of conclusions about them was conceived brilliantly by the Arab historian Ibn Khaldûn, adviser on organization and political action to kings and caliphs in North Africa and Spain during the fourteenth century. Some of his ideas are, perhaps, still applicable.

Khaldûn ran into the usual vicissitudes encountered by consultants; he was ousted by rival consultants, and he worked for rulers who did not appreciate his sage counsel (one of them had his head chopped off when he failed to heed Khaldûn's predictions). He instructed the feared Asian conquerer Tamerlane and kept him at bay. Then he retired and put his experience down in writing, together with his reflections on the then existing literature, the works not only of the Arab writers, but of the Greek philosophers.

Ibn Khaldûn felt that an understanding of organization must proceed from external data, transmitted from the past or from personal experience, to the explanatory or demonstrable knowledge of their cause and nature. According to Ibn Khaldûn, organization could help to produce either a rational regime which worked for the common good or one which worked for the selfish goals of its chief. To find the most suitable organization, he believed, one has to proceed from the known (that is, self-evident or demonstrable truth) toward the unknown. Such knowledge would at first be purely practical and based on experience, acquired through repeated trial and error and long practice during which men would find the right ways of doing things—whether of producing goods or of ordering their political and social relations—and identify the wrong ways that should be avoided.

Methods of improving organization, he said, can be studied through "the science of culture," which examines different types of society in order to ascertain historical events and rectify historical reports. Studying the organizations of different societies, he found that "the final cause is different from the formal cause" (e.g., the informal organization from the formal, deeds from words). Substantial errors tend to creep into historical accounts of changes in societies or organizations, he pointed out, because of such things as partisanship, overconfidence in sources, failure to understand the intention of reports, credulity, failure to understand events in their proper contexts, and interest in gaining favor with the powerful and influential.

Once having ascertained the facts about a society or an organization, one could begin to make comparisons. Ibn Khaldûn advocated the most nearly perfect society or organization in existence as a yardstick for comparison with other societies and organizations. And he undertook numerous studies toward that end, trying to arrive at "principles" with the help of "rationally demonstrated" sciences, like psychology, geography, and climatology.

He concluded that one must study growth in organization and that in this way its future course could be predicted. Like natural organisms, an organization has a beginning; it grows and develops and comes to an end. It reaches an optimum point and a natural limit beyond which it cannot develop. "As the prophet dies and the generation which had known him and was directly influenced by him passes away, the miracles are forgotten and impact of the extraordinary feats starts to decline ... once the inner impulse vanishes ... dynamic reality ceases to exist ... the regime is bound to degenerate into natural rule serving the lower impulses of whoever happens to be the stronger." [14]

But, Khaldûn pointed out, predicting the future course of organization is difficult because of the multiplicity of causes and because of chance and fortune, which are really only names given to hidden causes.

One of the first American examples of comparative-organization analysis was the work of Henry Varnum Poor and Daniel C. McCallum on organization of railroads. Poor was editor of the *American Railroad Journal* from 1849 to 1862, and McCallum was superintendent of the Erie Railroad from 1854 to 1857. The following is drawn from A. D. Chandler.[15]

[14] Muhsin Mahdi, *Ibn Khaldûn's Philosophy of History*, George Allen & Unwin, Ltd., London, 1957, p. 268.

[15] A. D. Chandler, "Henry Varnum Poor: Philosopher of Management" in William Miller (ed.), *Men in Business: Essays in the History of Entrepreneurship*, Harvard University Press, Cambridge, Mass., 1952.

The railroads, which were expanding rapidly in the mid-nineteenth century, were the first business organizations to find that operations on a large scale posed problems different not only in degree but in kind from those encountered in smaller enterprises. The principal problem, Poor and McCallum agreed, was that on a railroad 500 miles in length some sort of system must replace the personal attention a superintendent could give to a small road 50 or 60 miles in length. "We believe that the science of management is the most important in its bearings upon the success of the American railroads—that it includes facts and principles which are deserving of a full statement and elaborate discussion," Poor wrote in the *American Railroad Journal*. And he identified three principles, which he called "organization," "communication," and "information," pointing out that organization, or the careful division of work, was the most fundamental of all. The system should be designed, he said, to ensure that each man's time was fully utilized and the railroad's capital equipment kept in service as much of the time as possible. "Communication" was defined as a reporting system that would keep management informed of the way in which operations were proceeding; "information" as the knowledge that analyses of the reports would provide on possible methods of improving operations.

Poor and McCallum were close personal friends, and as superintendent of the Erie, McCallum was in a position to put Poor's ideas, which were drawn from his own experience, into full effect. He was, perhaps, the first man in American business to draw up an organization chart. This he constructed in the form of a tree, with the president and the board of directors as the roots, the five operating divisions and the service departments as branches, the subordinate superintendents and employees as the leaves. He provided for "communication" by instituting a system of daily reports from conductors, engineers, and station agents, from which monthly reports were compiled by division superintendents and analyzed to provide "information" as Poor had defined it.

McCallum also laid down the duties and powers of the various positions and determined their grades, which in turn determined the salary levels. He set forth the so-called "scalar principle," or need to follow the chain of command by prescribing that subordinates could communicate with the top executives only through their immediate superiors. He also developed the "principle" of "unity of command" by insisting that "all subordinates shall be accountable to and be directed by their own immediate superior only; an obedience that cannot be enforced where the foreman in immediate charge is interfered with by a superior officer giving orders directly to his subordinates."[16]

McCallum's system did improve efficiency remarkably. It eliminated duplication of work and made it possible to cut down the number of employees. Systematization also made possible a considerable reduction in the number of engines lying idle.

There were, however, some offsetting difficulties. The subordinate managers and employees found the system restrictive, and the Erie suffered more from strikes than other roads. This led Poor to consider the possible ill effects of too much routine and to urge greater flexibility. He also concluded that part of the difficulty stemmed from the fact that the higher executives were ill-informed about the jobs lower down and unacquainted with the actual operating techniques.

Carrying these ideas even further, he suggested a revolutionary change in organization. Since the stockholders and their representatives, the directors, had neither the time to acquire the necessary technical knowledge nor any interest in acquiring it, he suggested that the owners lease the roads to technically competent managers for a fixed rent and allow the resulting gain or loss to accrue to management. He also favored publication of complete financial data, similar to those later required by the Interstate Commerce Commission (ICC) and the Securities and Exchange Commission (SEC).

The railroads, however, were governed by financiers who were not disposed to issue revealing financial statements. McCallum was forced to resign in 1857.

Another contributor to the comparative study of organization

[16] *Ibid.*, p. 262.

also drew on railroad experience. This was Harrington Emerson, who was active some fifty years ago. Like Poor, he was an erudite and scholarly man who wrote widely and had much influence. He was independent of the scientific management movement, but had done extensive work on railroads as an efficiency engineer, and his testimony in the Eastern Railroad case to the effect that roads could save "a million dollars a day" made him nationally known.

His important contribution to organization arose in part from his studies in Germany, where he was greatly impressed by the German General Staff's planning of the successful campaigns of 1866 and 1870–1871. In his book on efficiency [17] he concluded:

"It is Von Moltke's greatest claim to fame that he perceived the deficiency of line organization in the army and supplemented it with the general staff which made the Prussian army the marvellously supreme organization it became after 1860. The theory of a general staff is that each topic that may be of use to an Army shall be studied to perfection by a separate specialist, and the combined wisdom of those specialists shall emanate from a supreme staff." [18]

But Emerson admitted immediately the need for adaptation of the military general staff to the different needs and circumstances of other activities:

Yet even Von Moltke's marvellous combination of old line and modern staff could not be adapted without change to railroad or manufacturing activities. Its deficiency lies in the fact that the members of the line, who are many, are excluded from intimate relations with the staff, which is numerically so weak.... In the last analysis the man in the line, the man down at the bottom of the line, meets with the difficulties, and he is the one who most needs staff assistance for his special case. [19]

In addition to this special staff assistance, Emerson observed from his many studies of the military, the railroads, and manufacturing the need for coordination of these staffs:

[17] Harrington Emerson, *Efficiency as a Basis for Operation and Wages*, 4th ed., The Engineering Magazine Company, New York, 1919, chaps. 3 and 4; see also his chap. 16 of *The Twelve Principles of Efficiency*, The Engineering Magazine Company, New York, 1912.
[18] Emerson, *Efficiency as a Basis for Operation and Wages*, pp. 59–60.
[19] *Ibid.*, pp. 63–64.

Modern organizations are defective because they individualize instead of generalize their staffs. The president of a railroad or of a manufacturing plant apportions duties among several vice presidents, each of whom takes up a line of duties. This is necessary, but in the old days in the Palace of Pharaoh it is not stated that the chief butler organized a staff with a head baker, or that the head baker organized a staff with a head butler. Each vice president, of course, requires a staff of his own for his special line of duties, but there are general needs which are the very fundamentals of strong organization, and these needs should be under general staff officers, all of whose aggregated wisdom should be available to guide, not only the president and vice president, but also each subordinate official down to the lowest man on the line. Because there is no general staff of this kind, each official down to the worker attempts, more or less awkwardly, to create his own general, as well as his particular, staff.... One of the defects of this kind of organization is that the staffs of the different officials are not correlated.[20]

At a later point Emerson compared the maintenance expenses of two railroads, one with staff assistance, the other without it. He found that the costs of the former were less than 50 per cent of those of the latter and the staff costs were only $10,000 on a total outlay of $305,000.

Then, in our own day, Elton Mayo's influence on organization through his famous Hawthorne Studies has spread as far as that of Ibn Khaldûn did earlier. Like Ibn Khaldûn's, Mayo's theories were comparative in origin. It was experience which disproved one hypothesis after another. (Mayo's typology of experimentation had been initiated by Max Weber in a textile factory before World War I.) The final conclusion was unexpected and profound in its impact. All the changes deliberately introduced to influence the output of a group of girls were as nothing to the spontaneity of cooperation in a group working informally together, a group whose attitude toward work completely changed when its members ceased to be separate cogs in a machine. Like Ibn Khaldûn, Mayo emphasized the primacy of the social function; the relationship of rulers or managers as one to groups rather than to individuals; the need for recognition, security, and a sense of belonging as

[20] *Ibid.*, pp. 64-66.

more important in determining morale than physical conditions of work.

Mayo's researches remain revolutionary and are extremely important to the study of organization. His findings are well known and have been tested many times by different investigators, in different countries. His method was, as he described it, "knowledge of acquaintance" based on direct experience rather than "knowledge about" based on reflection and abstract thinking. But even though he seemed to deny it, he did have a frame of reference. It is his omission to state it and his implied values or objectives that make him subject to criticism. For, to summarize very roughly, Mayo preferred the noneconomic to the economic values; he preferred to work in an atmosphere of peace rather than one of disagreement, even if the disagreement was peaceful. He seemed to be concerned with maintaining and strengthening the role of entrenched management as a more or less unassailable elite. Beyond that he largely ignored the role of higher management, disdaining its formal relations and omitting its informal aspects. These omissions and others were remedied to some extent by Chester I. Barnard in his *Functions of the Executive*,[21] Herbert Simon in his *Administrative Behavior*,[22] Kenneth E. Boulding in *The Organizational Revolution*,[23] all very considerable contributions to organization. But they were based largely on "knowledge about" rather than on the direct experience which Mayo advocated. That gap was filled for the first time—and very helpfully for management—by a rather neglected group of British medical psychologists and analysts under the leadership of the medical psychologist Dr. Elliott Jacques.

Curiously, his book [24] has not been given much attention in the United States. (Chris Argyris' extensive survey *Personality and Organization* [25] gives only a mention to its successor volume, quoting its title incorrectly.) Yet it is based on profound under-

---

[21] Harvard University Press, Cambridge, Mass., 1938.
[22] The Macmillan Company, New York, 1957.
[23] Harper & Brothers, New York, 1953.
[24] Elliott Jacques, *The Changing Culture of a Factory*, Tavistock Publications, Ltd., London, 1951.
[25] Harper & Brothers, New York, 1957.

standing of the technical problems of the organization of a company and the splits produced by changes in technique, size, personality, and specialization. The analysis is conducted partly in terms of individual and group psychoanalytic theory within a sociological (Parsonian) framework. Solutions are based in part on past historical experience and a comparison of what executives say and do and of outward manifestations with unconscious springs of action, as well as on a systematization of formal corporate policy and organization structure.

Elliott Jacques' follow-up work on *Measurement of Responsibility* [26] similarly avoids the usual pitfalls of supposedly mechanistic (and hence scientific) systems and the effusion of good will. It approaches organization directly, in terms most likely to be operational for all parties concerned. Briefly, Jacques recommended that the level of pay and the organization level of an executive be determined by the length of the intervals during which he is free to act, i.e., does not have to check with his superior. This system of salary administration is likely to minimize the unconscious resentment aroused by the lack of equity and measurability inherent in other approaches. It therefore goes to the real rather than the superficial root of some problems of organizational and economic relationships.

The most powerful support for the comparative approach has recently come from the study *Business Enterprise*.[27] This is probably the most thorough study of business organization so far made. It is based on more than ten years' work and partly on evening seminars on problems in industrial administration held at the London School of Economics. The seminars included among their members top thinkers on organization—university professors, postgraduate students, businessmen, and government officials. Their backgrounds ranged from science and technology to accounting, economics, law, marketing, and personnel, and they had worked with companies of varying sizes, from small firms to the largest

[26] Tavistock Publications, Ltd., London, 1951.
[27] R. S. Edwards and H. Townsend, *Business Enterprise*, Macmillan & Co., Ltd., London; St. Martin's Press, New York, 1958.

international companies. Some two hundred papers reviewing the development and organization of particular firms or groups of firms were analyzed.

After a tremendously detailed and thorough analysis, the authors conclude [28] that there are no universal patterns of organization (for a similar conclusion see R. V. Clements' thorough study) [29] and that:

The existing state of the literature gives little reason for thinking that the answers are just around the corner. We know of no "principles" of industrial organization that are both right and useful. Yet there will be many points of similarity [among business problems] and it is possible to learn from the experience of others—this book is designed to be helpful in making firms aware that there are many ways of doing things and that their own choice may not necessarily be the best.

As one of many examples, the authors show how two groups of outstanding writers on and practitioners of organization arrived at diametrically opposite conclusions on the problem of balance between centralization and decentralization as applied to the coal and electricity industries.[30]

That they weighed the gains and problems [of bigness] differently merely illustrates the very great difficulty of reaching final conclusions on organizational questions. Organizational studies should make them [firms] aware of dangers not immediately apparent in their own course of action, but which could be seen lurking in the background of similar decisions taken by others in the past.... The usefulness of professional consultants, lawyers, and accountants to their clients must surely be based largely on their background of accumulated experience.

The weakness of the comparative organizers is, of course, that they tend to assume that their successful experience in one type of activity over a certain period of time will continue to be applicable to that activity and to other activities and other companies; in other words, they tend to become universalists.

[28] *Ibid.*, pp. 574–575.
[29] *The Managers; A Study of Their Careers in Industry*, George Allen & Unwin, Ltd., London, 1958.
[30] Edwards and Townsend, *op. cit.*, p. 504.

This weakness can be overcome only by refining the canons of experience, testing them and stating the conditions under which they may hold. To some extent this condition has been met by the safeguards and limits of application of the comparative method which the comparative organizers set themselves. Tentative generalizations that may be drawn from the work of the great organizers described in this book are illustrative of the type of conclusion that may be arrived at by the comparative approach.

Most of these great organizers developed their ideas in response to a specific challenge. In a number of instances they took over organizations at a time when one-man control had ceased to be adequate. Either the founder-genius of the organization had passed away and it was necessary to make systematic organization serve as a substitute for genius, or the tasks had grown beyond the capacity of the genius to meet them. The success of their companies after reorganization is at least partial proof of the value of the work.

Some of the generalizations that may be drawn from a study of the work of these men may be stated in the form of a description of their approach:

1. They had definite *objectives* that were subject to rough measurement. They were usually highly rational in that they had clear-cut goals and ordered their resources so as to be able to reach their objectives within the framework of the law and existing social, human, and public conventions.

2. They did not regard the division of work and work assignment as predetermined, but rather as dependent on their objectives. For them, organization was like a road to market or a tool with which to build.

3. They treated organization as an art rather than as a science. True, they tended to classify types of work and to postulate hypotheses or "criteria" of organization. But their classifications and hypotheses were based on the technology of the industry, on the environment of the company, and especially on the changing personalities of top management. Their hypotheses are approxima-

tions and guides, applied with flexibility, rather than universal principles enforced regardless of circumstances and objectives. They are frameworks designed to meet change and in practice were continually modified.

These practitioners may have combined organization theory and practice at their best if we judge them by how nearly their organizations met the objectives they set. If they aimed at a maximum rate of return on investment, then we should evaluate their organization structures in that light. It is quite conceivable, though not necessarily true, that they might not score the highest marks on morale or community relations. But then criticism on these grounds should be leveled against the goals they set rather than against the organizations they designed to achieve these goals.

The great organizers devised some "principles," or rather guiding criteria, of their own. (It should be noted that these were conceived and applied mostly "without benefit of clergy," that is, without reference to a great book on organization and without the influence of a "guru," or crusading missionary.) These criteria were developed through the challenge of specific problems and possibly are not applicable beyond them. True, some of the criteria, such as the limited span of control, were similar to those developed by the writers on organization (though conceived independently), yet within the broad limits imposed by the declining efficiency of a fixed quantity of management they were not too strictly applied. Criteria that may be drawn from their work include:

1. Profitable control may be achieved by responsibility accounting: linking organization structure to a planned rate of return on investment and controllable expenses. This results in a high degree of correlation between effort and results (Donaldson Brown at Du Pont and GM).

2. Decentralization of operations and coordination of control—organizing different activities to operate as separate groups that conflict as little as possible yet work toward a common end (Du Pont, GM)—may provide a means of utilizing the advantages of both large- and small-scale enterprise.

3. Substitution of control by a group for one-man control works

best when members of the group have homogeneity of outlook, egalitarian status, and heterogeneity of ability (Du Pont and GM).

4. Organization of "rebuttal power" through substantial minority stockholders can act as a valuable check on absolute power and ingrown management and provide a means of developing freedom of expression, which can lead to better decision making (GM).

5. It may be possible to develop a "lifetime plan" embodying a regular and profitable rate of expansion (Weir at National Steel) over a long period of time.

6. When a company changes over from a centralized to a decentralized organization structure, the immediate, short-run, and long-run results are likely to differ (Westinghouse):

   a. The immediate impact tends to be an increase in profitability.

   b. The short-run impact may be expected to be an increase in administrative expense that will more than offset the gains.

   c. The long-run impact, however, will tend to be an increase in revenue that will more than offset the increased costs.

It would be, of course, extremely convenient if universally applicable principles of organization could be discovered that could be applied like a formula to all organizations, or even to all business organizations. But hope for this is dim, for a principle broad enough to cover all situations is necessarily so broad as to tell us little we did not know before. And if it is made definite—like the span of control—its validity may be questioned, because many successful organizers can be found who ignore it completely.[31] There is no way of knowing whether they are successful in spite of or because of this, or whether the principle is simply irrelevant, at least up to a point.

The comparative approach, therefore, seems to be the most helpful to those who must meet organization problems here and now. It would be interesting to analyze many more different structures, but this is a task for which the contributions of many

---

[31] A study by the author of 100 large companies (over 5,000 employees), many of them leaders in their fields, found that the median number of executives reporting to company presidents was eight, and in some cases there were as many as twenty or more. *Op. cit.*, p. 77.

are required. To study and evaluate even one organization is an extremely complex task, because of the many factors involved and because a large number of years of operation must be examined to arrive at a tenable conclusion. For changes may work out extremely well (or badly) to start with and show quite different results as the adjustments are made. In making organization changes, it is the long run that counts.

It is true that some of the universalists are outstanding men, and there is no doubt that they have made important contributions to the study of organization. They have drawn attention to the basic issues, and they have given us a vocabulary that is useful in classifying practical organization problems. Yet they have provided a field day for their critics because they have largely neglected to test and refine their "principles," because they have claimed too much, and because they seem unable or unwilling to deal with some important areas of organization.

In summary, then, we may conclude that "in spite of a general pattern, we find differences, and in spite of differences in setting, we find similarities" [32] in organizations. By using the comparative approach we may be unable to build up a universally applicable theory immediately, but possibly we can build up parts of a theory that are immediately useful and may ultimately become universally valid.

[32] Gunnar Heckscher, *The Study of Comparative Government and Politics*, George Allen & Unwin, Ltd., London, 1957.

2

Du Pont: Pioneer in Systematic Organization and Management[1]

> The human character, we believe, requires in general constant and immediate control to prevent its being biased from right by seduction of self-love.
>
> THOMAS JEFFERSON IN A LETTER TO
> PIERRE SAMUEL DU PONT DE NEMOURS

Before and during the years of Frederick W. Taylor's principal work on scientific management, the Du Pont organization, quite

[1] The author is deeply indebted to John Lee Pratt for suggesting that this study be undertaken, for encouraging it, and for helping at every stage. Much gratitude is owed to Lammot du Pont Copeland, who gave access to many of the original documents and helpfully reviewed the manuscript at several stages. The author appreciates access to the reminiscences and experiences of Pierre S. du Pont, Irénée du Pont, Donaldson Brown, W. S. Carpenter, Jr., W. F. Harrington, James Q. du Pont, J. F. Daley, Alfred P. Sloan, Jr., E. F. Johnson, Amory L. Haskell, and L. R. Beardslee. Of printed sources on Du Pont, I have drawn especially on William S. Dutton, *Du Pont: One Hundred and Forty Years*, Charles Scribner's Sons, New York, 1942. I am also indebted to Dr. C. G. Jung (Zurich University), Isaiah Berlin (Oxford University), Sir Dennis Robertson (Cambridge University), and Henri Fayol (Paris).

31

independently, introduced many management techniques and skills that were original contributions. Unlike Taylor, Du Pont systematized not only in technical matters at the foreman's level, but particularly at top levels. In the process, the company developed a group of men who created the largest and most successful chemical company in the world. It also provided some of the key men who helped to save General Motors from disaster in 1921 and then to make it the world's largest automobile company. And over the past twenty-five years the skills of management developed at Du Pont and General Motors have been adopted by many other companies.

"CAESAR" MANAGEMENT

The beginnings of systematic management at Du Pont can be traced in large part to the company's attempt to solve the problems of succession that arose when General Henry du Pont died and it became necessary to substitute system for the "Caesar" type of management.[2]

Probably more than any of his predecessors, General Henry was responsible for the dominant position of Du Pont as the greatest explosives manufacturer in 1889. Starting in 1850, after sixteen years as a powder maker, this second son of the company's founder took over a firm with a debt of over half a million dollars and made it the leading company in the industry.

In his earlier years he was an outstanding example of the innovating entrepreneur, demonstrating what it means to change, to combine, to think, and to plan ahead. He completely reorganized Du Pont's manufacturing facilities, introduced real economies, built the most modern powder-making machinery. He emphasized

---

[2] "Caesar management" may be said to be a comparative term in administration. The founder of a business may be likened to the founder of any organization—political, social, religious, or educational. These "Caesars" are usually unique in their talents applied at their particular time and opportunity; they create original organizations, difficult to explain, impossible to teach or to imitate. Their successors may be compared to "kings" who need to use a systematic administrative approach in order to survive.

production in quantity to make lower prices possible without sacrifice of quality. He reorganized Du Pont's selling completely, setting up agents in all parts of the country. He anticipated the development of new demand (in the coal fields of Pennsylvania, the gold fields of California, and so on), enforced speedy collection of accounts and strict terms of payment, stressed service and prompt delivery. Du Pont was the only company in the industry to survive the after-effects of the Civil War without financial difficulties.

The General's biggest stroke was the formation of the Gunpowder Trade Association, which in 1872 brought together all the major and minor companies in an agreement to minimize competition. The companies assigned trade territories on the basis of most economic service, restrained the destructive practices of their agents, and pledged themselves not to compete in the market for their major raw-material requirements. This move gave the industry long and profitable protection against price cutting and the unsettling effects of free competition. Gradually, the General acquired the majority of votes in the association, and largely by skilled financial manipulation he acquired other gunpowder firms. He frankly stated his firm's policy as follows: "We are every day dictating to our agents as to prices, terms, and conditions to govern them; but we do not allow anybody to dictate to us as to what prices, terms, and conditions we shall dictate. We do our own dictating."

The General's method of management was one-man control. For almost forty years he made all the major decisions and many minor ones. He determined the distribution of profits, at times putting as much as half of the total profits back into the company, and he enforced a large rate of savings among his partners. Manufacture of black powder was once assigned to his brother and partner, Alexis, and his nephew and partner, Irénée. But Alexis was killed in an explosion, and Irénée died at an early age. Both left their authority to the General, who had all executives of Du Pont report to him personally. At meetings with department heads he received information in answer to his questions but gave little or none in return. No minutes were kept of the daily 8:30 A.M. meetings, and nothing was disclosed of what was discussed. The General personally supervised the company's several hundred selling agents and initially traveled all over the country to keep in touch with them. Even each worker had access to his office and could consult "Mr. Henry" on any problem. The General himself tried to be completely informed of the quality of the work of each of his employees (he went on a personal inspection tour of his farms in the morning and of the powder mills in the afternoon); he kept the workers' valuable papers in a special compartment in his office and knew who was sick, celebrated a birthday, had a baby, or was drunk on Saturday night.

The company's policy was to do as much in its own shops as possible rather than leave anything to outsiders. "We build our own machinery," wrote General Henry, in turning down an offer from an engineering consultant. "We draw our own plans; make our own patterns; and have never employed anyone to design or construct our mills or machinery, dams or races, roads or anything else; being our own engineers and superintendents of all work done at our mills."

The "master's eye" was seemingly everywhere. Of all the family, the General lived closest to the mills (and his home was the one most exposed to the danger of explosions). He occupied an office of five rooms built by his elder brother, the former president of the company, Alfred Victor du Pont, on the lawn in front of his house. He still used the desk and chairs that his father had brought over from France. He wrote all the checks and signed all the contracts; he received and distributed the mail. He personally answered all letters addressed to him. He probably wrote over a quarter of a million letters in his almost forty years of tenure; writing with a quill (even when steel pens were available), using candlelight (even when coal-oil lamps, gaslight, and electric light existed), blotting the pages with sand, and taking the low-burned candles home. When typewriters became available he would not have one. When he was seventy-two years old he refused secretarial help: "We have no use for a stenographer." Every day he appeared in a high black stovepipe hat, accompanied by his greyhounds and riding in his buggy—with storm curtains always up—to make his daily inspections. On his rounds he might collect a bundle of willow twigs dropped from wagons and deliver it at the charcoal ovens or use his trowel to eradicate weeds on his expanding properties.

In addition to being head of the business and very active in politics, General Henry was also head of the family; he handled its financial affairs and housing and even its daily transportation. Family councils were held so that he could advise on emergencies, schooling, and marriage. In the French fashion, family and business affairs were intermixed, but in the interest of the business rather than that of individual members of the family.

General du Pont was thus engrossed in thousands of details, yet he did not lose sight of the firm's over-all goals. Though the modern administrator might argue that success could not be gained in this way, the General proved that it could be. He found in the daily immersion in details a relaxation from the tension of big things; it enabled him to indulge interests he could not have satisfied if he had devoted himself entirely to the broad view. In fact, detachment from the details might have left him highly dissatisfied and ineffective. And his care for even the smallest problems made for the long-run reputation of his firm. Moreover, he had the physique to carry these burdens. He was cautious, conservative, and thrifty. On his tombstone appear the words of the Psalmist: "Mark the perfect man and behold the upright; for the end of that man is Peace." But, as Marquis James noted in his biography of Alfred I du Pont, the peace that had come to the "perfect man" did not pass on to his surviving partners.

THE COLLAPSE OF SUCCESSOR MANAGEMENT

Eugene du Pont was the logical third-generation successor to General Henry, being the oldest son of the youngest son of the founder. At forty-nine he had a background in chemical research and works management but lacked the business experience of his uncle, Henry. Yet he persisted in running the business in just the same way. As head of the firm, he exercised absolute control, making not only the major decisions but also handling the same immense amount of detail, down to the personal opening and answering of the mail. He gave a good deal of advice but took little himself and wrestled alone with the hopelessly intertwined affairs of company and family.

But Eugene was not Henry's equal, and he faced many more difficulties. Where Henry had grown with the problems of Du Pont, Eugene was thrown into them without real training or guidance. Where Henry had been dealing with a small firm during most of his life, Eugene had to start at the point where Henry had been overwhelmed, and this in face of further acquisitions of powder companies. Where Henry had permitted margins of safety for maneuver, Eugene did away with some of them. For example, he abruptly dismissed the "never-sweats." (These were carpenters and bricklayers who built "$4,000 stone walls on $2,000 properties," stand-by labor ready to repair immediately any damage to the powder mills. It is suspected that the resentful artisans took revenge by starting fires on the property; the company was plagued by arson for several years.) Where Henry had had the physical capacity to master details and relax in the process, Eugene was overwhelmed by them. And where Henry dominated the Gunpowder Association, Eugene was constantly threatened by rising insiders who challenged his authority.

In spite of initial incorporation in 1899 and some attempts at delegation in selling and the addition of a new office and clerical staff, Eugene could not handle the burdens, administratively or physically. In 1902, at the age of sixty-one, a bout of illness overcame him, and within a few days he died. To his potential successors the words of Jethro to Moses in the Exodus in the Wilderness were a warning: "The thing that thou doest is not good. Thou wilt surely wear away, both thou, and this people that is with thee; for this thing is too heavy for thee."

The partners were indeed wilting away. Two of them, vice presidents Alexis and Francis, were in poor health; they died within three years of Eugene (in 1904 aged sixty-one and fifty-four, respectively), while Charles, the secretary-treasurer, was even worse off and passed away within the year while still in his thirties. The remaining partner and vice president, Colonel Henry, was a military man, not a practical powder man. He had his eye on the past—he remembered how hard his father and his cousin had worked—and on the future, in which he planned to enter politics. He decided to turn down the offer of the company presidency, became a United States senator, and lived to be eighty-eight.

These four survivors of Eugene reluctantly decided at his death that since there was no du Pont to take his place, it would be best to sell the company to a competitor, Laflin and Rand. It was at this point that thirty-eight-year-old Alfred I. du Pont (the youngest partner, who was not as a rule consulted) dissented sharply. He offered to buy the firm, and he persuaded his cousin, T. Coleman du Pont (thirty-nine), to join him. Coleman became president. He had never worked for the company (he had made a considerable fortune in steel, coal, and electric street railways). He in turn, persuaded their first cousin, Pierre Samuel, to rejoin the firm. The three cousins "purchased" the Du Pont Company for $2,100 cash and $12 million in notes and reincorporated the business. It was they who introduced systematic management.

NONCONFORMIST MANAGEMENT

Some of the beginnings of systematization, however, can be traced back to a nonconformist. Lammot du Pont, Sr., was probably the most brilliant executive this remarkable family has produced. A "master chemist," he combined the ability to rethink the fundamentals with the capacity to complete the experiments necessary for their successful application. He was a dreamer entranced by the broad sweeps of technology, yet he nursed his work with the care and intensity of a mother looking after her child. As a young man of less than thirty, he inveigled the redoubtable Lord Palmerston into releasing essential Indian saltpeter supplies of which he had cornered the London market to aid the North in the Civil War, even though the British Prime Minister felt he acted against his own best interests. And while he could deal successfully with the great, he associated easily with the lowliest workman. He considered the consequences of every action and planned carefully, yet he could easily handle the unexpected. He summed up his own philosophy: "As in rowing—perfect timing, never a splash."

Lammot du Pont was the inventor of "soda powder," the first notable change in the composition of black powder for six hundred years, which became the most powerful yet cheapest black-powder type on the market. He was also one of the inventors of "mammoth powder," which revolutionized naval warfare. He made successful experiments with dynamite, based in part on the work of Alfred Nobel and others. But when he proposed to General Henry that Du Pont manufacture dynamite, he was bluntly told "No." Henry began to work actively against its use, lending his name and his power of pungent expression to squelching the new product: "No man's life is safe who uses dynamite ... it is only a matter of time until that man loses his life."

At this point Lammot du Pont decided to throw all he had—his personal fortune, his full time, and ultimately his life—into the building up of dynamite. Leaving the Du Pont Company in 1880 to set up the Repauno Chemical Company, he predicted, "We have begun here what will some day be the biggest dynamite plant in America."

Lammot was the first du Pont to move away from Wilmington. He did so partly because he wanted to run his own show, in order to demonstrate that physical decentralization could lead to delegation of decision making—though the General rationalized this by saying that the new dynamite plant might blow up everyone if it were located on the Brandywine—and partly to let a non-du Pont become superintendent of a plant, something that was just "not done."

More important even than his contribution to product mix was Lammot's establishment of a separate system of management at Repauno, which became the *fons et origo* of the du Ponts' industrial supremacy. When there was little more than the shell of the parent company left in 1902, it was the men of Repauno who supplied executive talent for the three cousins. While on the Brandywine General Henry worked by candlelight and wrote laboriously by hand, the newest was none too modern at Repauno. Lammot permitted a high degree of participation in decision making. He set up a systematic approach to manufacturing and selling. He was one of the first to install an experimental laboratory at the plant, even staffing it with a few Ph.D's. He strove for improved safety and worked on the complete mechanization of the dangerous operations so that the workmen would not be exposed to them. He had started experiments on the utilization of by-products when he was killed in 1884, at the age of fifty-three. A small quantity of nitroglycerine exploded and blew up one of his manufacturing units, burying him under a bank of earth.

The essential contribution of Lammot du Pont was his refusal to accept things as they were, to proceed merely by trial and error, or to be conventional and authoritarian. He gave to the company the speculative and philosophical approach of his French great-grandfather Pierre Samuel, a "total" point of view. He introduced *a priori* deductive reasoning into management; he formulated hypotheses and tested, adapted, and controlled them. Being a theoretician and willing to follow his reasoning wherever it might lead, however different and unacceptable the result might be to his associates, he set a pattern for nonconformity.

His work was taken over by his cousin and old ally, William du Pont. But when William resigned in 1892 there was no du Pont available to head the dynamite enterprise, and J. Amory Haskell was brought in to become president.

PIONEERING MANAGEMENT IN HIGH EXPLOSIVES

Scarcely thirty-one years old, Haskell was at this time general manager of a coal and iron company and had produced harmony and profits during a period of labor troubles and depressed business, and he made the equally able Hamilton Macfarland Barksdale his general manager. Member of an illustrious Southern family, Barksdale had completed the civil engineering course at the University of Virginia in three years instead of the usual four and had been hired by William du Pont, who met him when he was building the B & O railroad line through Wilmington.

Neither Haskell nor Barksdale was a powder man or a chemist, but both had been users of explosives in their work on railroads and in mines. More important, through this experience in the two major large-scale industries of their time, they had perforce learned the systematic approach to management and the close control of expenses required by the large investment in the one and the keen competition in the other. Both men were first-class organizers.

They found plenty of scope in the powder industry, where production methods were rudimentary, organic chemistry was an occult art, organized research was nonexistent, and the whole works were liable to blow up at any moment. On the sales side, the manufacturer sold dynamite, as black powder had been sold ninety years before, on consignment to agents. He knew little or nothing about the use of his product or the ultimate consumer, and he jealously guarded trade secrets, special customer lists, and hidden understandings. The sales department consisted of order takers who did the packing and shipping. The location of mills and the placement of magazines were a matter of guesswork; slow delivery gave a strong advantage to the neighborhood manufacturer.

Within three years Haskell and Barksdale had seized the opportunity to introduce systematization. They set up a holding company, called Eastern Dynamite, which included the Repauno, Hercules, and Atlantic Dynamite Companies, and took steps to ensure that improvements introduced into any one company were immediately introduced into the others. They were guided by the then pioneering criterion "low prices, large volume." Among innovations in the sales area were the appointment of a sales manager and the development of trade reports from the salesmen on customers and prospects. They also set up a sales service for large contractors to supply information on prospective construction and idle machinery and to provide supervisors and workmen if they were needed. On the technical side they mechanized wherever possible in order to reduce the number of accidents. Rather than learn exclusively by doing, they brought in scientists and other technically trained men and sometimes gave them time off to continue their studies. An experimental laboratory was set up, and in addition they began experimenting with a bonus system. Earnings quickly improved.

J. A. Haskell left the company in 1895, and seven years later, after the death of Eugene du Pont, the du Pont partners asked Barksdale, then forty-one, to become president of the Du Pont Company. He was the second man not named du Pont to receive such an honor in a hundred years. Barksdale refused, saying that only a du Pont should occupy the office. Then he was asked to negotiate the sale of the company to Laflin and Rand. It was at this point that Alfred I. du Pont dramatically intervened. Some months later, when Coleman du Pont heard of this, he roared, "Sell to Laflin and Rand! Well, here's an idea. Why not buy Laflin and Rand?" Coleman did—for $4,000 and bonds.

With the new spirit infused by the three cousins, Barksdale's plan for systematizing the management of Du Pont was reaffirmed. It was never terminated, so great was the impact of his work.

Barksdale was probably the single most important influence on the development of systematic management at Du Pont. He was a thinker and teacher of the first order. He believed in the value of each individual and the need to give the greatest possible opportunity for individual development. Therefore he strove to maintain freedom of opportunity for the individual, to give each man opportunity to realize himself through the display of initiative in coping with the problems at hand, and opportunity to qualify for ever-expanding responsibilities along the ladder of promotion. With these objectives in mind, Barksdale hired a good many of the young men who were later prominent in Du Pont or GM. He took a great personal interest in them and helped train them (in the ability to express themselves concisely and grammatically, among other things). He made possible their attendance at the management meetings, where he played a major role. And he advocated decentralization to provide the opportunity for development which he sought for Du Pont's young men.

Barksdale used the superintendents' meetings of the High Explosives Department (the operating department of Eastern Dynamite) as the medium for systematization. These HEOD meetings (referred to here as the High Explosives Group), as they were known, began on a small scale; in 1904 they were held monthly in Wilmington with only ten executives attending. A few years later they became large semiannual affairs. Originally they were devoted mainly to papers written by the chairman, Barksdale, and some of his associates. Later on the papers were prepared, printed, distributed, and read in advance, so that the meetings could be devoted to discussion. There was full participation, and disagreement was permitted. Eventually a disputed point would be embodied in a resolution and put to a vote. The decision was then binding on all participants.

Unfortunately, only the proceedings of the years 1909 to 1914 are available now, but they indicate that the hundred-odd papers must have been an extraordinary collection, one of the earliest expositions of systematic management. As illustrated below, there are advanced attempts at generalization based on observation and experience combined with *a priori* hypotheses, as well as papers dealing with the highly technical arts of powder making.[3]

Standardization of Best Experience

The principal impetus for the development of administrative thinking came from the lack of organization at Wilmington headquarters where "everybody mixed into everything," the independence of the various works and plants, the consequent lack of over-all objectives, and the possibility of duplication of facilities. "We started with the feeling of the superintendents that the conditions in their plants were peculiar to them; and relationships were impersonal," H. G. Haskell (J. A.'s brother) once said. This feeling of separateness became more pronounced as more plants were bought up and operations became more widely dispersed.

---

[3] The papers were divided into two categories, general, or qualitative, and statistical, or quantitative. A perusal of the voluminous private papers of J. A. Haskell from 1890 to 1925 reveals additional important insights into the process of management.

The early meetings of the High Explosives Group were devoted to the development of uniform objectives and policies and their effective coordination through standardization and control. Best practice was determined and written up as standard. The best, it was said, could be determined only by scientific trial. "How much better can we do?" was the underlying theme.

It is extraordinary how modern the titles of the papers and their contents sound today, fifty years later. As the major problems arose, a systematic approach was developed to solve them. At first, the greatest difficulty was the heavy loss of life and property through explosions. Following the basic rule, "No economy which is accomplished at the expense of safety should be considered at all," Barksdale and his men skillfully identified the causes of accidents and rates of injury. Precisely, through the use of statistics, they worked out the safe distances between powder mills, set them down in writing, and taught and enforced the most detailed and minute safety procedures. Each worker was searched for matches, at irregular intervals, and the findings were tabulated by plants, by seniority, and by the type of pants worn by the workers. Recognizing the importance of frameworks, or "engines of thinking," the group drew up abstract models as a basis for the solution of practical problems. For example, the vital subject of barricades strong enough to withstand explosions was treated in a scholarly paper on "The Theory of Barricades." (Some of the safety measures were refinements of early rules regulating powder yards going back as far as 1811.)

Barksdale next proceeded to an analysis of manufacturing methods, checking results through an advanced system of detailed comparisons of expenses, evaluated by refined statistical methods. At each meeting detailed operating reports were presented showing money saved or lost in each plant's operations; competitive comparisons of cost savings in different plants; explanation for divergences from standards; customer complaints; and the goals to be sought. The detailed comparisons appear to have formed the basis for Du Pont's present system of department reports and charts.

Even organization structures and manning tables for different-sized powder mills were drawn up, in terms of the ideal and the actual. Barksdale stressed "thorough instruction in all essential matters, no uncertainty as to whose duty it is to look after things." Gradually staff functions were separated from line functions and a clearinghouse was formed for an exchange of information. Engineering, chemical, works accounting, and finished-products departments were organized, and in 1911 a labor-efficiency department was set up. Technical problems that no plant could solve entirely by itself were discussed by "commissions" on nitroglycerine, machinery, and similar subjects, manned by the superintendents or their plant technical experts.

The second major contribution by Barksdale and his associates was their stress on the human factor. This concern was expressed in many papers dealing with problems of wages, work satisfaction, training, and safety. The employees' bonus system was launched in 1905 under Coleman's regime. He started salary surveys of Du Pont and outside executives in 1908, the use of psychological tests in 1910! In 1912 there was a fascinating paper by Dr. W. G. Hudson on "The Living Conditions of the Workmen," with lantern slides for illustration and a report on experiences in other companies to emphasize variations in conditions. Hudson raised and answered the question, "Why do men work?" and then asked constructively, "How can we help workmen?" He counseled that wage increases should not be considered a complete solution to workmen's problems, adding to the list of their requirements protection from accidents, greater purchasing power, steady employment through inventory accumulation, advancement and promotion, welfare plans, hospitals and doctors, and better use of spare time. The studies of working-class expenditure patterns of the U.S. Department of Labor were used as a base for determining the cost and the size of housing projects for employees.

In another paper in 1912 the Labor Efficiency Division set out four principles of "Scientific Management in Powder Making":

1. Find the best way to do a thing.
2. Make this way standard as to both method and time.
3. Teach employees how to reach the standard.

4. Give them the right incentive to do it.

(Shades of Job Methods Training thirty years later!) The author even showed how differences in the volume and character of the work made it necessary to modify scientific management when it was applied to office rather than production work.

In those meetings, too, some of the beginnings of the famous Du Pont bonus plans were developed. Bonuses were used as a means of disciplining the men in their general behavior and observance of rules, especially safety rules, and of holding the men from temporarily more lucrative employment. Most important, perhaps, was the expression of Barksdale's own reflections on a systematic approach to human relations. Space and absence of documents prohibit a detailed analysis of his thinking, but the following excerpts from the proceedings on the ever-present problem of communications will give some insight into the management philosophy of this remarkable man.

Before we part I want to talk to you a little while upon a side of our work which affects me personally. It isn't possible in so large an undertaking as we are carrying on for the individual upon whom rests the responsibility for directing the work to do anything more than direct in a general way. To go into details is impossible. He performs his duty best when he succeeds in working out an organization—a scheme of organization—and then placing in each position to be filled the best available man and then endeavoring to see that in a general way the objects sought for by the organization and by the personnel are achieved. . . . I know of no point at which there is failure, except to appreciate the full importance of cooperation, and unless that cooperation is achieved—the organization as a whole can't reach a full measure of success, and I, consequently, as an individual [will] fail. . . . To appreciate that importance [of cooperation] it is necessary for us to appreciate the magnitude of the operation ($1¼ to $1½ million per month cash expenditure). That expenditure takes place at a large number of points scattered from the Atlantic to the Pacific and from the Great Lakes practically to the Gulf. . . . I readily understand that men placed as superintendents must of necessity find it more difficult to get the broad point of view. I have been similarly placed —I have been in charge of important works far distant from headquarters. I have gone through all the sensations you gentlemen have. I have dubbed many things as red tape which I would not have considered as such if I had taken the broad view. I was performing my duties as well as I knew how. I was at them every working hour my strength would permit. I was being called upon for information and data that seemed to me quite unnecessary. . . .

Now it may be that these reports are unnecessary. A year ago we felt this might be the case and a committee was appointed to go into this and everything was eliminated that could be. I can readily understand that these reports cannot always be gotten off as the main office wants them to, but I don't understand why, when a man finds that he cannot do that, he doesn't come forward and say so and give the reasons, and not let the man who is 1,000 or 2,000 miles away, and trying his d—— to help in the work of successful operation of the plants, remain in total ignorance.

Personally, I am entirely satisfied that each superintendent who so departed from standard practice had a good reason for doing so. The mere fact that he had a good reason for doing it made it important from the standpoint of the welfare of all of us this reason be stated. We have accomplished what we have only by a combination of all our brains . . . combined experience and combined observations. It isn't possible to continue an organization as large as ours if the individuals are going to, without advice, without any explanation, depart from standard methods adopted. The whole object of the organization is to get cooperation, to get for each individual the benefit of all the knowledge and all the experience of all individuals. If it isn't accomplished, the organization is a failure, and that is where this thing hurts me. . . . I am going to make a personal plea to you gentlemen to make it a point to take the broad view, not to look upon your own plant as the only thing to which you can render assistance, but to place yourself more in the position of one of several who are working for a common end. If you will bear those points in mind . . . I certainly would appreciate it because I certainly don't want to make a failure.

CONTROL

Each HEOD meeting devoted much of its time to the presentation, comparison, and appraisal of results. The object of the "new accounting" was put in a remarkably modern form in the 1911 meeting:

In the first stage of development, recording was the only purpose of accounting, but at present that is only one of its features, and the most important purpose is to analyze the business and guide the management in its future policy and permit it to discover and remedy any unsatisfactory conditions which may exist. The object of accounting is to record expenditures in such a way that the cost of any division of the Company's business may be known and the profit and loss resulting from such division determined. The divisions may be general such as for departments only, or they may be refined so as to show the most minor operations.

Of the many accounting innovations and improvements, one of the most interesting was the "construction appropriations," developed in the ten years before World War I. Its object was described as follows:

Good business requires that some systematic method be followed in order that there may be no expenditures or additions to earning equipment if the same amount of money could be applied to some better purpose in another branch of the company's business.... Three things influence the Executive Committee in authorizing these expenditures—
1. Is the addition or improvement desirable?
2. Is the proposition submitted the best way of accomplishing the object desired?
3. Do financial conditions warrant investing money in it?

Other contributions were made in papers on "The Systematic Control of Materials," on tying wage increases to increases in yield, on labor cost analyses and savings, on purchase analysis, on the "systematic analysis of additional power consuming units," on profitable utilization of idle land, on analysis of administrative expenses, and so on. Each HEOD meeting ended with an especially popular session on "Complaints against the Wilmington Office."

It is not surprising that Harry G. Haskell, chairman of the 1912 meeting, summed up the results of HEOD as follows:

Some plants are born efficient, some achieve efficiency, and some have efficiency thrust upon them. What was an abbreviation [HEOD] now inspires respect and affection and stands for what is best at Du Pont. One is not considered transferred but promoted to HEOD. Where the Chair [Barksdale] used to do most of the lecturing and the superintendents the listening, the problem now is to stop the superintendents from talking.

ADAPTIVE MANAGEMENT, 1902–1921

As we have seen, the beginnings and development of systematic management at Du Pont can be clearly traced to the Repauno Chemical Company and its successor, the Eastern Dynamite Company. Its founders were Lammot du Pont, Sr., H. M. Barksdale, the two Haskell brothers, and their associates. This High Explosives Group had been set up separately from the parent company, and even though a part of the stock of the firm was owned by some of the du Ponts, this group and its management system had developed independently. The group had hired college graduates and had personally given them a thorough training in administration. It had developed management skills and made possible exchange of the best experience among managerial personnel. And it was this group that provided a large number of the executives on whom the three cousins drew to rebuild the Du Pont Company. Without these management pioneers the parent company might not have survived; certainly it could not have developed as it did.

It was to the great credit of the three cousins that they reorganized the company effectively and took over the ideas and the system of the High Explosives Group and gave many of its members outstanding opportunities. They brought in some of their own men and attracted others. They also contributed greatly to the improvement of the financial fortunes of their company through amalgamation and concentration, through integration and diversification into products other than explosives, and through new combinations in marketing and finance. Lack of space, lack of the original papers and records, and perhaps lack of sufficient historical perspective make it impossible to deal fully with the contributions of the three cousins. We can merely indicate the framework which they created for the development of systematic management in terms of their personalities and the change in corporate structure which they effected. The latter was one of the major contributions of the High Explosives Group and one or two newcomers; its theory and plan (but not the execution of it) will be dealt with in some detail to indicate the merger of the thinking of the pioneers and their successors. But in order to comprehend the background of the organizational change, and the framework and climate in which it was attempted, a word needs to be said about some of the top personalities at Du Pont in the first twenty years of this century.

And there is another reason for introducing the personality factor: no system, however good, is completely predictive and hence measurable. Intangibles always play a role, and their impact is determined by the nature of the personalities dominant at the time. Hence we may get a small insight into the nondeterministic element of the Du Pont management by picking out some of the relevant personality features.[4]

The principal figures of "adaptive management" during most of this period 1902 to 1921 were the following:

"The three cousins":

Coleman du Pont (president, 1902–1915) was prominent in overall direction, acquisition, and mergers with other firms. He operated successfully in the pattern of other trust builders of his time.

Pierre S. du Pont (treasurer, 1902–1915; vice president, 1915; president, 1915–1919) was the real guiding head of the company during most of the years under consideration. His principal contributions were in finance, long-range planning, and organization.

Alfred I. du Pont (vice president, 1902–1916) continued his interest in production and devoted himself largely to the direction of black-powder manufacture.

"The three brothers" (sons of Lammot du Pont, Sr.):

Irénée du Pont (president, 1919–1926) was the "visioneer" for the company.

[4] An even approximate analysis of the personalities of Du Pont's top executives must await the opening and release of the personal papers of these men. Furthermore, the Du Pont effort was a collective one, and it is impossible today to identify precisely the contributions of each member of the group or to mention them all.

Lammot du Pont (chairman of the executive committee, 1919–1921; president, 1926–1940) provided much of the leadership and was above all "operational." He applied and carried out the principles and plans of systematic administration.

(The third brother was Pierre, described above.)

Some associates:

Walter S. Carpenter, Jr. (prominent member of the executive committee) was the counselor and guide of product expansion.

John J. Raskob (personal assistant to Pierre and later treasurer) was the financial promoter and probably the most highly successful "assistant to" ever to work in an American company. As an example of his financial analysis and foresight, there may be cited his famous memorandum of Dec. 19, 1917, on the future use of Du Pont profits: "The United States holds greater possibilities for development in the immediate future than any country in the world.... An attractive investment is afforded in what I consider the most promising industry in the United States.... The General Motors Company with proper management will show results in the future second to none in any American industry." Against strong opposition, Raskob persuaded the du Ponts to put $25 million and a year later another $24 million into General Motors (an investment later worth $2.5 billion).

Donaldson Brown (treasurer, 1918–1921) played a major part in the development of financial principles and tools, such as the "rate of return" analysis of investment and the incremental approach to costing and pricing.

It was this group that initiated the consolidation and the rationalization of the powder business and, with others, guided it into the chemical business within two decades. Coleman du Pont began with an analysis of the operating companies and their merger with the firms affiliated with the Gunpowder Trade Association. His plan was for one supercompany holding them all, setting policies and fixing prices and eliminating uncertainty as far as possible. It was Coleman who formed new companies, absorbed others, manipulated the owners, swallowed still others as subsidiaries, and generally kept the industry astounded with the speed and finesse of his financial juggling.

Amalgamation of Going Concerns

Magical and effortless as the amalgamations of Du Pont with other powder companies might have appeared on the surface, they were carefully planned and executed. When the assets of Du Pont were acquired in 1902 and the first inventory in probably forty years was taken, it was found that the five companies were owned directly, comprising 40 per cent of total assets. Fifteen other companies were under the joint control of Laflin and Rand and Hazard, and those in turn controlled some further fifty-odd companies. A plan was drawn up to acquire as full control as possible of these minority and majority interests and then to acquire other strategic powder producers. Coleman kept a strategy chart in his office on which he checked off the various acquisitions as they occurred. To safeguard its current holdings, Du Pont bought up Laflin and Rand first. Then other powder concerns were acquired in rapid succession, until within a short time Coleman had acquired almost all the companies that were members of the Powder Association, including Repauno and Eastern Dynamite.

Integration

The second step was the efficient integration of these separate concerns. Each was run as an independent operating unit. Each had its own sources of supply; production facilities differed, and products varied in quality. Each had its own sales organization and branch offices. All that the Gunpowder Trade Association really did was to coordinate sales practices, which made it possible for all the duplication to survive. There was no attempt to improve products, to introduce new ones, or to do serious research ("it could always be bought in Europe"). Even the weakest could survive in this cartel arrangement, but its legality became doubtful after the passage of the Sherman Antitrust Act and the vigorous speeches of Theodore Roosevelt.

The most important step toward the integration of these different groups was undoubtedly the formulation of objectives and policies and the coordination of controls through the Du Pont executive committee of 1903, one of the earliest in any company. Its members were four du Ponts: Coleman (chairman), Pierre, Alfred, and Francis I. (still under thirty and a brilliant chemist), J. A. Haskell, H. M. Barksdale, and A. J. Moxham, Coleman's old mentor (described as "an old-fashioned, homely type of capitalist, who carried an umbrella on sunny days and put his money to one hundred uses"). Members of the executive committee were vice presidents and served on the board of directors. Coleman formed the executive committee to encourage executive participation and coordination. With his change of interest and illness a few years later, the power of the executive committee rose, and slowly it made an increasing number of decisions, while the president merely recommended changes in policies. From the very beginning of its existence the committee ended sole control by one member of the du Pont family.

The executive committee began by making general the policies, practices, and procedures developed at Repauno and established later by Barksdale and his associates through the HEOD. Essentially these were put into effect by establishing central staffs, which developed the policies and controls that were enforced through the president and executive committee. Much of its work during these years was codified in the Du Pont "bible" or "how to" manual. For example, a central sales board was established which set up price schedules and rigidly enforced them, ending price cutting, rebates, secret agreements, and so on. Industrial explosives were now sold for different specific needs. Agents were superseded by the company's own salesmen, assisted by technical experts who helped customers in installations and by the promotion of multiple usage, safety, and economy. A Trade Record Bureau was set up centrally, and each cartridge of dynamite or pound of powder sold anywhere had to be reported in duplicate to this bureau so that continuous analysis could be made of actual and potential sales to each customer.

Another staff department of growing importance was research. Repauno's Eastern Laboratory (founded in 1902) and the Experimental Station (1903) hired outstanding chemists and pioneered important contributions to more effective powder. Location of plants, production efficiency, standardization, simplification, safety, and cost reductions were promoted toward a high degree of uniformity by Alfred I. du Pont and his staff in black powder, by J. A. Haskell in smokeless powder, and by Barksdale in high explosives.

Development

The third major Du Pont innovation was J. E. Moxham's establishment of the Development Department. Its first head was W. B. Dwinnell, who was followed by Irénée du Pont, R. R. M. Carpenter, and W. S. Carpenter, Jr. Its task was to find new outlets for the products of Du Pont factories and to make the company independent of, or at least less dependent on, outside sources of supply. (Du Pont was among the first to initiate purchase analysis, with the rule that if someone else could manufacture more cheaply than Du Pont in the long run, it would buy rather than make.) The Development Department was also to go beyond explosives into fields that could logically be entered with currently available technology and manpower. One of the guiding rules at that time was that the company preferred to buy a going concern rather than start from the beginning. The acquisition of the International Smokeless Powder and Chemical Company in 1903 provided Du Pont with its first nonexplosives business because of International's diversification into lacquers. But this aspect of the acquisition was an accident. Actually, it was in 1908, when Du Pont had excess nitrocellulose capacity, that Coleman appointed a committee to investigate ways and means of disposing of larger amounts of nitrocellulose for nonexplosive use. It was on this committee's recommendation that the firm in 1910 purchased the Fabricoid Company, the country's largest artificial-leather concern, to absorb the surplus nitrocellulose.

When Du Pont lost an antitrust suit begun in 1907, which culminated in the 1912 dissolution order, the parent firm was resolved into three (Du Pont, Hercules, and Atlas) and its growth in explosives was curtailed. As Lammot du Pont explained: "The dissolution was notice to the Du Pont Company that it could not expand in the explosives field, having already been dissolved for being too large, and that was a very powerful influence for branching out into other lines." As it began to branch out, Du Pont's basic policies were (1) the entry into new fields or old ones with a prospect of improvement, (2) the accompaniment of Du Pont dollars with Du Pont–trained men, and (3) investment aimed frequently at ownership or control.

World War I added greatly to the pressures for diversification. The company acquired huge surplus funds for investment because of its great sales expansion, and the executive committee felt it would "be able to invest [those funds] for greater benefits to our stockholders than by handing them out as a dividend and having these stockholders try and invest it for themselves." The company also was looking for utilization of likely excess capacity. As Raskob put it, "After the war it will be absolutely impossible for us to drop back to being a little company again; and to prevent it, we must look for opportunities, know them when we see them, and act with courage." The company was also anxious to utilize its expanded staffs. According to Irénée du Pont, "We had trained personnel, and we were in a position with the know-how we had ... to find industries to which we could contribute something and utilize the personnel which we had trained, especially the upper brackets of the company." There were many other advantages for Du Pont in diversification, such as economies of buying, acquisition of new markets, and so on. Finally, an economist was added to the staff during World War I in recognition of the growing interdependence of the firm with the national economy.

Organization

But the very attempt at readjustment, diversification, and further expansion on top of the great wartime growth led to serious organizational problems. The Du Pont losses on diversification were heavy soon after each acquisition. From 1917 to 1921 the company lost $18 million on dyestuffs, $2.4 million on paints ("The more paint and varnish we sold, the more money we lost"), $2.5 million on lead and pigments, $2.1 million on chemicals, and $5 million on artificial leather (1920–1921 only). In addition, in November, 1920, General Motors came to the verge of bankruptcy. Of course, the change from inflationary expansion to deflation was a major cause of trouble. But the basic difficulty was the lack of adjustment of organization to growth. This was the conclusion of the company's subcommittee on organization, reporting to the executive committee, Mar. 19, 1919, as follows:

It must be recognized, that while adopting the principle that all major decisions on organization are made by the president, we have defeated the principle to a partial extent by allowing the Executive Committee to act for the president as the immediate superior in an executive way to whom the department heads are held responsible. [Members of the Executive Committee running line departments found it difficult to avoid a parochial view.] The interposition of a committee charged with the duty of performing executive acts better done by an individual is, we believe, responsible for most of the minor inefficiencies, inconveniences, wasted effort and unnecessary duplication, which are matters of common knowledge to those engaged in carrying out the daily routine. These are usually small matters with relation to the business as a whole, and for this reason rarely impose themselves on the attention of the higher officers. Nevertheless, in the aggregate they are of no mean importance.

In establishing from time to time certain departments more or less inflexibly defined, we have forced the company's business into artificial channels instead of arranging that the business could adapt itself to what might be described as its natural course. It makes no difference that when the limits were fixed they were truly the best limits, for owing to the law of change of all living things, necessarily those limits would be different the next minute. Since our business is a large one, all sorts of expedients have been resorted to in the way of compensations, and parts of departments have unofficially overflowed their fixed and theoretical boundaries. But this usually did not occur until conditions became intolerable.

As an analogy, if we imagine that at some date the company's different units were defined and assigned a certain office space, and thereafter left for two or three years to their own devices except as to office space, what would happen? Certain units would grow to a greater degree than the others and the result would be that the stronger, larger units would stay within their office limits as long as possible, and then beg, borrow, or steal space from other departments. No one would be entirely satisfied, and the distribution of space under these conditions would be unlikely to be the most economical arrangement. This, in a different way, is somewhat the experience of the artificially created and permanently fixed and limited departments. Change and growth have taken place constantly and when the channels were full they burst their bounds.

We must not lose sight of the fact that the last four years have been emergency years and that departments as well as individuals have gone out of their way and exceeded their natural duties. Furthermore, the conditions were such that there was no time for ordinary savings and business efficiencies, for the reason that those would be far less than the profits represented by a small increase in production. . . . Our task is now to handle the [fixed] volume of business with the greatest economy.

The subcommittee's recommendations, set down in two reports, were based largely on the thinking and experience of Donaldson Brown, F. W. Pickard, H. G. Haskell, and W. C. Spruance, and their colleagues at Du Pont. Visits to the top executives of U.S. Steel, Westinghouse, International Harvester, Armour, and Wilson & Co. also influenced them. The resulting documents may well be the most complete exposition of organization principles made up to that time; they were certainly more systematic and better tested than the work of Taylor, Gantt, or Gilbreth, the pioneers of scientific management. The Du Pont principles applied to the top levels of management as well as to the supervisory level. Some of the thinking appears to be pioneering even today. Most basic, perhaps, was the linkage of the object of organization, defined as "the process of disposing or arranging constituent or inter-dependent parts into an organic whole" with "the attainment of maximum results with minimum effort." This linkage between economics and organization is frequently overlooked today, when organizations are often judged in terms of organizational "principles" based on the apparent orderliness of the charts, or in terms of rules of thumb drawn from other companies, or in terms of sociological or human-relations objectives. The originality of the Du Pont organization objective was that it rested on the accomplishment of the most efficient results at least expense through a process of organization which is made operational, or economic, in the following criteria, summarized from the documents developed by the committee on organization.

First Criterion: Coordination of Economically or Market-Related Effort

The basic "industries" or principal subdivisions of work at Du Pont should be arranged through *coordination of related effort and segregation of unrelated effort.*

As the authors of the organization memoranda put it:

It is often more necessary to combine related efforts which are unlike. For example, in developing business, such as dye stuffs, before it was more or less standardized, it is decidedly wise to have one individual in control of both production and sales, because the relation of the product and its qualities is so mixed up with the demand of the market for the product that to divorce them and segregate the business into a clearly defined production department and an independent sales department would be detrimental to the business.... While the production of dyes is quite unlike the sale of dyes, nevertheless the union between them is so close that union is *more economical* than segregation.

The Du Pont organizers effectively opposed the notion of putting all like things together, often advocated on the ground that duplication is eliminated in this way:

For instance, it is natural to think that all engineers and engineering work should be grouped in an engineering department. Now surveying a farm, designing and building a bridge, running a locomotive, or operating a power house are all "engineering," but it is quite obvious that they are so unrelated that to group them under one head would be uneconomical.

Instead of the usual functional organization of production, sales, purchasing, and so on, five manufacturing departments were set up; a general manager had full responsibility and authority for results in his own department.

Second Criterion: Undivided Responsibility

A unit once defined—for example, the Sales Department or a plant or branch office—is placed in charge of the best available individual, who as head of that department has direct and complete authority and is held *responsible for results*. He can in his official capacity arrange every detail in his department according to his best judgment, subject only to the alternative of having someone replace him if his official judgment is not good.

Third Criterion: Clearly Defined Superior-
    Subordinate Relationships

The relation of officials to each other should be such that each shall have undivided authority over those subordinate to him, and conversely each official, be he high or low, subject to some officer next higher up, until a single head is reached ... subject only to the business being conducted according to the principles and methods laid down by the authority higher up.

Influenced by Barksdale's management concepts the sub-committee concluded that a decentralized form of organization was most suitable, with both responsibility and necessary authority delegated down the line.

Fourth Criterion: Drawing Economic Advantages of
    Specialization from Centralized Staff Services

Directors of staff should be able to establish and maintain general policies, procedures and correlation of the functional activities of like-named units of the departmental organizations to a degree sufficient to insure proper uniformity and efficiency.... It is assumed that advisory functional staff officials will employ periodical and special meetings of appropriate officials of the line departments to establish and maintain general policies and procedures,... passed on to Executive Committee,... and [will] discuss and advise regarding special major problems....

The Service [staff] Department [is] responsible for the conduct of the special duties which are common to two or more of the line departments and which for purposes of economy and efficient control are to be performed by [the] Service Department for and in a manner satisfactory to the Line Department.... Their activities would be governed by established procedures and policies and any radical departure would require the prior consent of appropriate officers in the interested line departments.

Thus eight general or staff departments were set up, each of which was characterized by closely related activities.

Fifth Criterion: "Rate-of-Return" Criterion of Unit's Performance

The proposed type of organization affords more direct and logical control of the investment of Working Capital [separated for each department].... Monthly reports would reach the Executive Committee directly from the General Manager, each report covering all matters pertaining to a given industry.

The executive committee would act somewhat like a banker in appraising loan applications and watching their use. It would request budget information from each departmental general manager regarding his projected profit on the total investment in his department, broken down by different sales categories and types of expenses, varying with volume. The executive committee would compare promise and fulfillment, forecasted and actual rate of profits to investment, and promotions and bonuses would be partly determined thereby.

Sixth Criterion: Ultimate Control by Group Management

The Board of Directors governs all the Company's affairs and lays down the policies and principles to be followed in the conduct of the business. Our Board is too large and diversified to function as an executive body, and therefore selects from its members a few who comprise an Executive Committee of the Board to represent and act for it, carrying out the details of general policy laid down by the Board and in general functioning for it and subject to its approval from time to time. The Executive Committee should be comprised of those members of the Board most conversant with the details and daily needs of the Company's business. The proper function of such an Executive Committee is to exercise general supervision over the Company's affairs, to decide all questions of policy, and in general to act in the Board's stead.

The members of the executive committee were divorced from the departments, except in an advisory capacity: "They are to be free to give all their time and effort to the business of the Company as a whole so that they will be able to consider all questions and problems without bias or prejudice." Individual membership on the executive committee was fairly long, and new members came up from inside the company. Thus the viewpoint of the company as a whole was confined to coordination of its varied interests and to the adaptation of policy to change. This was distinguished from the specialized departmental viewpoint, which looked at an industry's specific needs and special problems in a particular field. There has been no fundamental change in this organization concept.

Seventh Criterion: Knowledge of General Business Principles Requisite for a General Manager

The objection has been advanced that some of the grand divisions are too large and too diversified to be under the control of one individual. The answer is that the controlling individual need know not every detail of the business, but requires only a good mind, sound judgment and knowledge of general business principles. He will never have occasion at one time to need to know all conditions—what he will have to do will be to examine the facts affecting certain portions of his domain and make his decisions accordingly. It is no more impossible to find such a man than it is impossible to select a man for Justice of the Supreme Court on the ground that no one can have knowledge of all the cases that are likely to come before him.

Eighth Criterion: Multiple Truths in Management

On many points differences of opinion arose [among members of the subcommittee] and in fact many things can be done in more than one fashion without loss of efficiency.

Ninth Criterion: Adaptation to Change

The organization of a company should be sufficiently elastic to adapt itself to the needs of the business, as fast as those needs assert themselves.

Since the character of effort throughout the company is continuously changing, the authority to correlate effort should be sufficient, and should be available all the time.

Tenth Criterion: The "Ideal Organization"

The ideal condition is one in which every unit or group is so coordinated and controlled that each functions to the best advantage with respect to its own work and the work of the whole Company....Each unit should be so organized as to contribute to total organic unity.

Referring to these principles and the detailed organization charts and job descriptions, Pierre S. du Pont as president wrote to the board of directors of the "new form of organization carefully thought out and based upon past experience." Interestingly, he separated the question of "form or relationships" from "the selection of individuals for the performance of selected duties" and urged that the selection of the personnel of the two top committees (executive and finance) should precede the final determination of the form of organization.

SOME RESULTS, 1902–1921

The period 1900 to 1904 witnessed Du Pont's greatest growth in terms of assets (with the exception of the founding years 1811–1814), while the period 1915 to 1919 was the second fastest in growth. Income accounts for 1904 to 1912 (before the dissolution of the powder trust) and for 1916 showed tremendous advances (Table 2-1).

TABLE 2-1

Year	Gross receipts (millions of dollars)	Net earnings	Accumulated surplus	Dividends (% of common stock)
1904	26.1	4.4	5.0	.5
1912	34.5	6.5	15.1	12
1916	318.8	82.0	28.6	100

In the early years, 1902 to 1909, Du Pont put its earnings largely into over thirty acquisitions, valued at about $43 million. The wartime performance was astonishing largely because capacity was multiplied more than twelve times in two years.

"The Du Pont Company is entitled to the credit of saving the British Army," said General Hedlam, chief of the British Munitions Board. On Mar. 7, 1918, Moody's Investor's Service commented: "Admittedly the war brides [munitions and other war shares] look a little fagged and worn after their lively downhill honeymoon of 1917, but they are apt to look a great deal more fagged when peace comes, and hundreds of other managements begin following the example of the Du Pont powder."

The immense earnings of 1915 to 1918 ($213 million) made possible participation in GM and many chemical ventures. By the end of the World War I period, John J. Raskob could truthfully say that Du Pont was now the biggest financial industrial aggregation in the United States.

Most noteworthy for managerial evaluation was Pierre S. du Pont's comment in 1918 that of the ten members of the executive committee and the six department heads, supported by ninety-four assistants, nearly 90 per cent had advanced themselves during the four years of war and "none has failed to make good at the work allotted to him." Most of the top Du Pont executives in 1919 ranged in age from thirty-five to forty-five! And in January, 1921, the principal top executives of General Motors were all Du Pont men (P. S. du Pont, J. J. Raskob, J. A. Haskell, J. L. Pratt, E. F. Johnson, and D. Brown), with the exception of Alfred P. Sloan, Jr., and C. S. Mott.) Finally, in 1922, P. S. du Pont reported that "the new [decentralized] organization is definitely yielding very good results."

CONCLUSIONS: ONE REASON FOR DU PONT'S SUCCESS

If one were to select any *one* major reason for Du Pont's success, it would clearly be the group aspect of its management. A closer examination would show, however, that it was not group work *per se* that made for Du Pont's success. It was not simply that a group of men got together in a democratic manner, showed a lot of good will, worked high-mindedly toward some ideal goals, communicated them to others, and permitted a large amount of participation on the part of those concerned in reaching these goals. On the other hand, it was definitely not the "great man theory" that prevailed or the rugged individualist "Caesar" type of management that put the company on a long-run successful basis. While some of both elements were present, it was a much more complex and sophisticated set of conditions that made for Du Pont's success. There is a near analogy to the Du Pont objective of the "organic unity of all its parts." It would perhaps be appropriate to liken Du Pont's group management and its efficiency to the biological efficiency of collective life. In the origin of life

sometime, somewhere, a few cells stuck together and formed a colony with a community of interests, a sort of *collective egotism*. With regard to other living beings, the community still behaved like an egotist; but it was in the interest of each cell within this colony that the other members also had to strive, because the strength of the whole depended upon all its parts.... In the course of the struggle for survival, cells found it useful not only to stay together but to rely ever more upon each other. Eventually, large numbers of them learned even to share a single life.[5]

A number of definable elements and conditions were essential to the successful group approach at Du Pont. Among these elements were the development of a philosophical approach and the quality of adaptability. There seemed to be two main strands in Du Pont's philosophical approach—rationalist and pragmatic.

The rationalistic approach was of French heritage through Pierre Samuel du Pont de Nemours, physiocrat, economist, and statesman, father of the company's founder, Eleuthère Irénée. He passed on through his successors the methods and ideals of the writers of the Enlightenment. The efforts of the French *philosophes* to reduce all problems to scientific terms; their belief in reason, observation, and

[5] Hans Selye, *The Stress of Life,* McGraw-Hill Book Company, Inc., New York, 1956, pp. 282–283.

experiment; their clear formulation of central principles and application of them to concrete situations; their war against obscurantism and irrationalism; their search for the truth, sometimes narrow and pedestrian but always confident and fanatically honest; the lucid prose in which they expressed themselves—all this he admired, made his own, and passed on. Lammot, Sr., Pierre S. du Pont, and Barksdale were the outstanding examples of the rationalist approach in the period we have been considering.

This rationalist approach was balanced with the pragmatic approach of attention to, and examination of, the concrete results of action. The pragmatic method is really an attempt to interpret each notion by tracing its practical consequences. William James asked, "What difference would it practically make to anyone if this notion rather than that notion were true? . . . What experiences will be different from those which would obtain if the belief were false? What is truth's cash-value in experiential terms?" His answers are to be found in a number of general concepts:

1. *Common sense:* "Our fundamental ways of thinking about things are discoveries of remote ancestors."

2. *Adaptation to reality:* "Our theories are instrumental rather than revelations."

3. *Truth:* "Truth is made up largely out of previous truths, experience funded, the sum total of experience, and becomes matter for the next day's funding operations . . . everlastingly in the process of mutation. . . . The true is that which works."

4. *Verification:* "Direct face-to-face verifications. . . . All things exist in kinds and not singly."

The criteria of action developed in the pragmatic approach are thus based on the principle of experience. "The mere fact that things have been found in experience to be thus and thus gives a valid reason for holding that they will continue to be thus and thus for the time being." [6] Hence the validity of commonsense business decisions depends on the validity of inductive inferences, that is, upon arguing logically from experience.

[6] Roy Harrod, *Foundations of Inductive Logic,* The Macmillan Company, London, 1956, p. 56.

The du Ponts have always had a strong tendency to adhere to values learned from experience. Hence they have thrown their influence against deductive notions not substantiated by experience. Yet the management held on to the basic rationalist fundamentals, such as the rules and standards of private capitalism; the physiocratic belief in a large and growing "net product" promoted by "natural laws" of competition; the identification of risk and control. ("There where the risk lies there also lies the control.") These standards were applied both to the untrammeled conduct of the enterprise and to the supervision of its investments. The rational calculus of return on investment was a basis for choosing among alternatives; the attempt was to maintain organic unity within the system and between different systems. Mutuality of public and private interests was rationalized on the experience and needs theory of the Physiocrats.[7] These fundamentals served as a framework for criteria of management and organization which were developed rationally, founded on and verified by experience.

Again, it was experience in relation to standards of accomplishment which determined management development and management succession. Thus at Du Pont the words "Many are called, but few are chosen" are particularly appropriate. Rather than permit the fairly indiscriminating participation advocated by many of the believers in the cooperative process, the du Ponts carefully selected and trained for leadership. The charge of nepotism is not often leveled at them, and yet the family's survival in business leadership for so many generations has not been explained adequately. A parallel might be drawn with a constitutional monarchy. The chances of capable leadership are on the whole better than the odds in an autocracy; the dictators succeeding Caesars often do so on nothing more than the worst form of Machiavellianism. But the du Pont principles of selection for leadership are superior to the simple one of automatic succession of the eldest son. In order to be

---

[7] N. J. Ware, "The Physiocrats: A Study in Economic Rationalization," *American Economic Review*, 1931, pp. 607–619. There exists a fascinating correspondence between P. S. du Pont and A. J. Moxham on the ideas of the Physiocrats in relation to Henry George.

accepted it was usually necessary for a du Pont to have studied physical science at one of the top universities in the country. Out of some one hundred potential competitors, only those du Ponts who attained a degree had a long-run chance in the company. A substantial number were then eliminated by the test of job performance. A program of cross-fertilization, or directed movement of family and nonfamily personnel, among different functions and product departments tested potential leadership; also, candidates were often given varied assignments in manufacturing, sales, and research or served as line and staff officers, as "assistants to" and "assistant managers." They tried out, and benefited from, the counsel of older men with differing ideas regarding different types of management. It was originally Barksdale's idea that the work of a manager could be established only by trying him out in different groups and not permitting him to take his staff with him.

Yet even after this rigorous selection process there were additional requirements for belonging to the inner ring, the finance and executive committees. The basic requirement may be summed up as "homogeneity of outlook and heterogeneity of ability." The latter requires different types of technical competence. The former could be acquired only by long association with Du Pont management and by the acceptance of rationalist and pragmatic management principles tied in turn to profitability, the ability to adapt to changing experience, and a belief in the traditions of the family that proudly counted not only business leaders and scientists among its forebears but even had its own martyrs, notably Lammot, Sr., and Alexis du Pont. Tradition has carried down to the present generation the maxims of the founder Eleuthère Irénée, as set out in his twelve volumes of letters, such as perfect workmanship, absolute honesty, courtesy to all, a lively sense of trading, the 20 per cent rate of return to be aimed at over the life of an investment, etc.

In the years 1902 to 1921 there was an increasingly large group of du Ponts to draw upon for developing executive talent, since the various branches of the family were large and intermarriage frequent. Able executives married into the family and in this way increasingly obtained equal consideration with those bearing the du Pont name. There was also, in those years at least, some degree of homogeneity in the personalities of the Du Pont management. Common to all of them was a *vocation*, a devotion to the company. Jung [8] describes vocation as an "irrational factor that destines a man to emancipate himself from the herd and from its well-worn paths. True personality is always a vocation and puts its trust in it as in God.... He *must* obey his own law, as if it were a demon whispering to him of new and wonderful paths."

Another common characteristic of members of the top Du Pont committees was a high degree of extroversion—a keen interest in events, people, and things; motivation by outside factors; and the tendency to be influenced by environment. But different types of extroverts contributed to Du Pont committee deliberations. Thus the "extroverted intuitive" type was perhaps best personified by Coleman du Pont. As Jung said of this type:

He dislikes anything that is safe, familiar or well-established. He is no respecter of custom, and is often ruthless about other people's feelings or convictions when he is on the scent of something new; everything is sacrificed to the future.... He often looks like a ruthless adventurer, but he has, in fact, his own morality based on his loyalty to his intuitive view. For him not to "take a chance" is simply cowardly or weak,... yet it is almost impossible for him to carry a thing beyond the point where success is established.

Among other Du Pont executives the "thinking extrovert" dominated, as for example in Pierre S. du Pont:

He undertakes most important actions on the basis of motives intellectually or rationally conceived. He orients himself on hand of objective facts [that is, he has a factual approach] or generally valid ideas. This set of principles and facts serves as yardstick for most actions.

[8] In the following I have drawn on and quoted from the studies of C. G. Jung, "The Development of Personality," Bollingen Series XX, Bollingen Foundation, Inc., New York, and *Psychologische Typen*, Zurich, 1950, pp. 451–558. While there are, of course, no pure types in real life, Jung's analysis has been helpful in describing some of the psychological characteristics of business leaders at Du Pont, 1902 to 1921.

Thus the du Ponts and their associates from High Explosives made great and original contributions to the advancement of systematic management in the first twenty years of this century. Their thinking and plans were based on a combination of general principles and lessons drawn from experience. The execution of their work was undertaken by carefully selected men who reached powerful positions at a young age, who had the incentives of family tradition and highly tempting individual rewards, who had mastered some of the art of successful group work, who retained much that was good in the old-line entrepreneur method of operation, who were guided by a mission, and who passed on their fortunes, their ideas, and their young men to build the biggest industrial empire of the first quarter of this century.

BIBLIOGRAPHY AND SOURCES

Brown, Donaldson, and W. C. Spruance: "Du Pont Organization Study," Wilmington, 1920 (typewritten).
────── et al.: "Report of the Sub-committee on Organization," Wilmington, 1919 (typewritten), including H. F. Brown.
du Pont, Bessie Gardner: *E. I. du Pont de Nemours and Company: A History, 1802–1902*, Houghton, Mifflin Company, Cambridge, Mass., 1920.
du Pont, E. I. de Nemours and Co: *Annual Reports*, Baltimore, 1904–1922.
HEOD *Superintendents' Meetings*, 1909–1914.
du Pont, Philip F., et al., v. Pierre S. du Pont et al., record of the suit over the so-called Coleman du Pont stock, 1915–1919.
du Pont, Pierre S.: Testimony before the U.S. District Court, in Civil Action No. 49 C–1071, *United States of America v. E. I. du Pont de Nemours & Company, General Motors Corporation, et al.*, U.S. District Court for the Northern District of Illinois, Eastern Division, Chicago, 1953 (stenographic reports).
Dutton, William S.: *Du Pont: One Hundred and Forty Years*, Charles Scribner's Sons, New York, 1942.
Harrod, Roy: *Foundations of Inductive Logic*, The Macmillan Company, London, 1956.
James, Marquis: *Alfred I. du Pont: The Family Rebel*, The Bobbs-Merrill Company, Inc., New York, 1941.
James, William: *Pragmatism*, Longmans, Green & Co., Inc., New York, 1943.

Jung, C. G.: "The Development of Personality," Bollingen Series XX, Bollingen Foundation, Inc., New York, 1954.

———: *Psychologische Typen*, Zürich, 1950.

Kerr, George, H.: *Du Pont Romance*, Wilmington, 1939.

Lundberg, Ferdinand: *America's Sixty Families*, Vanguard Press, Inc., New York, 1934.

Malone, Dumas (ed.): *Correspondence between Thomas Jefferson and Pierre Samuel du Pont de Nemours, 1798–1817*, Houghton Mifflin Company, Boston, 1930.

Mueller, W. F.: "Du Pont: A Study in Firm Growth," unpublished doctor's dissertation, Vanderbilt University, Nashville, Tenn., 1955 (microfilm).

United States v. E. I. du Pont de Nemours & Co. et al., record of the Sherman Antitrust Act suit, 1907–1912.

Van Gelder, Arthur P., and Hugo Schlatter: *History of the Explosives Industry in America*, Columbia University Press, New York, 1927.

Wertenbaker, Charles: "Du Pont," *Fortune*, Nov. 10, 1934, pp. 65–75, 198–207, 213.

Winkler, John K: *The Du Pont Dynasty*, Reynal & Hitchcock, Inc., New York, 1935.

3

Contributions to
Organization and Administration [1]
by Alfred P. Sloan, Jr., and GM

> "Oh Youth! The strength of it, the faith of it, the imagination of it...."
>
> JOSEPH CONRAD, *Youth*

One of the best examples of a solution to the problems confronting the successors of founding geniuses is seen in the work of Alfred P. Sloan, Jr., former president and later board chairman of the General Motors Corporation and his principal associates.

The founder who preceded Sloan at GM, in the years 1916 to 1920, was William C. Durant. By dint of his financial flair and

[1] I have drawn on the reflections of and interviews with Donaldson Brown, Walter S. Carpenter, Jr., Irénée and Pierre S. du Pont, R. S. McLaughlin, James D. Mooney, Charles S. Mott, John L. Pratt, Alfred P. Sloan, Jr., George Whitney, and Charles E. Wilson. The contributions to administrative theory and practice made by GM in the early 1920's were, to a large extent, the result of a group effort.

sales-promotion ability, Durant brought together a large number of enterprises.

One of his acquisitions was the Hyatt Roller Bearing Company, purchased in 1916 for $13.5 million, and with it he acquired the services of Alfred P. Sloan, Jr. At Durant's request, Sloan became president of United Motors, a service company that provided accessories for GM. United Motors was absorbed into GM in 1918; later that year Sloan became vice president in charge of a group of accessories divisions [2] and shortly after that a director of the corporation and a member of its executive committee.

Durant and Sloan respected each other and had in common an unbounded faith in the future of the automobile business. Their outlook and management philosophies were quite different, but perhaps because of this very fact they complemented each other in a unique way. Durant was the man who invented the idea of General Motors, but it was Sloan and his associates who made it work.

Durant carried his business information in his head. He worked by hunch, intuition, and brilliant flashes of insight. He had vivid imagination, foresight, and charm. Many of his ideas were pathbreaking; often his results were outstanding; but he was prone to error because of hasty and inadequate analyses of facts. While Sloan and his group did not disdain risk taking and chance (in cases where the ultimate uncertainty could not be removed), they believed in the factual approach to the solution of business problems.

Durant used largely a "one-man" method of making major decisions, and he preferred executives who agreed with him. He might never forgive a man who, like Walter Chrysler, crossed him in public. Sloan, on the other hand, believed that General Motors had to be a group organization. He was one of the first to realize that the major obstacle to organization growth is the limited capacity of management and that, as companies increase in size,

[2] Specifically, Sloan had charge of the divisions that sold parts and accessories to outside companies as well as to GM. Another group of parts divisions sold only to GM.

problems of coordination, communication, and outside representation increase faster than the ability to cope with them. Sloan felt that one-man control was vitiated by the excessive danger of mistakes it entailed; he recognized that no human being can be infallible. He felt that each executive, including the man at the top, must realize that he needs help and that every person in a position to make a contribution, or to obstruct, should be consulted before a decision is made. Where Durant relied on personal loyalty and personal inspiration, Sloan tried to enlist *all* executives in a real partnership in the interests of the corporation as a whole —by utilizing their abilities to the full, by a fair policy of promotion, by offering real incentives, and by using persuasion rather than command.

Durant placed emphasis on finance and maximum sales; one of his associates recalls that he appeared to think of volume of sales as an end in itself, more important than profits. Sloan realized the necessity for balance and the wisdom of attempting to achieve optimum results for all those connected with the corporation. Where Durant went so far as to counsel certain individual investors to add to their GM holdings, Sloan gave each inquiring stockholder a professional reply. He held that a director should represent the interests of all the stockholders as distinct from any segmented group, which was also the Du Pont concept. (Planned stockholder relations were initiated when Sloan found one day that Durant was issuing statements to the stockholders and the public without certification by outside public accountants, a practice Durant later agreed to stop. Sloan also set an example with the detailed and professional annual reports he issued.)

Durant's qualities were highly effective in the early days of General Motors. Its growth was fostered by the flexibility and informality encouraged by his method of doing business. And the mistakes that occasionally resulted were more than compensated for by the seemingly continuous growth of automobile demand and the upward phase of the business cycle.

After some years of Durant's management, chinks began to

appear in the armor of General Motors. This occurred when the difficulties of readjustments after World War I were imposed on a less than first-class management.

One of Durant's major shortcomings was his failure to understand how accounting could be used to improve performance. One of his associates, John Lee Pratt, has said:

No one knew how much money had been appropriated. There was no control on how much money was spent. Durant's executive committee consisted of the plant managers and when one of them had a project, he would get the vote of his fellow members; if they would vote for his project, he would vote for theirs. It was a sort of horse-trading. In addition, if they didn't get enough money, when Durant visited the plant, he would tell them to go on and spend what they needed without any record being made.[3]

A second shortcoming of Durant's later management was the lack of inventory control. As John Lee Pratt explains it: "Durant set up a 'correlation committee,' but there was practically nothing in the way of correlation." The only record of purchases might be the suppliers' invoices in the plant managers' pockets.

As the automobile business expanded rapidly (especially between 1918 and 1920), GM division managers started to hoard materials in anticipation of an even greater demand during the latter part of 1920; they made long forward commitments and incurred more and more debt. There were no statistics to show them how inventory stood in relation to demand, or how prices should behave in relation to supply and demand. Sloan recalls:

Prices were largely determined by the initiative of the different managers. ... I remember one executive committee meeting at which one division manager said to another, "I see you raised your price $150 the other day." The other one said "yes," and the first one said, "I guess I'll do the same thing tomorrow."

---

[3] One of the contributions of Walter P. Chrysler to the Buick division was the introduction of better accounting. He borrowed Du Pont's controller and assistant controller for that purpose.

When the inflation turned rapidly into deflation, much of the raw material could not be used. Furthermore, a part of the inventory was not appropriate for the kind of cars needed in the changing markets. There were no field reports of car sales, and production was left to the discretion of each manager. Reduction of surplus materials and write-offs from property disposals resulted in a large loss and dangerously high bank debts.

Thirdly, Durant failed to take expert advice, especially technical counsel. Engineering, general construction, and precision of most of the car lines were poor. He made major errors in investment. Some acquisitions were largely gambles, because Durant was not sure which course the industry was taking. The Elmore Manufacturing Company was purchased in 1909 for over half a million dollars because "maybe a two-cycle motor was going to be the thing for automobiles." Seven years later GM sold this company for $50,000. (Nearly thirty years later, GM applied the two-cycle principle to diesel engines and in a short time became the world's largest supplier of diesels.) Durant invested $140,000 in the Carter Car Company, because it had a patented friction drive; it proved to be a total loss. The Scripps-Booth car division bought in 1918 or 1919 was liquidated in 1923 or 1924; the Sheridan car project was also liquidated. The Sampson Tractor Company had to be sold in 1921 at a loss of $12 million, written off because the concept and price of the tractor were wrong. A contract was negotiated with the President of Mexico to drill oil in Mexican property covered by water. Although it was decided not to go through with the contract, Durant persuaded one of the negotiators, John Lee Pratt, to leave Du Pont and become his assistant.

Another example of Durant's haphazard methods of decision making, as told by Sloan, was as follows: One day Sloan left his office at Forty-second Street near Times Square in New York (his headquarters were above a bar). He was walking up Broadway when he ran into Durant, who told him of his newest idea—to put up a big office building in the heart of the Detroit business district. Sloan demurred and after some prodding from Durant (who really

did not like disagreements) suggested another location at West
Grand Boulevard and Cass. Real estate would be less expensive; GM
executives from many of the outlying plants would save a lot of
time in getting to the head office. Durant was impressed and invited Sloan to inspect his proposed location. As soon as Durant
saw the empty land, he rapidly measured the ground and asked
Sloan to handle the financial and real estate problems involved
(of which Sloan knew nothing). But once GM set up in the new
location, suppliers and dollars moved in. In this way, Detroit's
second most valuable real estate parcel was created!

Finally, the organization of GM was inadequate. As the late
Pierre S. du Pont told it: "Durant had operated as a one-man concern. He was really the head of the company and attended to everything. The other men were subject to his direction; there was very
little incentive for the men themselves to operate independently."

Durant might have as many as forty or fifty individuals who
could go to him for a wide range of decisions. He had no inter-
mediaries between himself and the managers of the large car
divisions, except Sloan, who was head of the accessories divisions.
Durant did bring in Walter Chrysler from Buick as general manager, but the two never agreed on the division of responsibilities
since Durant would not give up direct dealings with the division
managers.

Walter Chrysler has told of the difficulties he had with Durant's
methods of management. For example, at one time Durant sold
the Detroit Buick branch without consulting him. On another
occasion Durant hired one of Chrysler's principal superintendents
without telling him anything about it. As Chrysler told it:

A number of arguments on matters of that kind occurred during our
three years together. I remember I went to see him once and said, "Billy,
for the love of —— please, now, say what your policies are for General
Motors. I'll work on them; whatever they are, I'll work to make them
effective. Leave the operations alone; the building, the buying, the selling
and the men—leave them alone, but say what your policies are."

Billy laughed at me. "Walt, I believe in changing the policies just as
often as my office door opens and closes."

I wagged my head and said, "You and I can never get along." That's the kind of fellow he was, though; we'd fight, and then he'd want to raise my salary. [Durant was paying Chrysler $500,000.] Then I'd speak as gently as I knew how: "Billy, I'm getting all the money I want. Salary be damned! Will you please leave the Buick organization alone?"

Once I had gone to New York in obedience to a call from him [Durant]; he wished to see me about some matter. For several days in succession I waited at his office, but he was so busy he could not take the time to talk with me. It seemed to me he was trying to keep in communication with half the continent; eight or ten telephones were lined up on his desk. He was inhuman in his capacity for work. He had tremendous courage too. He might be risking everything he had, but he never faltered in his course. He was striving to make completely real his vision of a great corporation. Men, big men, came and went at his command. "Durant is buying" was a potent phrase in Wall Street then. During a lull I gained his attention for a minute. "Hadn't I better return to Flint and work? I can come back here later." "No, no. Stay right here." I waited four days before I went back to Flint; and to this day I do not know why Billy had required my presence in New York.[4]

In 1919 I believed we were expanding too fast by far. [GM's capacity in 1918 was 223,000 cars.] During that year, the authorized capital stock was increased from $370 million to $1,020 million. Less than a third of the common had been issued. However, all my feeling, all my complaints, had to do with the physical expansion. Besides the tractor business, the company was taking over a variety of manufacturing enterprises. The corporation was getting many of its own sources of supply, of bodies, differential gears, and many other items. We were building new factories and putting up houses for employees. They were putting up a $20 million office building. They kept buying things and budgeting this and budgeting that, until it seemed to me we might come to a dismal ending. Buick was making about half the money, but the corporation was spending much faster than we could earn. So I quit—this time for keeps—saying, "Now Billy, I'm done." Alfred Sloan and one other came to see me. They tried to talk me into staying. "No, I'm washed up. I just can't stand the way the thing is being run. All I'm anxious about now is to sell my stock." Yet the auto-

---

[4] Durant might call a meeting of top executives at 9 A.M., so that Chrysler and others had to get up at 5 or 6 A.M. to get to Detroit in time. The men might find Durant busy on the telephone buying and selling, wait all day, and go home without even talking to him.

mobile industry owes more to Durant than it has yet acknowledged. In some ways, he has been its greatest man.[5]

The actual end of the Durant regime came late in 1920, when the finance committee, which included Pierre S. du Pont and John J. Raskob, of Du Pont, and representatives of banking interests,[6] were shocked to learn that Durant was in distressing financial circumstances because of his stock market operations. The day was a holiday, but it was inevitable that the next morning would bring a deluge of calls for more margin. Durant's only collateral was his large blocks of GM stock, and a forced sale of his holdings might well bring on a general collapse. GM had large loans outstanding and might be thrown into receivership.

Du Pont, Raskob, and representatives of Morgan and Company wrestled with the problem far into the night. As Pierre du Pont tells this episode:

Since my first acquaintance with Mr. Durant some years ago he had never up to Thursday, Nov. 11, 1920, said anything to me concerning his personal affairs. I am quite sure that if Mr. Durant was a borrower on the

---

[5] Walter P. Chrysler, with Boyden Sparkes, *Life of an American Workman*, New York, 1950, pp. 148, 152, 161; quoted with permission of Dodd, Mead & Company, Inc., publishers.

[6] The Du Pont Company had acquired a financial interest in GM a few years earlier, and Pierre S. du Pont and Raskob became directors in 1917 at Durant's request. Du Pont and Raskob had recognized some of Durant's shortcomings and were particularly concerned that GM gain better recognition and acceptance in the banking and investing world. Mainly through Raskob's energetic influence, the following outstanding bankers and industrialists joined the board in 1919: Owen D. Young, Clarence Wooley, William H. Woodin, E. R. Stettinius, Seward Prosser, and George F. Baker. The last three made up the banking group. In the banking and industrial world of the time, the automobile industry had a questionable status. Entry of the six men just mentioned furthered acceptance of the industry, and of GM in particular, by the banking fraternity and the investing public. Had this move not been accomplished, it is doubtful whether GM could have weathered the storm. In 1920 the banking group engaged the services of a nationally known engineering firm to make a study of GM and recommend changes that seemed desirable. An exhaustive examination was made over a period of months, and late in 1921 the consultants came through with a report and recommendations. One recommendation was that the Sampson Tractor division be scrapped—a move determined months before—and another that the Chevrolet division be dispensed with.

GM stock at the time, nothing was said about it. I have supposed that he owed no money. I have felt quite certain up to Nov. 11 that Mr. Durant was not operating in the stock market and was not a borrower of money. A meeting in Mr. Morrow's office in November, 1920, at J. P. Morgan & Co. Mr. Durant left us with the impression that his holdings were as clear as our own.

On Nov. 11, 1920, Mr. Durant asked us (P. S. du Pont and Raskob) to lunch with him. Mr. Durant stated that he was worried about his personal accounts but made no definite explanation. In answer to Mr. Raskob's question as to the condition of Mr. Durant's affairs, he replied he would have to look up the matter.

On Tuesday, Nov. 16, Raskob and I went to Mr. Durant's office to find out his true position as we had agreed in conversation with Durant. Durant's personal affairs, if seriously involved, might indirectly affect the credit of General Motors Co. Mr. Durant was very busy that day, seeing people, rushing to the telephone, and in and out of his room so that, although we waited patiently for several hours, interrupted only by lunch time, it was not until four o'clock that afternoon that Mr. Durant began to give us figures indicating his situation. He had pencil memoranda of the number of loans at banks. The total memoranda, as written down by us from what he said, showed an indebtedness of twenty million dollars, all presumably on brokers' accounts and supported by 1.3 million shares of stock owned by others and by an unknown amount of collateral belonging to Durant, also $14.9 million which Durant estimated he owed personally to banks and brokers, against which he held 3 million shares of GM stocks. Mr. Durant stated that he had no personal books or accounts and was wholly unable to give a definite statement as to the total indebtedness; what part of it was his personal and what part was indebtedness of others on which he had lent collateral without other commitment. Apparently, he had no summary of brokers' accounts on hand. However, the whole situation, besides being very involved, seemed very serious. Mr. Durant promised to ask his brokers for accounts in order to make some positive statement.

Meantime the statements already given appeared so indefinite that Mr. Raskob and I were loath to believe the accounts in any way accurate. However, the situation seemed serious enough to warrant speculating on a plan of relief. We decided that, in order to avert a crisis, it might be possible to organize a company to take over Mr. Durant's holdings, issuing $20 million of notes which would be offered as collateral to the holders

of obligation and that the du Pont interests might invest $7 million or even
$10 million in securities of the company, in order to furnish cash to liqui-
date pressing accounts and make payments, in part, to others.

[On Thursday, November 18th there was still no complete statement of
Durant's obligations and Durant refused to make one. Finally late that
afternoon Durant made a statement of his obligations to three Morgan
partners, Morrow, Cochran, and Whitney] ... then ensued a discussion
of the whole subject, in which the Morgan partners outlined their opinion
of the extreme seriousness of the situation and the panic that might result
in the event of Mr. Durant's failure, which might possibly involve the
failure of several brokers and some of the banks. ... Mr. Morrow stated
that he would give up an engagement and return at nine o'clock [in the
evening] and I agreed to break an engagement and do likewise. I returned
to the hotel and, together with Mr. Raskob, went to the office at the
appointed time, where three Morgan partners had assembled. Mr. Raskob
outlined to Mr. Morrow our rough plan of giving assistance. Mr. Morrow
stated that he thought the plan impossible of execution because of the
very critical condition of the market and recommended that we place a
loan of $20 million among the bankers, in order that an offer of cash for
all of Mr. Durant's indebtedness might be made. Mr. Raskob and I agreed
on part of the Du Pont interests that we could furnish $7 million and
sufficient additional collateral toward the project. The Morgan partners
were very complimentary as to the willingness of Du Pont to help in the
situation, Mr. Cochran using the expression that "there are two firms in
the country who are real sports, viz., Du Pont and Morgan." The Morgan
partners stated that they must go as carefully as possible into Mr. Durant's
accounts before any attempt was made to float a loan. We therefore went
to Mr. Durant's room and checking of the accounts was carried forward
and the proposition of relief presented to Mr. Durant by Mr. Morrow
(40% of Mr. Durant's equity was to be returned to him). Checking of
accounts and discussion of the subject continued without interruption
until about 5:30 Friday morning, about which time Mr. Durant and I
signed a memorandum. Messrs. Morgan & Co. arranged a loan of $20 mil-
lion with the principal banks in New York before five o'clock that evening
(Nov. 19). Announcement was not made till Monday, Nov. 22. The Morgan partners acted with remarkable speed and success, the whole deal in-
volving $60 million or more, having been planned and practically com-
pleted in less than four days, in which are included a Saturday and Sunday.

The Du Pont Company considered the one-year banking accommodation merely a stopgap. Before the end of the term a ten-year bond issue was placed and the obligation paid off. In connection with this "lifesaving" procedure, Durant was allowed 20 per cent of the stock of Du Pont Securities in return for his GM holdings. He realized on his equity holdings in 1921; they yielded him something like $6 million, which he said "was enough for a man 60 years old."

With the passing of the years Durant has become identified as "the man who practically bankrupted General Motors." Such an image would facilitate a contrast with the knights in shining armor who subsequently saved GM. But careful organizational analysis reveals that the situation was neither wholly black nor wholly white. It was mostly gray, and the analyst has to determine its varying shades.

The principal blame for the difficulties of GM must be ascribed to the sudden downswing of general business conditions and GM's inability to adapt. This hit all the automobile companies, including GM, whose sales dropped from July to August, 1920, by 25 per cent, in October by 60 per cent, and in November by 75 per cent from the peak. GM, like many other companies, had undertaken a big expansion program. Its most important aspect was the expansion of producing capacity. Durant, on his part, disclaimed responsibility for overexpansion. According to the automotive-press writer W. A. P. John, who interviewed Durant at length in 1922, "for one solid hour I read document after document, bearing the signatures of over twenty men, stating that Mr. Durant had not only *not inaugurated the program*, but had emphatically cautioned against it in meeting after meeting. And not all those men are 'Durant men' either!" John then asked Durant why as chairman of the executive committee he had permitted the program to be carried out against his repeated warnings. Durant's reply was that "he owed them much for their aid [although by permitting him to handle for them a single investment of $24 million they had made over $70 million]; they had a reputation for being con-

servative businessmen; and they were supremely confident." [7] Durant
was apparently under the impression that the du Ponts had seemingly unlimited funds as far as GM was concerned and were willing
to employ them.

As in most reconstructions of the past, the actual causes of
troubles were a good deal more complicated than appears on the
surface. Certain acquisitions Durant opposed initially, such as
Kettering's Delco Labs. Certain investments were proposed by
Durant but expanded by Raskob, such as the huge GM office
building, which Durant feared would remain partly empty for a
number of years (as it did). Durant wanted to clean up Frigidaire
before expansion; he wanted to stop the Cadillac expansion.

Basically, the finance committee controlled the purse strings, but
it did not stop Durant's requests. The efforts to slow down expansion came from the GM executive committee rather than the
finance committee. It attempted in March, 1920, to reduce inventory requirements. In May, 1920, it appointed an inventory
allotment committee, which did not fare any better. In both cases
GM's top management was unable to enforce its requests on the
operating divisions. It was Durant's failure to coordinate these
separate "empires" and his method of paying division managers on
the basis of output that led to the rapid rise of inventories as
compared with declining sales (which accounted for 70 per cent of
the Corporation's borrowing).

Again in July, 1920, Durant tried to tighten up, and in the period
August to October, 1920, Durant recommended to the executive
committee that it disallow all appropriation requests over $1 million.

Even at the worst point in November, 1920, GM's position
was not bad from a long-run point of view. The fixed capital
expansion had been soundly financed. Working capital was strong
(current assets were $2\frac{1}{2}$ times current liabilities). Full interest payments were made on debentures and preferred stock.

Thus the basic cause of GM's difficulty was its inflexibility in
facing the sudden and severe postwar recession. GM's actual
trouble came from (1) lack of foresight; (2) lack of unity of com-

[7] *Motor*, January, 1923.

mand [three power centers—the finance committee (du Ponts), executive committee (Durant), and the automotive divisions]; (3) the lack of speedy feedback and control of the divisions; and (4) Durant's excessive confidence in the value of GM's stock, his feeling of *noblesse oblige* to his friends, his attempted one-man organization, with certain failings which showed up in a downturn. Thus organizational shortcomings were predominant in the GM disaster.

To Durant his departure from the GM presidency was merely one more of the inevitable valleys of high finance. On Dec. 1, 1920, he appeared in his office for the last time, shook hands with all his associates, and invited them to a dinner. He had lost almost one hundred million dollars within a few weeks, but his exit line could have been written by Dostoievsky in *The Gambler:* "Well," he said without a trace of rancor or regret as he glanced about the room, "May 1st is usually national moving day. But we seem to be moving on December 1st."

He moved on "to enjoy life with his wife," but he could not keep out of the automobile business. He bet everything on the "Durant" car and lost. Durant's "final coup" was in 1929 when he started a national chain of bowling alleys and restaurants in Flint, again ahead of his time.

The du Ponts, however, had learned their lesson, because they followed the rationalist and experimental bent of their founder. They had looked into the abyss and were firmly resolved never to let it happen again. They sought to set up an organization and control which would not be at the mercy of the vagaries of one man or even a national holocaust. Within a dozen years, when General Motors was much larger and much more vulnerable in terms of potential decline, they survived easily when sales dropped more than 80 per cent from their peak.

But their first problem in 1920 was to avoid too sharp a break of continuity in the management.

When Durant left, it was feared that the entire character of General Motors might change and that the very real advantages it had acquired under his leadership might be lost. To avoid this, the bankers on the GM finance committee appealed to Pierre S. du Pont (former president of Du Pont and then head of the du Pont family) to assume the presidency. Since du Pont had already retired from his own company and was loath to leave his home in Wilmington, Delaware, he desired a role no more active than that of close counselor. But the bankers, through their spokesman Seward Prosser, persuaded him to accept the post for a limited time.[8] He stipulated that he should be allowed to relinquish the presidency as soon as a qualified man could be found.

THE NEW GM MODEL

Long before Durant resigned, Sloan—who had always been interested in management problems and had been studying the GM organization since he joined the company—had become very much concerned with the managerial shortcomings he observed. He had almost all his funds invested in the corporation, and he did not wish to sell his stock while he was close to Durant. Moreover, he held a top position and he loved the work.

In May, 1920, Sloan had prepared an elaborate report on the GM organization, embodying a plan for the systematization of management and the introduction of administrative skills. Sloan's memorandum on organization appears to a considerable extent similar to a plan developed before at Du Pont and discussed by him with Du Pont representatives on a trip to France. John Lee Pratt presented it to Durant for him, and later he recalled: "Durant glanced at it and said it would take some time. So far as I know, that was the end of it."

Sloan was quite discouraged, worried about the future, and upset physically. So he took off a month during the summer to go to Europe and think over his position. On returning to the States, he heard that Durant opposed lowering the price of GM cars in the then falling market. That, apparently, made Sloan decide to resign; he had received a handsome offer to act as industrial rep-

---

[8] Du Pont also took over the management of the Chevrolet division until William S. Knudsen was brought in from Ford.

resentative of the New York banking company Lee, Higginson and was inclined to take it. But since there was no time limit attached to the offer and Durant was unprecedentedly on vacation, he waited a while to watch developments.

Then, in December, 1920, Pierre S. du Pont presented Sloan's reorganization plan to the board of directors.[9] (It had been incorrectly assumed that since du Pont himself came from what was then a centralized organization, he would not favor the decentralized pattern Sloan recommended.) Sloan's plan was accepted, largely in its original form, on Dec. 30, 1920. Sloan was made vice president in charge of the advisory staff, and a short time later he succeeded J. A. Haskell as operating vice president. Of the original nine on the executive committee, four had left GM.

The GM executive committee at that time was a temporary stop-gap, pending evolutionary processes. Although the way was left open for any contender who displayed the necessary knowledge and ability, all concerned thought of Sloan as the natural successor to Pierre du Pont, and du Pont himself leaned heavily on Sloan during his period in office. Sloan was chairman of a group known as the operations committee, which evaluated broad policies before they were passed on to the executive committee; du Pont and Raskob attended when they could or whenever something of importance was under consideration. (After Sloan assumed the presidency, a new executive committee was created, which functioned more fully in the usual way.)

Sloan received a high and increasing degree of responsibility. On Apr. 25, 1922, he was appointed a member of GM's finance committee; on May 10, 1923, he was made president of General Motors; and that same month he became a member of the Du

[9] It is impossible to describe and appraise all GM's contributions to administration and organization in a single chapter. Some of the old group are no longer alive or no longer accessible. Hence the following is devoted to some examples drawn from the original GM organization plan, to a partial summary of its initial execution and implementation, and to some of its results from 1921 to 1925. An adequate history of GM during those years might require some volumes. Our emphasis is on an evaluation of some of Sloan's contributions to the body of administrative knowledge and those of his principal associates.

Pont board, though he was not able to attend the meetings very frequently.

Sloan's organization study—the report on which the GM reorganization was based—is a remarkable document. Almost entirely original, it would be a creditable, if not a superior, organization plan for any large corporation today. Succinctly and clearly written, with no unnecessary language, it presents his program for GM in twenty-eight pages (plus a comprehensive organization chart) that must be read and studied carefully to discover its manifold implications. It is a landmark in the history of administrative thought. Most remarkable of all, as Sloan has said, "the basic principles of management to date that I have outlined in the original study I made in the spring or early summer of 1920 still hold in General Motors today, [although] there have been changes in the shape of the organization chart [and] in nomenclature."

As happens in the systematization of a great enterprise, the reorganization was made possible by the conjuncture of a group of outstanding individuals who fitted together just at the right time.

Of these, *Alfred P. Sloan, Jr.*, appears to have been the great empiricist who rose to the many challenges by providing the model, the system, the methodology, and the proper distribution of the equities among the various groups affected by GM. He was a complex personality and a tireless worker who made GM his all-embracing interest. He let time, persuasion, and an incisive appeal work for him.

Pierre S. du Pont was distinguished as a profound mind, a man who recognized the essentials and backed the great risky decisions to the hilt. He studiously kept out of details. He stayed in the background to give more leeway to the younger men.

Donaldson Brown was probably the most brilliant of the group. He made the great contributions in the areas of basic objectives, policies, controls, and systematization of ideas. He was selfless and professional to an extraordinary degree. His associate (and later successor) in this work was *Albert Bradley*.

John J. Raskob was the financial genius, promoter, and risk taker who undertook the great coups for the corporation.

John L. Pratt was the general-staff officer par excellence, who counseled and represented his chiefs on many hazardous missions. He was the "balance wheel." John T. Smith was the counselor of common sense and moderation. *James D. Mooney* guided the corporation's foreign affairs and presented its organizational image through his writings.

It is impossible to separate the contributions of each of these individuals to administrative thought, and in the following pages the work of Sloan is intermixed with that of the men named above, unless the contrary is stated.

The recommendations of 1920 rested on two principles, which are stated as follows:

1. The responsibility attached to the chief executive of each operation shall in no way be limited. Each such organization headed by its chief executive shall be complete in every necessary function and enabled to exercise its full initiative and logical development. [Decentralization of operations.]

2. Certain central organization functions are absolutely essential to the logical development and proper coordination of the Corporation's activities. [Centralized staff services to advise the line on specialized phases of the work, and central measurement of results to check the exercise of delegated responsibility.]

The definite objectives Sloan hoped to attain by the plan included:

1. To definitely determine the functioning of the various divisions constituting the Corporation's activities, not only in relation to one another, but in relation to the central organization. [Clear division of work on the basis of specialization.]

2. To determine the status of the central organization and to coordinate the operation of that central organization with the Corporation as a whole, to the end that it will perform in its necessary and logical place.

3. To centralize the control of all the executive functions of the Corporation in the President as its chief executive officer.

4. To limit as far as practical the number of executives reporting directly to the President, the object being to enable the President to better guide the broad policies of the Corporation without coming in contact

with problems that may safely be entrusted to executives of less importance. [Concentration of the chief executive's work on innovation and
representation through delegation of operating functions down the line
with coordination and planning by general advisory staffs.]

Two major segments of organization are distinguished, major
control and executive control. *Major control* was viewed as a line
of authority running from the stockholders to the directors to two
major committees to be chosen by the latter:

1. The *finance committee*, which would formulate financial
policy for the corporation as a whole and pass on appropriations
for capital investment recommended by the executive committee.
A chart dated January, 1921, shows that the committee included
John J. Raskob, Pierre S. du Pont (then president of the company),
and seven other directors, including J. A. Haskell, who with Sloan
had charge of operations. Raskob was chairman.

2. The *executive committee*, to be headed by the president
and to include representatives of the operations. The same chart
shows du Pont as chairman, Raskob as financial representative,
and Sloan and Haskell as vice presidents in charge of operations.

Executive control was to rest with the president, who would act
within the framework laid down by major control. Under him
would be the *operations*, which were grouped on the basis of common characteristics: commercial and manufacturing with outside
distribution, manufacturing only, common geographical bases.

General managers of operational units received absolute administrative control ("as great as the chief executive of an independent
administrative corporation") over their own manufacturing, sales,
financial, and engineering staffs, and in practice they were seldom
overruled. Related operations of lesser importance were grouped
together under a single head, which cut down the number of
people reporting to the president and relieved him of detailed
administration.

Divisions within the corporation were encouraged to compete
among themselves in engineering accomplishments, styling, and
service to public wants and tastes. In the transfer of products from
one division to another, company policy attempted to make prices

competitive with those of outside suppliers; in fact, purchases from outside suppliers were known to have been made for the purpose of keeping division management on its toes.

Coordination was provided through an *operations committee,* on which the heads of the operating divisions would be represented. A *general advisory staff* was provided to help the decentralized divisions with specialized problems: purchasing, engineering and research, insurance, legal problems, real estate, sales and advertising, and so on, but the staff was *specifically* denied authority over the line. "The advisory staff," Sloan wrote, "is practically consultant to the operations. . . . While it may develop and disseminate information and stands ready to be called upon for advice . . .operations are free to accept or reject the advice as . . . judgment may dictate, subject to the general supervision of the president."

Another central group was the *general financial and accounting staff,* under the direction of the chairman of the finance committee, who would also be a vice president of the corporation. (In 1920 this was Raskob.) The province of this group was the finance and accounting of the corporation. Its activities were coordinated, through the president, with the financial activities of the divisions.

The president was also given a personal staff consisting of a number of "assistants to" and an *appropriations committee.* The latter was to investigate the desirability of proposed property improvements or purchases recommended by the operating divisions. It could draw on specialists in the general advisory staff for technical data and advice.

ADMINISTRATIVE SKILLS

The work on the organization structure was followed rapidly by the introduction of new administrative skills. Sloan vividly explains the reason:

There are two ways of running any kind of business. They are the "hunch" method and the scientific way. By temperament and education, I have always followed the latter. It has paid me big returns and it will for others.

Often in thinking of 1920 and in thinking of what developments have taken place, I liken General Motors to a great big ship crossing the ocean. In the spring and summer of 1920 here was this great ship going along at full speed, just every ounce of steam that could be put into the boilers was there, and the sun was shining and people on the bridge seemed to feel no possibility of fogs, shoals or anything of the kind, but it was just going on forever. The storm came suddenly and we found ourselves in a position of inventories increasing, lack of business, shutting down our plants.

Now it seemed to me that there was a much better way of doing things —we had to have a different method of operations. We would have some sort of signals so we would be able to know exactly where we are at all times and would have to have some plan of forecasting to look ahead as far as is possible. So little by little we have developed indices. ...We have such control over this ship that we know exactly where we are at all times.

In the desperate situation that existed, Sloan's achievements and those of his collaborators at GM were remarkable. They saved GM from destruction, a fate suffered by so many competitors before and since. They systematized the government of the corporation, shifting it away from management by hunch and intuition. They inaugurated operational controls and mechanisms for speedy adjustments. The work that went into each administrative change was enormous. Yet results were accomplished with amazing speed.

The introduction of the following administrative skills represented merely a fraction of the work involved—and of the results accomplished.

Forecasting

The forecasting program at GM was described by Albert Bradley, assistant treasurer of the corporation in the mid-20's, as "nothing more than systematic planning applied to the conduct of the business." It grew up largely in response to the overproduction of automobiles in relation to market demand and the subsequent overstocking of dealers.

The most important purpose of the forecasting function was microeconomic: to keep production schedules in line with changes in ultimate consumer demand. To a lesser extent, it was designed to provide a means of establishing an operating program geared to provide a desirable rate of return on capital, plus income for expansion.

Prior to 1921, inventories had gotten completely out of hand throughout the divisions and were in a highly unbalanced state. The operating divisions had been proceeding more or less autonomously, with no control exercised from the central office over material commitments and purchase. In the latter part of 1920 the finance committee appointed a central inventory committee, headed by John L. Pratt, to gain control over the situation.

The emergency-committee plan which had been established could not satisfactorily meet the corporation's requirements over the long pull. No such committee could possibly have sufficient familiarity with the detailed considerations involved in the orderly purchase and procurement of materials for all divisions. Instead, each division had to be counted on to gauge its own commitments in the light of reasonable expectancy of movement of finished products into the hands of consumers.

At the same time, it was recognized that effective central-office control was necessary to ensure orderly purchase of materials and to safeguard against the bad inventory situation which had prompted the establishment of the central inventory committee late in 1920.

Discussions led to a plan submitted to the finance committee under date of Apr. 21, 1921. It was approved unanimously by the finance committee and became the basis of central-office control. The report set down the fundamental principle that "the operating units themselves must of necessity be looked to as the primary seat of control of inventories." The interposition of an inventories committee, with its delegated powers, "affords a condition of dual responsibility which in normal conditions is unwholesome and objectionable."

Two chief aspects of inventory control were pointed out: first, the necessity of holding stocks on hand and en route to a minimum point calculated to afford measurable assurance against shutdown for lack of materials; and second, the hazard of basing commitments on inaccurate forecasts and of losses from price changes or obsolescence. Among major considerations bearing on such commitments are the degree of confidence that may reasonably be placed in requirement estimates, the probable price trends, the condition of suppliers, and the form and conditions of contract commitments. The memorandum stated:

All [of these] are essentially operating problems and can be best dealt with by the operating organization. Insofar as the whole involves the matter of working capital requirements, the Finance Committee must have its voice reflected in the control, but this had better be by way of rules covering points of general policy rather than by any attempt at direct action. Moreover, it would seem logical and sound in organization principle for the Vice President or Chief Executive in charge of operations to be looked to to see that the divisions effectively control inventories in accord with Finance Committee policies or good business practice.

The plan required the divisions to submit monthly forecasts of production schedules four months ahead, and it prescribed limitations on commitments and procurement of materials to the approved schedule. Such planning by the divisions required forecasts of sales, to which production schedules necessarily must be tied. Opportunities were provided for central-office scrutiny of sales forecasts. Procurement of materials for needs beyond requirements of the four-month forecasts was classified as "forward commitments" and required advance submittal to the governing committee of the board for approval.

Principles adopted in that 1921 report, and the inventory-control methods it established, including the monthly forecasting, have remained in effect in General Motors to the present day. The top financial officer had to scrutinize monthly forecasts and raise questions when estimates of future sales appeared out of line with basic trends and conditions. Discussions were held, and attempts made to rationalize forecasts of retail sales. Frequently these discussions led to revisions of forecasts and to corresponding adjustments of production schedules, but always the final determination was left to each division. The central office did not presume to impose revisions of forecasts.

Dealers were induced to report on their sales every ten days so that the rate, seasonally considered, at which new and used cars were passing into the hands of users could be determined. It was also recognized that overzealous sales representatives might be forcing cars on dealers, making distress merchandising necessary to clear inventories; therefore an attempt was made to obtain data that would reflect whether individual dealers were operating at a profit. Eventually this led to the introduction of standard accounting practices throughout the dealer body.

The importance of obtaining accurate reports from dealers was demonstrated in the spring of 1924, when Sloan made his first field trip to call on dealers across the country. The first cities he visited were St. Louis and Kansas City, where he found conditions of oversupply, just as had been expected. After leaving Kansas City, he sent a telegram instructing William Knudsen, then head of Chevrolet, to cut back production schedules and stating the extent of the cutback. This was the only time in the years of Sloan's regime when instructions were laid down flatly, he observes. This single exception to the rule points up clearly the observation that GM's management was free of dictation from the top.

Macroeconomic forecasts were based on an appraisal of economic growth (taking account of population, wealth, and income), business-cycle trends, industry trends and competition, and seasonal variations. Some of GM's statistical data were of a pioneering character—for example, the estimates of wealth and population trends. Path-breaking also were some of the basic calculations of return on capital, the gearing of price policies and utilization of operations to desired profitability, the careful estimates of consumer demand, and the gearing of expenses to sales to produce the desired profits. Some of the pioneering work was summarized by Donaldson Brown in a 1924 memorandum, "Pricing Policy in Relation to Financial Control." Divisional and corporate forecasts were made for three contingencies: "pessimistic," representing minimum expectations, "conservative," representing what was likely to happen, and "optimistic." Stressing that a theoretical approach was essential to successful planning, Brown postulated that "a price reduction would be desirable, if the added volume affords an increase in aggregate profit in excess of the economic cost of the additional capital required." Illustrating this thesis profusely in relation to utilization, Brown was thus a pioneer of "marginal analysis" and also in the detailed analysis of the strategic revenue and cost factors determining rate of return on capital investment.

Policy Making

Absence of policies had made for inconsistency, red tape, mistakes, and losses—the haphazard price making was one of the more flagrant examples. Under the new system, the statistics developed by the forecasting function were used to determine the income of various consumer groups and to develop a line of products for each income bracket. The policy was to produce "a car for every purse and purpose," "just as a general conducting a campaign wants to have an army at every point at which he is likely to be attacked."

The basic price policy of the corporation was designed to provide an optimum return on investment over a period of time; the standard price was set in line with a standard volume, and the relationship between rate of operation and capacity was fixed, although with a certain amount of flexibility.

Relationships [10]

At a time when there was little knowledge of "the human factor in industry," Sloan had already proclaimed that "no matter what the value of any business is, measured in bricks and mortar, that part is negligible compared with the value of every man in his place coordinated into an effective whole."

From the beginning he realized the tremendous importance to employees of personal contact with the chief executive and the

---

[10] "Relationships" here refers solely to executives and dealers; employee and public relations are outside the scope of this chapter.

inspiration derived from it. In order to devote at least half his time to personal contact, he passed on detailed planning and co-ordinating work to his staff.

He did not confine his contacts to the GM headquarters. After the new organization was properly established, he devoted a large part of his time to dealer relationships. He probably had personal contacts with more dealers than any other executive in the industry. Traveling at night, interviewing during the day, he talked to thousands of dealers a year—well over a hundred on any one trip. He used personal contact as a means of "short-circuiting all the great distances between ourselves, the executives who initiate a program and the dealer who is making the final contact with the customer."

Sloan's visits were unannounced. He took one half to three quarters of an hour to establish confidence. Then he would talk about the product and methods of improving and selling it. Dealer meetings were held at which bankers were invited to give financial support or reluctant men were persuaded to become dealers; newspapermen were persuaded to provide publicity.

Sloan was an extremely patient listener. Detailed notes, taken at the meetings, were analyzed at home, and the GM accounting department was enlisted to help the dealers by providing accounting systems for them, making interdealer comparisons, and helping them cut expenses. The GM sales promotion department was established to make customer surveys (a major factor in the greater acceptance of GM cars) and to improve sales efforts, advertising, and so on. But most important was Sloan's personal work of introducing the dealers to systematic methods. Watching the progress buoyed him up and sustained his faith in systematization of the business. Sloan used to say:

If I could wave a magic wand over our dealer organization, with the result that every dealer could have a proper accounting system, could know the facts about his business and could intelligently deal with the many details incident to his business, I would be willing to pay for that accomplishment an enormous sum.... It would be the best investment GM ever made.

Sloan was able to place before each dealer bogeys showing the proper relationship of each expense item to the business as a whole, and with very profitable results to the dealers. They were so grateful that years later they collected a large donation for the Sloan-Kettering Institute for Cancer Research.

In his relationships with his executives Sloan placed stress on their contributions to corporate objectives and professional performance, rather than on "politics" or personal loyalty. He attempted to make partners of his principal associates and to encourage their participation in policy making.

The partnership idea was buttressed with a systematic bonus plan "designed to develop good officials." This highly ingenious plan not only served as a means of rewarding good performers, but also helped top management to discover and develop them and reduced "pirating" of executives by other concerns. The plan in existence at GM today is substantially the same.

A bonus plan had been inaugurated by GM in 1919, under the urging of the Du Pont representatives on the board, but during the Durant days some of the division managers had specific contracts providing for definite percentages of the output of their divisions. The Du Pont people regarded contracts of this kind as unsound, since they placed no emphasis on contributions to the corporation as a whole. These contracts were all canceled through separation or settlement shortly after Durant left.

The plan was then modified so that individual awards from top to bottom were designed to reward individual contributions to the over-all success of the corporation. Division allotments were made on the basis of return on investment considered in the light of surrounding circumstances, and individuals were rewarded on their superiors' recommendations and on the approval of higher authority.

Even this brief analysis indicates that the GM bonus plan of thirty years ago still ranks among the best designed today. Note the emphasis on divisional evaluation tied to the general organization plan and the profit objectives of the company, the attempt to set up separate "little General Motors companies" evaluated in terms of their own performance and in comparison with other divisions. Since division heads were held responsible for the performance of their units in terms of money results, they were anxious to receive the necessary authority—a prime factor in expanding decentralization. Note also that individuals were to be evaluated on a commonsense basis, with a check provided by group opinion. There is neither dependence on quantitative measurements alone nor emphasis on such largely subjective factors as "integrity" or "loyalty."

Clearly, this bonus plan exhibits a great advance in rationalizing executive compensation plans. It is definite in areas where knowledge is advanced, such as accountancy; it relies on common sense in areas of speculation, such as psychology. The method, procedure, and the financial obligations of the corporation are always unmistakably clear.

RESULTS

One criterion for evaluating Sloan's reorganization of General Motors is the opinion of management generally, both within the corporation and outside it.

If imitation is the sincerest form of flattery, that opinion is high. The GM organization plan has been adopted by a considerable number of very large corporations and many medium-sized firms, as well as by government agencies. Though there have been important variations in individual cases, the essence of the programs and the basic principles are the same. Henry Ford, apparently with the GM reorganization in mind, derided it as follows:

To my mind, there is no bend of mind more dangerous than that which is sometimes described as the "genius for organization." This usually results in the birth of a great big chart; showing, after the fashion of a family tree, how authority ramifies. The tree is heavy with nice round berries, each of which bears the name of a man or an office. Every man has a title and certain duties which are strictly limited by the circumference of his berry. It takes about six weeks for the message of a man living in a berry on the lower left-hand corner of the chart to reach the President or

Chairman of the Board, and if it ever does reach one of these august officials, it has by that time gathered to itself a pound of criticisms, suggestions, and comments. Very few things are even taken under "official consideration" until long after the time when they actually ought to have been done. The buck is passed to and fro and all responsibility is dodged by individuals—following the lazy notion that two heads are better than one.

Now a business, in my way of thinking, is not a machine. It is a collection of people who are brought together to do work and not to write letters to one another. It is not necessary for any one department to know what any other department is doing. . . . It is not necessary to have meetings to establish good feelings between individuals or departments. It is not necessary for people to love each other in order to work together.[11]

But when Ford's grandson found that the respective shares of market had been almost reversed and that his own company was losing heavily, he hired some of the best GM executives and installed a method of organization substantially that of General Motors.

Pierre du Pont, not given to exaggeration, stated in his first report to GM stockholders for the year 1921: "Much has been accomplished and many plans laid that will develop to the future advantage of the corporation. Systematic study has been given to the relations of the several divisions to each other, and duplication or conflict of effort has been avoided. . . . Benefits are already accruing." In his report for 1922, du Pont felt that the results of the reorganization were such that "the recurrence of the 1920–1921 disaster would seem unlikely, if not impossible." On his retirement, he summed up the two years' reorganization efforts with the opinion that "the greater part of the successful development of the corporation's operations and the building up of a strong manufacturing and sales organization is due to Mr. Sloan."

C. S. Mott, one of the largest GM shareholders, recognized Sloan as "a crystallizer of corporation policies for the benefit and protection of the customer, the stockholder and the members of

[11] Henry Ford (in collaboration with Samuel Crowther), *My Life and Work*, Doubleday & Company, Inc., New York, 1926, pp. 91–92.

the GM organization...an ideal man to direct affairs of GM." But it is not necessary to rely on opinion alone to appraise the success of the reorganization. Facts and figures tell the story.

Short-Term Profits

Even while there were losses from the inevitable disturbance of change, the liquidation and scrapping of inventories, the abandonment of unsuitable car, truck, and tractor models, benefits were accruing, and they increased during subsequent years.

In the first year after Sloan became president, the corporation nearly doubled its manufacturing capacity, and it did so entirely out of its current earnings. At the same time, GM sold the largest number of cars in its history, and by 1927 sales had risen almost 100 per cent—from 800,000 to 1.5 million cars. Dollar volume of sales nearly doubled between 1923 and 1927, and a loss in 1921 was changed to a profit of $235 million in 1927.[12] The bank loans had been paid off by 1922.

Production schedules, which had been one of the least efficient aspects before 1921, became more stable with the elaboration of current operating controls. By 1925 operations were at a more nearly level rate, and closer scheduling of materials made it possible to manufacture a larger quantity of cars with a smaller amount of money tied up in inventories.

The turnover of inventories was also favorably affected. For example, the turnover of total inventory rose from one turnover annually in 1920 to over six in 1925. End-of-the-month investments dropped from $160 million in December, 1920, to $110 million in December, 1925. There was an equally great improvement in the turnover of "productive inventory" (total inventory less finished product). It turned over $1\frac{1}{2}$ times in 1920 and more than nine times in 1925.

Before the reorganization there was a great gap between GM

---

[12] As in other reorganizations, GM lost money initially. In 1922, John J. Raskob was able to declare the usual dividend only because a physical inventory check at Buick revealed several million dollars' worth of stock not found in the books!

sales to dealers and dealer sales to users. This saddled the dealers
or the corporation or both with considerable inventories and heavy
extra expenses. The difficulty of the problem is indicated by the
fact that the initial attempts to lessen the gap were not always
successful. For example, in 1923 almost 10 per cent more cars
were sold by GM to the dealers than the dealers sold to the public.
This period of "oversupply" lasted from August, 1923, to March,
1924. But in 1925 there was almost perfect equilibrium (only a
1 per cent gap), and this was maintained in subsequent years.

Better scheduling of inventories and production resulted in
steadier employment. In 1925 the maximum number of employees
varied only 11 per cent from the average, the minimum only 18
per cent from the average. While this was still a substantial variation in employment, it was a great improvement over past practices, the best performance in this area the corporation had ever
achieved, and considerably better than the performance of competitors. It was also the basis for further substantial improvements.

Long-Term Results

Subsequently, General Motors grew to be the largest manufacturing corporation in the world, with sales of more than 10 billion
dollars—more than General Electric, Westinghouse, Du Pont, and
U.S. Steel together. Its total profits, after taxes, were greater than
those of any other manufacturing corporation—and greater than
the sales of any corporation except the few members of the "Billion
Dollar Club" for several years in the 1950's.

ADMINISTRATIVE THOUGHT

Sloan and his associates began their work in response to a specific
need or problem. They did not evolve their plan in a vacuum; rather
it was a pragmatic response to what appeared to be a series of
overwhelming challenges. They had to win acceptance from divergent interests—from the financial interests of the Du Ponts and the
Morgan bankers and from a group of highly ambitious executives
whose interests were largely operational. Persuasion of the latter,

they knew, was necessary if results were to satisfy the financial interests.

As one means of attracting and holding outstanding associates, Sloan and his group developed what might be called an "administrative ideology." Essentially it was a method of thinking about the administrative process. Fundamental was the thought that the process of administration should be decentralized but review or control should be centralized.

The decentralization theory was based on a concept somewhat akin to the theory of atomistic competition—each self-sufficient activity of the corporation would operate on its own within the over-all framework of the rules of a free-enterprise system. Freedom of operation would make it possible for each activity and its leadership to contribute to the maximum of their abilities in the light of their superior knowledge of the local situation. Freedom of operation was tempered by veto power, but a coordinated control system set the framework within which the veto would be exercised, and this system provided for accountability.

This ideology was put in the form of statements, speeches, and letters and was frequently repeated and reinforced by example. Undoubtedly "decentralized operations and coordinated controls" had a powerful appeal to able men. It was inspirational, because it gave promise of greater opportunity for the individual. It convinced intellectually because it pointed out a way of overcoming the problem of diminishing returns from management as size increases.

Sloan's ideology helped to keep most of the good men at General Motors, since it gave them scope for their talents. Yet it kept within bounds that individualistic and separatist group which had forever threatened to break asunder in Durant's day.

"Scientific" Methodology

But the ideology alone would not have been sufficient to rescue the corporation. It had to be translated into a general framework for guidance and a series of dimensions which could be tested like a scientific experiment or which might at least be developed to such a point through increasing systematization or rationalization (like the German *Rationalisierungsprozess*). The methodology developed was never scientific in the sense that experiments in the physical sciences are, nor was it intended to be more than a systematic or factual approach that could be checked in a very rough fashion by results. Sloan's contributions to the methodology of the administrative process are essentially three: the planning process, the administrative framework, and the administrative skills.

Sloan developed the *planning process* in immediate response to the challenge of Durant's chaos and on the basis of his training as an engineer. In the debacle of 1920 he knew he would lose his job, his reputation, and his savings unless he produced results. He had to plan in such a way as to assure the reasonable fulfillment of his promises and the board's expectations.

Promise and fulfillment was, therefore, the keynote of the tremendously detailed, complex, and highly original method of planning for the future that was developed. This explains the independence and originality of GM's pricing policies (the base price of Chevrolet is said to be the one that all others follow), of its labor policies, public relations policies, and dealer relations policies. It explains Sloan's shift of emphasis from preoccupation with financial and technical problems to general administration, human relations, and, above all, sales (for example, the model changes which beat the predominance of the Ford Model T; Sloan is fond of recalling that the automobile industry started as a sports car industry).

And the "scientific" test of the plan is considered to be its results, which often show little deviation from the plans. Sloan the engineer, who had learned the importance of precision in every detail, transferred it to the planning process and eliminated, or at least greatly reduced, the uncertainty. As Sloan himself describes it:

> I instituted a system that provided scientific means of administration and control whereby the corporation would be able to project itself as much as possible into the future so as to discount changing trends and influences and also to be prepared at all times to alter its course promptly and effectively if the necessity arose.

The GM plan requires above all an *administrative framework*. This is a most carefully thought-out series of conventions, maintained thoroughout by an oral tradition. Freedom and control are closely balanced:

1. Central management determines short- and long-range plans for the corporation as a whole as well as the scope within which each division operates, considering such factors as long-term growth, cyclical and seasonal variations, capacity, and competition. While planning takes into account the ideas and suggestions of the divisions, it accedes to them only in so far as they fit into the over-all plans, and to that extent central management predetermines activities of the divisions.

2. Central management fits the divisions into a pattern of operation, set by the over-all plan, allotting to each division its role in the over-all scheme. It sets production goals, based on general economic factors and a minimum quota for each division, decides capital and current expenditure allocation, determines major appointments, salary changes, and bonus allotments, and makes major policy decisions affecting all the divisons.

3. Staff aid at various levels is provided to help the divisions meet the goals and to measure the results, and it worked by "factual persuasion."

4. Provision is made for integration of viewpoints and for teaching. In the formative days Sloan made frequent visits to the plants, particularly in the car and truck divisions, to contact those on the ground. General managers of these divisions were called into Detroit once or twice a month for meetings, and often representatives of the specialized staffs sat in. These sessions led to the creation of policy groups to contend with specialized phases of the business, such as sales and distribution, engineering, labor relations, styling. Group meetings took on the characteristics of seminars. Sloan generally sat in, and although he would explain his viewpoint on specific questions as they arose, he encouraged debate and different points of view and he delayed the final decison until the underlying concept was accepted by those who had to carry out the decision. This kind of procedure was calculated to

provide training and elicit contributions to fundamental policy from those down the line.

5. Division managers handle production and sales distribution in the plants and sales agencies of their divisions; appoint personnel except top executives; determine factory methods and equipment; handle most purchases, dealer contracts and franchises, and certain aspects of advertising and public relations, though their decisions may be subject to review and challenge by central management.

The *administrative skills* originated mostly from the factual observations of Sloan and his associates and were then evolved through what might be called an "integration of expert advice." Usually one man would think up the central idea in response to many pressures or as a result of group discussion.

The scientific methodology of GM depends on its over-all plans. But the build-up of the plans and their execution is only as good as the administrative skills which go into their development. Some of these skills have been highly developed—for example, forecasting and the controls. Others have undergone long periods of study, and Sloan and his associates have made major contributions to their improvement.

The development of organizational skills as described below is one example. Here the method of development was in part empirical, in part comparative.

The organization developed empirically in response to needs and experience. Thus decentralization of operations was a necessity in the beginning, because the new GM top managers were not familiar enough with the actual production and selling of cars. They were busy with over-all problems; hence the distinction between policy making and execution. They were forced to provide some immediate over-all objectives and consistent methods of meeting them; hence the development of central coordination and controls. Staffs developed in response to specific needs; for example, GM cars, like others of the time, were painted black. Fred Fisher (of Fisher Bodies) thought colors would make the product more attractive. That led to the establishment of an arts and colors department—a new staff activity. Similarly, the added management controls required "staffs" of various kinds.

The comparative method of organization development is illustrated by the line-and-staff concept, drawn largely from the military and adapted to the needs of GM. Though Sloan opposes the use of military methods, he says that "the advisory staff might be compared with the Army organization where you have line officers and advisory officers." He also followed the military distinction of general, special, and personal staffs. In addition, he may have drawn on his early (1906) experience with the New York Telephone Company and on special studies at Du Pont. The use of the hierarchical, or scalar, principle, the establishment of so-called semi-independent units, may be based on some of the thinking of the Roman Catholic Church, which has some of the same organizational problems experienced by a large industrial organization— large size, complexity, the need for perpetuation and channels of communication, and so forth. But though Sloan and his associates used the comparative method of study to determine the organization of GM, in each case they made allowance for major differences between institutions, and the final product was a highly original adaptation.

THE FUTURE

In any consideration of the future of General Motors, the basic question is, of course, the efficacy of Sloan's ideology and scientific methodology after his departure. His "system" was designed not only to provide a factual basis for managerial decision making, but to minimize dependence on any one individual by enabling the company to draw on the ideas of a large group of executives at several levels. If the system is to be considered entirely successful, therefore, it must not depend on the presence of the individual, Sloan.

A fortunate combination of outstanding individuals of diverse talents launched the new GM model in the early 1920's. There were some major differences of opinion among them—for example, between Sloan and the du Ponts over the nature and powers of the top committees and over such questions as the integration of organized labor in the corporate structure and its participation in corporate revenue—but they were bound together by similarity of outlook and personal friendship. The old leadership, men like Sloan, Kettering, Mott, Pratt, and some of the du Ponts, held substantial blocks of shares in GM. While these holdings were not substantial percentagewise, they were large in absolute dollar sums, running into millions of dollars and constituting a major part of each individual's savings, investments that he could influence for good or ill by his administrative actions. GM's ideology was originated and developd by men who might also be called owner-managers; it was partly forced on them in order to overcome the then existing independence of formerly separately owned companies. It was the coordination, control, and staff services that were novel.

Being "founding fathers" and collaborating over several decades, these men were able to maintain the framework of "decentralized operations and coordinated control" by oral tradition and to interpret, amend, and improve it as times and personalities changed. Those who built up the concept lived within its boundaries without too much difficulty.

But it is not evident that its intent is entirely clear to the successors of this group. There appear to be major differences among them in the concepts of delegation and final decision making. To what extent, therefore, will the GM executives of the future be able to work with an ideology that they did not create and may not entirely understand? How can they avoid the penalties of being first? Sloan foresaw this change earlier and pointed out that "initial success in business is often easier to achieve than to maintain competitive position and to survive as a successful enterprise. The feeling of real satisfaction concomitant with success may well stifle further initiative and generate resistance to change and to the new ideas requisite for continuance of the growth of a business and to keep it up-to-date."

Even though Sloan frequently made the final decision, he employed group management in the sense that he relied on research and scientific findings, listened to recommendations, asked questions, might refuse to overrule the decision of a subordinate until the latter had made a number of mistakes, and drew men out by the device of the chummy but inexorable "request for cooperation."

One of Sloan's successors, Harlow C. Curtice, chief executive of GM from 1952 to 1958, made an increasing number of decisions himself—a GM chart in *Business Week* showed him in seven different boxes; his "span of control" was greater than that of his predecessors; he no longer had a "chief of staff." It may be that the belated extension of dealer franchises and the delayed response to changing public taste showed some inelasticity of adjustment within the organization at the time. But some of the centralization moves, like that in engineering, could be justified on economic grounds; others, like those in labor and public relations, on the basis of legal and governmental changes.

Then, as "fact finding" by central bodies tends to cover more and more phases of operations, the work of the division managers at GM tends to become increasingly predetermined; one might almost say predestined. It will be hard to find justification for going contrary to "facts" centrally determined.

There appear to be other administrative changes that may lead to a less effective "system." Is the retention of the influence of some of the "founding fathers" beyond age sixty-five a partial indication of the difficulty of ideological transference? Is the specific involvement in operating details of selling, engineering, production, labor relations, and styling as practiced by successive chief executives going to be finally abandoned for general involvement in over-all management and public problems?

GM's scientific methodology is likely to prove more durable. The objective approach of the new management techniques, the ability to analyze events and explain them, the power of forecasting and controlling results are skills that can be acquired and constantly improved, and the application of them at GM constitutes a permanent contribution to scientific management. But these techniques can be and are being copied by competition all the time. GM's competitive edge can be maintained only by a greater rate of improvement of administrative thought and skill and by the introduction of newer techniques. It is planned that this will be done by the new generation at GM, possibly with three or four back-up men for each key job. But to what extent will there be some succession simply because of seniority and friendship? To what extent will there be frustration and resignations because of long waits for promotion? To what extent are the "middle-aged Turks" protecting their "intellectual investments" in the time-proven methodology against the criticism of the "young Turks"? How good are the successors to Sloan (picked in part by him through his influence as board chairman and member of the bonus committee)? Are they picked in his image or as best adapted to the circumstance? And, finally, how much of an independent contribution and inquiring mind is permitted today and how far down in the executive ranks? To what extent can GM continue its present product mix? Is GM at the point where it should stop growing in automobile market share and shift to other fields? Is GM placing too much emphasis on market share as compared with maximization of profits? To what extent will social and non-economic factors require consideration in future decisions? To what extent will there again be younger men at the helm of GM, as when Pierre du Pont made room for them by retiring from the presidency at the age of fifty-three?

Thus the organizer Sloan, who replaced innovating genius by an ideology and a scientific methodology, may have succeeded only partially in making his system deterministic beyond his own period of service. A new or more highly developed ideology and scientific methodology may be needed to replace Sloan's guiding influence in the required adaptations of the future.

This will be the task of the new organizers at GM. How will they make the transition as the organizing giants pass from the scene? What will be their performance relative to that of their competitors and their absolute contribution to the advancement of scientific administration and the clarification of social responsibility?

These will be the criteria for judging the success of the future organizers of GM.

BIBLIOGRAPHY

"A Day with Alfred P. Sloan, Jr.," *Fortune*, April, 1938.

"Autos—the First Target," *Time*, Sept. 24, 1945.

Bradley, Albert: *Financial Control Policies of General Motors*, Annual Convention Series, No. 41, American Management Association, New York, 1926.

Briscoe, Benjamin: "The Inside Story of General Motors," *Detroit Saturday Night*, Jan. 15, 22, 29; Feb. 5, 1921.

Boyd, J. A.: *Professional Amateur: The Biography of Charles Franklin Kettering*, E. P. Dutton & Co., Inc., New York, 1951.

Brown, Donaldson: Industrial Management as a National Resource, in *The Conference Board Management Record*, April, 1943.

———: *Decentralized Operations and Responsibilities with Coordinated Control*, Annual Convention Series, no. 57, American Management Association, New York, 1927.

———: "Pricing Policy in Relation to Financial Control," *Management and Administration*, February, March, and April, 1924.

Chrysler, Walter P., with Boyden Sparkes: *Life of an American Workman*, Dodd, Mead & Company, Inc., New York, 1950.

Dale, Ernest: *Planning and Developing the Company Organization Structure*, American Management Association, New York, 1952.

Douglass, Paul F.: "Alfred P. Sloan, Jr.," in *Six upon the World: Toward an American Culture for an Industrial Age*, Little, Brown & Company, Boston, 1954.

Drucker, Peter: "The Corporation as Human Effort," in *Concept of the Corporation*, The John Day Company, Inc., New York, 1946.

du Pont, Pierre S: Testimony before the U.S. District Court, in Civil Action No. 49 C–1071, *United States of America v. E. I. du Pont de Nemours & Company, General Motors Corporation, et al.*, U.S. District Court for the Northern District of Illinois, Eastern Division, Chicago, 1953, (stenographic reports).

Durant, Margaret: *My Father*, New York, 1929.

Durant, William Crapo: Collected papers (in possession of Mrs. W. C. Durant).

Epstein, R. C.: *The Automobile Industry*, A. W. Shaw Company, Chicago, 1928.

Forbes, B. C.: We Face the Future without Fear with Faith—Sloan, *Forbes*, Mar. 29, 1924.

———— and O. D. Foster: *Automotive Giants of America: Men Who Are Making Our Motor Industry*, B. C. Forbes Publishing Co., New York, 1926.

Ford, Henry (in collaboration with Samuel Crowther): *My Life and Work*, Doubleday and Company, Inc., Garden City, N.Y., 1923.

General Motors Corporation: *Annual Reports*.

————: *GM and Its People: An American Industrial Team*, Detroit, Mich., February, 1949.

Harbison, F. H., and Robert Dubin: *Patterns of Union-Management Relations: United Auto Workers (CIO), General Motors, Studebaker*, Science Research Associates, Chicago, 1947.

John, W. A. P.: "That Man Durant," *Motor*, January, 1923, pp. 70, 242–257.

Kennedy, E. D: *The Automobile Industry: The Coming of Age of Capitalism's Favorite Child*, Reynal & Hitchcock, Inc., New York, 1941.

Kettering, C. F., and Allen Orth: *The New Necessity: The Culmination of a Century of Progress in Transportation*, The Williams & Wilkins Company, Baltimore, 1932.

Mooney, James J.: *The Principles of Organization*, Harper & Brothers, New York, 1942.

Moore, Joseph A.: *Famous Leaders of Industry, Fifth Series: Life Stories of Men Who Have Succeeded*, L. C. Page & Company, Boston, 1945.

Mott, C. S.: "Organizing a Great Industrial," *Management and Administration*, May, 1924.

Pound, Arthur: *The Turning Wheel: The Story of General Motors through 25 Years, 1908–1933*, Doubleday and Company, Inc., Garden City, N.Y., 1934.

Quinn, T. K.: *Giant Business: Threat to Democracy*, Exposition Press, New York, 1953.

Rae, John B.: "The Engineer-Entrepreneur in the American Automobile Industry, *Explorations in Entrepreneurial History*, Harvard University Research Center in Entrepreneurial History, vol. 8, October, 1955.

Seltzer, L. H.: *A Financial History of the American Automobile Industry: A Study of the Ways in Which the Leading American Producers of Automobiles Have Met Their Capital Requirements*, Houghton Mifflin Company, Boston, 1928.

Sloan, Alfred P., Jr.: The General Motors Reorganization Plan, Defendants' Exhibit No. 300, in Civil Action No. 49 C-1071, *United States of America v. E. I. du Pont de Nemours and Company, General Motors Corporation, et al.*, U.S. District Court for the Northern District of Illinois, Eastern Division, Chicago, 1953.

————: Address to San Francisco and Oakland Chambers of Commerce, San Francisco, Calif., 1946.

————: *Importance of Management*, reprinted from General Motors Corporation *Annual Report*, 1946.

————: Address before Central Office Educational Conferences on the efficiency of GM's decentralized organization, May 23, 1945.

————, with Boyden Sparkes: *Adventures of a White-collar Man*, Doubleday and Company, Inc., Garden City, N.Y., 1941.

————: "Industrial Statesmanship," address before the National Industrial Conference Board, New York, 1940.

————: "A Great Corporation from Within," Van Rensselaer Lecture delivered at Drexel Institute of Technology, Philadelphia, June 6, 1939.

————: "Announcing Dealer Relations Board," message to GM dealers, June 6, 1938.

————: Address at first nationwide GM dealer coordination meeting, May, 1937.

————: "Development of General Motors Interests in California," message to GM stockholders, May 12, 1936.

————: "Business Bigness," message to GM stockholders, July 1, 1935.

————: *Fact finding as an Aid to Management*, New York, 1930.

————: "Acquisition of a Substantial Interest in Adam Opel, A.G., Germany," message to GM stockholders, Sept. 12, 1929.

————: "How Members of the General Motors Family Are Made Partners in General Motors," message to GM stockholders, May, 1929 (revision of a previous message of same title issued in 1927).

————: Address at opening of GM's Linden, N.J., plant, May 27, 1927.

————: "Principles and Policies behind General Motors," address before the Automobile Editors of American Newspapers at GM Proving Ground, Milford, Mich., Sept. 28, 1927.

————: "The Most Important Thing I Ever Learned about Management," *System*, August, 1924.

Smith, Edgar W.: "Organization and Operating Principles," in W. J. Donald (ed.), *Handbook of Business Administration*, McGraw-Hill Book Company, Inc., for the American Management Association, New York, 1931.

U.S. Federal Trade Commission: *Report on Motor Vehicle Industry*, 76th Cong., 1st Sess., House Document No. 468, 1939.

U.S. Senate Subcommittee on Antitrust and Monopoly of the Committee on the Judiciary: Stenographic reports of hearings on the study of the antitrust laws, General Motors, November and December, 1955.

4

Ernest Tener Weir:
Iconoclast of Management[1]

There are some ways in which I might begin life
with hardly any outlay, and yet begin with a good
hope of getting on by resolution and exertion ...
and a head to plan.

CHARLES DICKENS, *David Copperfield*

The fundamental qualities for good execution of
a plan are, first, naturally, intelligence; then dis-
cernment and judgment, which enable one to
recognize the best methods to attain it; then
singleness of purpose; and, lastly, what is most
essential of all, will—stubborn will.

MARSHAL FOCH

[1] The author had the privilege of working on this analysis with E. T. Weir on
a number of occasions, discussing his life's thoughts and plans. E. T. Weir
went over several versions of the draft of this chapter. Many of Weir's personal papers and speeches were studied and drawn upon. A number of visits
were made to Weirton. The charts were conceived and executed by R. S.
Weinberg, manager of market research of IBM. The author alone is responsible for the accuracy of the facts and their interpretation.

Most of the great organizers of American business have been the successors to the founders of the great corporations rather than the founders themselves. The entrepreneurial genius who seizes a unique

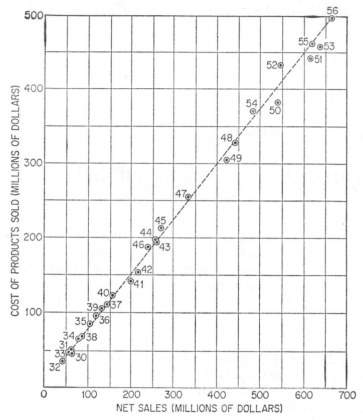

CHART 1. NATIONAL STEEL CORPORATION COSTS OF PRODUCTS SOLD AND NET SALES, 1931–1956

opportunity and builds an empire around it seldom has either the time or the inclination to plan in detail very far in advance.

Ernest Tener Weir, founder of the National Steel Corporation, was an exception to this rule. From the very first he planned his company in its entirety, and it grew according to his plan. When the physical plant consisted only of a run-down tin-plate mill, he had already envisioned a completely integrated steel company—self-sufficient even to ore sources—and had created the nucleus of an organization that could grow as the company grew without major restructuring.

Moreover, the organization plan paid off. In terms of size, National Steel is fifth among the steel companies of the United States, but in terms of profitability it was first for a long time by a number of tests. At one time during the Great Depression, National Steel made a profit while every other steel company—including the giant U.S. Steel—was suffering a loss.

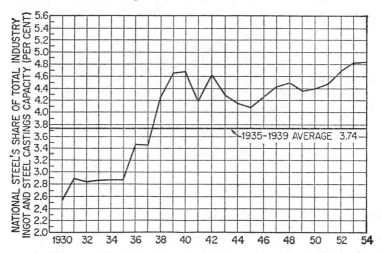

CHART 2. NATIONAL STEEL CORPORATION SHARE OF TOTAL INDUSTRY INGOT AND STEEL CASTINGS CAPACITY, 1930–1954

This profit picture was made possible not only by advances in sales that continued with remarkable steadiness, but by close control of costs, which were held strictly in line with sales. On the few occasions when sales dropped, costs were held absolutely in line. For example, when sales dropped more than $50 million from 1937 to 1938, there was an almost equal drop in cost. Similarly, when sales dipped after World War II, in 1946, 1949, and 1954, there were correspondingly lower costs; in 1949, in fact, the decrease in costs was greater than the decrease in sales. This remarkable correspondence is indicated by Chart 1.

In addition, the company's annual steel-ingot capacity rose more

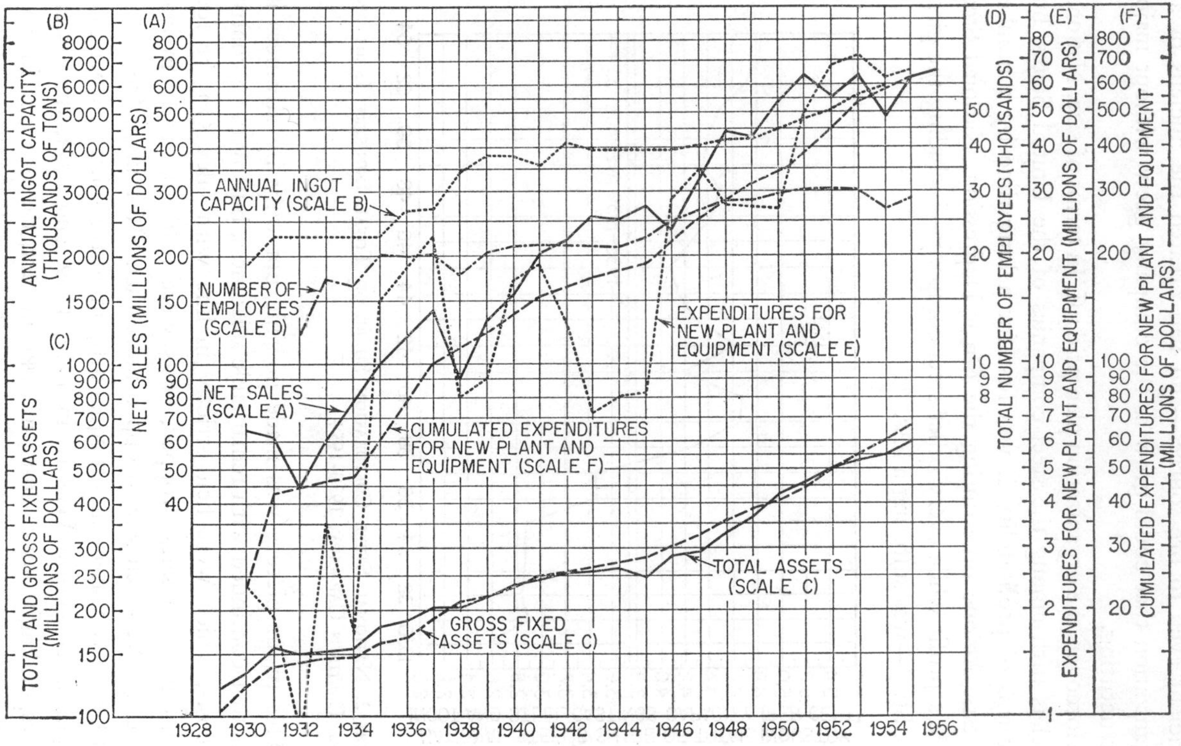

CHART 3. NATIONAL STEEL'S LONG-TERM GROWTH, 1929–1956

steeply than that of the industry, as is shown in Chart 2, which depicts capacity as a percentage of the industry capacity. The rise from less than 2.9 per cent in 1935 to almost 4.7 per cent in 1940 was particularly steep, and thus capacity added during a low-cost period could be taken full advantage of in World War II. The war itself led to a decline in percentage of industry capacity because

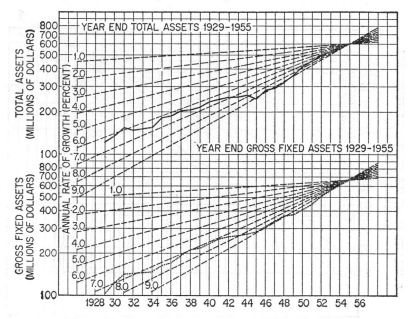

CHART 4. GROSS FIXED ASSETS AND TOTAL ASSETS, 1929-1955

the war restrictions were based on the 1935–1939 average, which in National's case was 3.74 per cent.

Chart 3 shows the extraordinary control which "E. T." had during his 27 years as chief executive at National. This is clearly evident from the principal strategic elements of his company's development. Lines show the development of net sales (scale A), annual ingot capacity (scale B), gross fixed assets and total assets (scale C), number of employees (index trend numbers scale D), expenditures for new plant and equipment (scale E), and cumulated expenditures

for new plant and equipment (scale F). At the right and left of
the chart (A) relates to scale A, (B) to scale B, and so on.

Charts 4 and 5 show the extraordinary regularity of increase, year
by year almost, of capital investment expenditures which are so
often subject to violent fluctuations, especially in the steel industry.
Chart 4 shows total assets and gross fixed assets from 1929 to
1956 at their annual percentage rate of growth. The growth rate

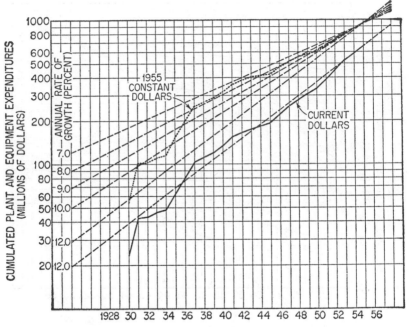

CHART 5. CUMULATED PLANT AND EQUIPMENT EXPENDITURES, 1930–1956

of the former fluctuated between 6 and 9 per cent, that of the latter
between 7 and 9 per cent per annum, and this includes the Great
Depression years.

Chart 5 shows the cumulated plant and equipment expenditures
from 1930 to 1956 in current dollars. These grew steadily at about 12
per cent per annum. Even in terms of "constant dollars," that is, current dollars deflated in terms of 1955 dollars, the fluctuations remain
between 7 and 12 per cent per annum.

While there are some breaks in the upward trend of the lines, on the whole there is a remarkable upward consistency, even in the darkest years, in an industry subject to considerable fluctuations. Weir first became nationally famous—infamous to some—in the 1930's, when he fought unionization more intransigently than his fellow industrialists. He defied government officials in the matter of a union election under the old National Recovery Act—and won his case when Section 7-A was declared unconstitutional. When President Roosevelt talked of "economic royalists," Weir picked up the phrase and announced that he was proud to be one.

Weir was not, however, entirely or even largely the arch-reactionary that some of his words and actions make him appear. For example, in 1932 he developed an analysis of the discrepancy between production and consumption that sounds remarkably like Thorstein Veblen's, though Weir had never read Veblen at the time (and probably not later):

The only reason for production is consumption demand, and there must be a balance between them. If the producer expects his goods consumed, he must do his share in having the consumer's income on an equitable basis. If the producer's profit is excessive, it must be taken from the consumer, and slowly but surely the power of consumption declines and production is not absorbed. Also the trouble is intensified by the producer from his excess share of earnings, using them to increase his plant and equipment, and his production. Thus there results a chasm between the requisites of prosperity—production and consumption—that eventually brings the collapse.

And these words, uttered in 1934, are hardly those of a reactionary: "If there had been some power which could have, by a stroke of the pen, taken some per cent from capital and given it to labor ten years ago, we might have had no depression. The over-expansion of industry would have been curtailed by this mythical reduction in the return to capital, and the purchasing power of wage earners would have been greater by reason of this increase to labor."

Moreover, to a large extent, Weir practiced what he preached. True, he went further than U.S. Steel in reducing wages after 1929, but in 1933 he notified the American Iron and Steel Institute that he was raising wages 15 per cent and forced the rest of the industry to follow suit. "Steel manufacturers," he said, "are not justified in even considering any further liquidation of labor. We have gone, if anything, too far along those lines."

In 1935 he criticized other companies for raising wages, saying the increase was economically unwise, but in 1941 he again forced a rise in industry rates. U.S. Steel, the pace setter for the industry, had not yet settled its union contracts, but Weir knew that the projected profit statements from the industry would show ability to pay and believed that haggling and delay were not justified. As the bickering went on, he told his associates: "It isn't enough— seven cents. When profit reports come later they'll make 'poor mouth' claims look ridiculous. And it will cost a lot of labor confidence." Then suddenly he stopped pacing up and down and called in his public relations man John Ubinger: "You can put out the word that we are raising ten cents an hour—no need to elaborate. We've told our workers."

The announcement dropped like a bomb on the bargaining table where Big Steel and the union leaders were arguing. In a few minutes their long disagreement was dissolved and all steel wages went up ten cents an hour. Weir said: "We felt ten cents the proper figure in view of the industry's earnings. We felt the men should share in that improvement."

Some time later, Weir opposed U.S. Steel's plan to hike prices, supported a wartime price freeze, and marched out of the American Iron and Steel Institute in token of his disagreement.

These contradictions have suggested to some observers that Weir might simply be an "old-fashioned nineteenth-century liberal" who believed that it would be possible to convince businessmen that it would be to their ultimate interest to pay higher wages and hold them to that course by moral suasion.

Certainly his basic philosophy was that of the liberal period in which he grew up, close to John Stuart Mill's principle of "framing the plan of our life so as to suit our character; of doing as we like, subject to such consequences as may follow; without impediment from our fellow-creatures so long as what we do does not harm them, even though they should think our conduct foolish, perverse and wrong." If he was harming his workers by fighting tooth and nail to keep the national unions out of his mills, Weir was not conscious of it, and he seems eventually to have won over the workers themselves to his point of view. (In 1950, when the NLRB held an election in his company, the independent union that had been organized in the meantime won hands down.)

All his life Weir drove his own way, though many of his fellow creatures of varying shades of opinion thought his conduct foolish, perverse, and wrong. In his fight against the unions he was clinging tenaciously to the past, but the ways in which he was ahead of his time are more significant. For it was by violating conservative traditions that he achieved his success.

YOUNG MAN WITH A PLAN

Basic in Weir's career were a lifetime plan and the goal of freedom of action, economic as well as political, social as well as personal. He never forgot his own experience of dependency. He never forgot the dependence of his father, a livery stablekeeper, on the whims of the wealthy who hired the horses. After his father's death, his mother and younger brother were dependent on his own meager earnings, which meant that he himself was dependent on his superiors. From his fear of dependency arose a desire for an integrated operation that would not remain in business "only at the sufferance of someone else."

(Weir's opposition to unions seems to have stemmed from the same cause, more so than from the simple fear that unionization would cost him money. He gained no profit advantage from forcing the industry to raise wages more than it had planned on doing in 1941. Nothing would have been easier for him than to wait for the rest of the industry to settle and then meet the same terms.)

Weir was born in 1875, and began his business career in 1890 when his father died and he had to go to work to help support his mother and his younger brother. He started as an office boy at

$3 a week and worked 10 to 14 hours a day to make that much. According to his own account, the family was so poor at this time that once he was almost unable to get to work because he lacked a penny for the toll bridge he had to cross on the way. (Just as he was later to talk bankers into lending him money for his business ventures, he talked the tollkeeper into lending it to him.)

Weir remained with his first employer, the Braddock Wire Company, only two years. When he was seventeen he moved to a clerical job with the Oliver Wire Company and managed to progress rapidly, acquiring considerable experience in several departments of the business during the seven years he remained there. In 1898, he left for the Monongahela Tin Plate Company, which was sold shortly after to the American Tin Plate Company. By the time he was twenty-five, he was an assistant manager. In this position his new superior was James R. Phillips, who, though he was a little older than Weir, became his friend and later his partner.

In 1901 the United States Steel Corporation took over the American Tin Plate Company, but even in the disruption that generally attends such an event Weir managed to land on his feet. In that same year he was placed in charge of the original Monongahela mill on the south side of Pittsburgh; and in 1903 he became manager of American's Monessen plant, largest in the Pittsburgh district.

The employee period of his life Weir regarded merely as a preparation. In preparation for his future career, he systematically acquired the necessary experience by studying various phases of the steel business and identifying the steps by which he would progress. He learned all he could about steelmaking technology, established important connections, and made himself known as a young man of high promise.

Also, he checked regularly on the progress of his plans. Even as a boy of fifteen at Braddock he had figured out that his company was making enough wire each year to stretch a line to the moon—about 239,000 miles. He doubted there was need in the world for that much wire and told his mother, "I guess I'd better look for another job. There's no future in this one." But his mother could not afford to lose his weekly income and persuaded him to stay. Ownership and independence were his ultimate goals, and in this he was entirely in conformity with the ideals of his time. Thus William Miller writes:

> In that era ... young men, whether professionally trained or not, who had no prospect of inheriting a business and yet clung to salary jobs ... merited as little regard in the business community as spinsters of the same age did at home. Roles of a sort, of course, were prescribed for both spinsters and employees, but for the latter at least, these were likely still to be such as cramp the spirit and cloud over the blue sky of aspiration.[2]

It was in the methods he used to achieve these goals that Weir differed from the majority. The industry was concentrated in Pittsburgh; Weir moved away from it. During the thirties, when the industry was holding up prices and operating at 17 per cent of capacity, Weir cut his prices and kept up volume. He adopted new processes before the rest of the industry considered them feasible, and at a time when large companies were hardening into bureaucracies, he allowed his managers an unprecedented degree of freedom.

Both Weir and his boss at U.S. Steel, Phillips, felt they could have no real future in so large an organization and constantly discussed establishing their own company, even though neither one of them had been able to save much money as yet. "We felt we would do much better in a business in which we would have a substantial share of ownership." But with the trusts gobbling up as much control as possible, it was not until 1905 that Weir and Phillips heard of a small tin-plate mill in Clarksburg, West Virginia, that could be bought at a comparatively low price, especially since its plant was poorly designed, had inefficient machinery, and, as Weir described it, was "horribly congested."

That they themselves had not a tenth of the money needed did not bother them. Phillips was able to get one bank loan, and Weir

[2] "The Business Elite in Business Bureaucracies" in William Miller (ed.), *Men in Business: Essays in the History of Entrepreneurship*, Harvard University Press, Cambridge, Mass., 1952.

went to the Farmer's Bank and talked the president into lending him $10,000 without any collateral, the stipulation being that his father-in-law, who had no collateral either, cosign the note. Because of their reputations as up-and-coming young men, Weir and Phillips were also able to convince others, including the head of the Bank of Pittsburgh, the president of the Fidelity Trust Company, and ten prominent Pittsburghers, each of whom had built his own business, that it would be profitable to put up money for the new firm.

The company had 250 employees and was capitalized at $250,000, $190,000 of which went for the purchase of the plant. Phillips, who became president, died shortly afterwards in a railroad accident near Harrisburg, and the investing group elected Weir to fill the vacant position.

Though the company made money almost from the start, its position was insecure for a long time. Since it was too small to issue bonds or sell common stock, each step toward expansion was marked by a new bank loan. As Weir put it:

We could have continued on a comfortable basis if we had been content with small operations and small profits. But that was never our idea. From our start, it was our intention to build a successful big company.... Our backs were against the wall many times in those early days. We operated on a shoestring budget. Too many mistakes, one big mistake, or even some accident beyond our control could have broken us.

Early in his career at Clarksburg, one event beyond his control nearly did break him. Weir solved the problem in the characteristically original and slightly ruthless manner that befitted a classical entrepreneur.

Weir had constructed a dam in the West Fork River near the plant, and under ordinary circumstances it would have ensured an adequate water supply for the plant processes. But in the summer and fall of 1908, an unprecedented drought hit West Virginia. No rain fell for months, and the water behind the dam sank dangerously low. The company used the same pickling solutions so many times that the packing on the pumps had to be replaced every day because it was eaten away by the acid. Weir got portable pumping equipment and started pumping out pools left upstream by the drying river, but as the drought dragged on, this source became more and more inadequate.

Finally, Weir cast his eyes on a reservoir commonly supposed to be owned by a nearby chemical company. Though it was pretty much of a forlorn hope, he took the trouble to investigate the title. He discovered that the chemical company actually owned only half of the reservoir. The other half belonged to a local farmer who was perfectly willing to sell. Weir bought the half interest and started pumping that night.

Next morning he got a call from the president of the chemical company in Cleveland. Employees had hastily notified headquarters when they arrived on the scene in the morning.

"I'm just pumping out my half of the water," Weir said innocently. "I bought it yesterday. By the time you can get here, I'll have my half."

The chemical company president called his attorney, John W. Davis, later Democratic candidate for the Presidency, whose birthplace was Clarksburg. Davis agreed that Weir was entitled to his half of the water, but suggested that cooperation in finding other sources might be more profitable than fighting over the division of the scarcity. Weir was willing enough to settle on this basis, and the two companies joined forces to prospect for supplies. By surveying the country for miles around, they found enough pools to carry them through until the drought finally broke early in December.

Meanwhile, in the sales field, Weir was bucking U.S. Steel. Instead of trying to beat the giant corporation on its own terms, he sought gaps in its sales efforts. He used a different price and discount policy and stressed personal attention to customers, providing a good deal of it himself. Gradually he acquired a number of small customers and became their personal friend. Later on, a strike at U.S. Steel's competitive tin-plate mills helped him to gain a larger foothold. From then on Weir took a leading role in selling, either personal or inspirational, following the Carnegie maxim: "Give me a market and I give you a mill."

EXPANSION AND INTEGRATION

The first large expansion movement was planned as a means of protecting the independence of the company. Weir bought his sheet-bar semifinished steel from the U.S. Steel Corporation, as did almost all the other independent tin-plate producers. But this principal supplier was also a competitor in the sale of tin plate, and he knew that the corporation had the power to put him out of business. So he went to Judge Gary, head of the corporation, and told him: "You can break me. You can close me out if you cut the price of plate and keep the price of sheet up or if you decide not to sell me sheet bar. I must know where I stand."

Judge Gary admitted that what Weir said was true. But as of that moment, he said, the corporation had no idea of doing any of the things Weir had mentioned. Then he added: "I cannot give you any guarantee against it. As I say, young man, we haven't any such moves in mind now. But who knows about the future?"

Weir did not choose to remain in business "only by the sufferance of someone else," even though the worst never happened. (In the end, U.S. Steel tried to "join" rather than "fight" Weir and offered him the presidency and an annual salary of $1 million, which he refused.) To assure himself a supply of sheet, he had to be his own supplier, "have a 'Little Steel' fashioned after 'Big Steel,' where you provided everything for yourself. For this reason we had to have an integrated steel operation from the very beginning."

So Weir borrowed another $300,000 and, after careful considera-- tion of alternatives, purchased 105 acres of apple orchard and wheat-- fields at Crawford Crossing, West Virginia, and called it Weirton.

The choice of the new location, away from the obvious spot, Pittsburgh, is an example of Weir's unorthodox approach. In Pittsburgh he would not have had to build up an entirely new community from scratch and there would have been certain "external economies"—suppliers and legal, financial, and accounting services would have been readily available.

Weir did not choose the conventional way because, as he put it, we had something else important in mind besides building an integrated plant. We knew that our location would become the main location for our company. We were convinced that the principles and process on which we operated our business would make a basis of peace and harmony possible if we could establish our own environment. Naturally, we could not do that in an existing industrial center. In such a center we would have to share the existing environment, including the attitudes, prejudices, and antagonisms that had built up during its entire previous history.

In order to get harmony and goodwill we were entirely willing to undertake the double burden of building a new community at the same time as we were building our new plant and to undergo the growing pains that such a venture involved. And that is why Weirton did not come into being through accident . . . it was deliberately selected and consciously planned as the location for both a steel plant and a community.[3]

In selecting this spot, Weir, who had no formal training in economics, could not have followed the dictates of the complex economic theory of location more closely if he had worked with a textbook in his hand. The site was close to coal resources, and the coal could be transported by river. Ore would also be transported cheaply, by water to the lower Great Lakes ports and then by rail transshipment. Heavy finished products could be delivered to customers along water routes at a relatively low cost as well as by rail. A "windfall revenue" could be obtained from some customers in the immediate vicinity of Weirton, since, under the old basing-point system, they paid Pittsburgh prices plus the freight rate to Weirton, though this was counterbalanced to some extent by freight cost to customers east of Pittsburgh. The new site was also advantageously near markets—half the population of the United States was within a 500-mile radius. There was adequate water supply; the plant location was free from the floods that threatened so many other sites; and, above all, there was plenty of room for expansion.

Weir built the first tin-plate plant at the lower line of the valley but close to the hills. If it had been his intention to build a finishing plant alone, this move would have been uneconomical. It was logical only in terms of a fully integrated steel plant.

[3] "Some Aspects of Our Personal History," speech given on Feb. 24, 1955.

The first plant, costing about a million dollars and necessitating further loans, was in operation before the end of 1909 and consisted of ten mills. Another ten mills were added in 1910, twelve more in 1911 (through the purchase of the Pope Tin Plate Company of Steubenville, Ohio), four more in 1914, two in 1915. In a few years the company had fifty mills: twenty-six at Weirton, twelve at Steubenville, and twelve at Clarksburg. It was the largest producer of tin plate in the country outside of U.S. Steel. The process of integration was furthered by World War I, which provided an opportunity to set up steel mills and blast furnaces, and in 1920 an up-to-date steel plant was completed. Prior to and during this time Weir purchased iron-ore properties in the Great Lakes region and acquired coal lands in Pennsylvania and West Virginia. Weirton Steel then had more than 5,000 workers and sales of more than $50 million annually. The growth of the company proceeded with remarkable steadiness over its first twenty years.

A real community to support and benefit the commercial venture was planned at the time Weirton property was purchased. Weir said many years later:

As we were walking over the vacant fields and looking over the land, if someone then could have opened a door to the future and made us see the panorama of mills, houses, churches, schools, stores and everything else that goes to make up the Weirton of today, naturally we would have been highly pleased—but I cannot say honestly that we would have been greatly surprised. Because when we came here, it was already a settled matter that we would build a completely integrated steel plant and the community to support it.

The original community, called The Cove, consisted of a few houses. Today Weirton has a population of 30,000, an area of 18 square miles, and 6,400 houses. The physical equipment of the city compares in quality and quantity with the best in the country.

Weir organized the town, as well as the company, according to his own ideas; much of the actual plan was conceived and carried out by Thomas Millsop, Weir's protegé and then president of Weirton Steel. There are only a few city employees; and the cost of running the city is said to be lower per head than that of any other city in the United States, and real estate taxes per head are among the lowest. Most services are contracted for on the basis of bids. All expenses—including postage—are published, so that the administration of all city affairs is indeed a "public" affair. Each householder undertook to pay for paving his part of the street and constructing part of sewers, and the city notes financing the payments were largely paid off on presentation. Ninety-five per cent of Weirton's employed population own their own homes.

Some of the community's feelings may be indicated by the fact that the man who succeeded Weir as president of the company, Thomas E. Millsop, was elected and reelected mayor, though the town is heavily Democratic in national elections and he is a Republican.

By 1929 Weirton Steel was almost twenty-five years old, an established company and an extremely profitable one. And it was still closely held in undisputed control by those who founded it.

But it had one vulnerable point. Though Weir had acquired coal and ore holdings before Weirton was ten years old, the company was far from self-sufficient in raw material. Fifty per cent of the Superior ore reserves, which at that time supplied four-fifths of the steel industry, were owned by U.S. Steel, and other large steel producers had bought up most of the remainder.

One of the few remaining independents was the M. A. Hanna Company, which possessed large reserves of ore, mostly in the Mesabi range. Under the competent direction of George M. Humphrey, later U.S. Secretary of the Treasury, who had helped to reorganize it in 1922, Hanna operated as an independent selling to independents, of whom Weir was one.

But there was a possibility that Weir might lose this source. Cyrus Eaton was then attempting to put together the country's second largest steel company, and it was not improbable that he, or someone else with the same idea, might come to dominate Weir's major independent source of supply. Weir decided that his investment would be better protected if he were "Mr. Humphrey's partner rather than Mr. Humphrey's customer." Humphrey, sensing the difficult years ahead, preferred assured markets to the insecurity of independence.

Weir was also anxious to expand his steel production facilities. Dependence on a single product (tin plate) seemed too dangerous. And he foresaw that the great markets of the future would be the Middle West in general and the automobile industry in particular. So he directed his attention to the Great Lakes Steel Corporation, at Ecorse, a suburb of Detroit.

Great Lakes Steel was itself something of a maverick in the industry. At that time the steel industry had an inhibition about construction in the Detroit area. To open a plant there was something that "just wasn't done." The company was the brain child of George R. Fink, who had sold sheet steel to the automobile industry and had good connections with it. Though a large steel company was said to have offered him a good position if he would desist from opening a plant near the big auto companies, he went ahead on a small scale. Then by 1929 he had done so well that he decided to expand, and selected a site on the Detroit River for a larger plant. Although he was able to raise $20 million, he needed more new capital, and this he could get from Weirton while still preserving the company's identity, which might have been lost had he merged it with a large concern. In becoming a part of the more diversified enterprise, he became less completely dependent on the automobile industry, and the ore resources and nearby blast furnaces of M. A. Hanna assured him of supplies and saved further heavy investments.

Agreement of the merger was reached just before the stock market crash in 1929, and the accord was formally ratified just after the break. Weir got a 50 per cent interest in the newly formed company, which was named the National Steel Corporation, and became its chief executive and chairman of the board. Fink got a 25 per cent interest and became president, and Humphrey got the remaining 25 per cent and became a member of National's Board and chairman of its executive committee. The M. A. Hanna Company did not itself go into the merger. Instead, it maintained its identity as an affiliated company and contributed the ore, the Detroit blast furnaces, and the freighters.

Weir brought in not only Humphrey's assets, but also one of the country's best business brains. As chairman of its executive committee, Humphrey took a prominent part in the company's affairs from the very beginning of his association with it. He became chairman of the board in 1957 after leaving his post as Secretary of the Treasury in order to smooth the changes caused by Weir's death that year. One of Humphrey's important planning contributions was his exploration of related investments and discovery of aggressive managements, which he very successfully combined with M. A. Hanna's investments, such as the Pittsburgh Consolidated Coal Company and the Iron Ore Company of Canada.

There was no new equity financing in the consolidation, no "water," and no promoter's profits. Weir asked banks for a promissory note of $40 million ("it was like asking for the National Debt at that time") and got it with no collateral other than his promise to repay and to issue bonds later as conditions might warrant.

INGREDIENTS OF SUCCESS

Born at the outset of the Great Depression, National Steel might have been expected to collapse almost immediately; from Hanna, Weir got no advantages competitors did not already have, and Great Lakes was handicapped by the worst automobile depression in the history of the industry. Instead, National Steel produced at 62 per cent of capacity while competitors were down to 25 per cent and below. In 1932 Weir made a profit while the rest of the industry was losing money. In 1933 he made a greater profit than all the rest of the industry. How was this possible?

1. National Steel's finishing capacity was considerably in excess of its furnace capacity. Hence it could adapt production to falling demand by the inexpensive method of shutting down a strip mill rather than by the costly process of shutting down a blast furnace.

2. Great Lakes Steel could supply large quantities of steel at low selling and transportation expense; even small quantities could be sold at a profit and supplied in a hurry. "This 'grocery store' busi-

ness did not make anyone rich but it kept Fink from becoming poor."

3. The world had to continue to eat, and much of the food it needed had to be conserved in tin.

4. Finally, the techniques of production were highly efficient, and though it was unostentatious and largely unpublicized, National's management was one of the most competent in America.

Technical innovations included the four-high continuous mill—Weir acquired the patents and built the mills in 1927 before anyone else in the steel industry had introduced the process, though he had to borrow $7 million to finance the construction. This converted a job that had taken a whole day into a three-minute operation. He was also one of the pioneers in another revolutionary technical advance, the electrolytic tinning of steel, building an experimental line in 1938 and going into production in the spring of 1943. In World War II his second-in-command, Thomas Millsop, undertook to roll brass on large steel equipment—a feat never before attempted and for technical reasons considered impossible. In a month's time, Weirton became the country's largest producer of rolled brass and was responsible for breaking a procurement bottleneck. Later the company devised methods of rolling magnesium sheets. In the production of an essential atomic-bomb material, Weirton solved problems that producers in other fields had refused even to tackle.

In the field of organization, Weir built a logical structure from the very first, observing—though he had never heard of them—two of the classical rules of organization: unity of command and authority commensurate with responsibility.

Though he was never much concerned with organization charts and manuals, and in fact operated for a long time without even a chart, he early laid out the broad outlines of the principal jobs, dividing the work logically so that the profitability of the various functions could be gauged.

At the very first, he did transgress the rule that authority should be delegated along with responsibility, but because—unlike many business geniuses—he permitted subordinates to disagree with him, he corrected this fault at the instance of one of the salesmen he hired when he found that he could no longer handle both the sales function and the job of chief executive.

Moreover, he introduced some ideas that organization planners in other companies began to approach cautiously only in very recent times; for example, he delegated both responsibility and authority as far down the line as possible, with control exercised through profit and loss statements rather than through rules regarding set ways of doing things.

From an engineering viewpoint, the individual mill was of optimum size for management; similarly, the optimum unit in marketing was a group of customers for certain specialties or a particular territory. In each case, the "middle manager," who was managing a unit just about large enough for one man to comprehend all the details, was charged with the basic decision making and stood or fell on results.

Weir went much further in this than do many companies that believe they have "decentralized decision making" today. A superintendent of a nearby company once commented:

I have never been able to understand why we do not have financial authority commensurate with responsibility. I have friends at a competitive company [Weirton] and I know that when they write a good order, they get what they need. They don't have to sit around writing justifications and explain why they need it to everybody. They are responsible people holding responsible jobs and they know it is up to them to make a good showing cost-wise, and everybody knows that they don't order things unless they are aboslutely needed. But when they say they want it, they get it immediately. A general superintendent [in our company] can make a mistake that will cost the company half a million dollars, yet he cannot authorize the purchase of a $5,000 tractor.

And middle management did not hesitate to insist on its prerogatives. One new higher-echelon executive who persisted in checking too closely on a lesser member of the management team was frankly told: "This is not the way we do things here. I am not a flunky. If you want to know how I'm doing, take a look at the profit and loss statement." The underling not only got away with it, but also won his point and was free from further interference.

Weir's strong belief in maximum freedom of operation for all managers, including foremen, is one explanation for his stubborn refusal to recognize international unions. He thereby avoided their severe restrictions on work assignment and change of assignments and so increased his supervisors' powers to meet company goals.

Moreover, Weir did not allow the staff men to proliferate as they have often done in other companies. Headquarters staff was kept small, and staff work was supplied where it was most needed, in the field helping with day-to-day problems. Staff men were flexible and could be easily and quickly shifted to new assignments. Central activities were confined to financing, purchasing, and coordinated control.

Since Weir delegated so much real authority, he had time to keep up personal contacts with his executives and through his own leadership imbue them with the company policies that had meant success: first-class personal service to all customers, punctuality (telegrams, even from overseas, were answered within a half-hour of receipt and the answers were equivalent to contracts), acceptable or more than acceptable prices, etc.

Putting together the resources of Hanna, Great Lakes, and Weirton was perhaps the most important of Weir's organization feats. It fitted perfectly into the natural tendencies and development of the steel industry.

Weir thought little of formal management training and appraisal forms. The very real delegation of authority and responsibility, combined with the full exercise of accountability, he believed, provides enough training and affords the logical means of appraisal through results.

In this, and in his view that the top manager needs considerable knowledge of all the technical specialties (a training he systematically acquired in his employee days), Weir may appear to have been lagging behind the times. Actually, he may have been ahead of them. The view that management is a "skill in itself" which exists independently of technological knowledge may have been somewhat overdone in recent years. Perhaps it has led to overdependence on certain types of staffs and consequently to growth in overhead. Undoubtedly, technical skill—in metallurgy, or sales, for example— may exist without the ability to plan and coordinate that is the essence of the management job. But the man who plans and co-ordinates, no matter how logically, is at a distinct disadvantage if he has no real knowledge of the things he is planning and co-ordinating.

Weir knew production, he knew financing, and he knew sales and sales problems; in fact, he continued personal selling to some extent almost to the end of his life.

Since Weir was a substantial stockholder himself, he placed prime emphasis on the best use of his and other stockholders' investment. The principal method of control was through a profit and loss system for the main organization units (Weirton, Great Lakes, etc.) and through regular examination of controllable sales costs for the units that were not so large. Much of the detailed control was exercised by the small "management company," which occupied only half a floor in Pittsburgh's Grant Building and contained few but extremely able minds in general management, law, and finance. Finally, banks played an important part in his controls. Weir was continuously in debt, and as soon as one loan was paid off, he entered upon an even larger one: "We've always been in debt and I hope we always will be. It keeps us working harder." Surplus was kept in inventories and fixed assets. "A big cash balance is a terrible thing. It encourages the idea that the company is rich."

It must be noted also that there were important elements of luck in Weir's success. He got into the tin-plate business (where food canning made for a stable or rising demand) more or less by acci-dent. He was raised to the presidency of his new company by the premature death of Phillips. And he was enabled to gather in new customers by a strike against his competitors in tin plate. Later, his company grew with the rising demand for steel from the auto-mobile companies.

But subtracting these nonrepetitive factors, the other ingredients of Weir's success may be instructive.

PERSONAL QUALIFICATIONS FOR SUCCESS

The achievement of Weir's plan was, of course, a highly complex affair, and an outside analyst can, at best, trace only some of the elements.

First among the elements were his own personal qualifications, consisting partly of traits often characteristic of other great founders and organizers, but to some extent underplayed in the selection and development of higher executives today.

Weir had a highly logical mind. He clearly recognized the basic and essential aspects in the business situations that confronted him, and he organized to meet them. His selection of the site at Clarksburg and the fitting together of the logical combination of National Steel were two examples. Another was his successful move in keeping up volume by cutting prices during the Great Depression.

Weir had an innovating disposition and the ability to face risk. He was an innovator in all phases of the business, not only in technical advances but in the location of his plant away from the steel centers, and in building his own community from scratch. He never "played it safe" by waiting to see what the rest of the industry would do. Instead, he obtained new bank loans and went ahead.

He had an absolute will to succeed and few and uncomplicated goals. He sought only business success in the nineteenth-century tradition in which he grew up and complete independence.

Weir possessed great technical knowledge. In his employee period, he systematically acquired knowledge of as many phases of the business as possible, including the technical advances. For this reason he was on surer ground in introducing his innovations than he would have been if he had had to depend entirely on the advice of others, however competent.

Weir's physical energy was prodigious. In his younger days he could work around the clock for several days together, or drive himself steadily for months at a time. Even in his old age he would sometimes have appointments all day in one city, fly home, and then have a long dinner conference on an urgent issue.

His words and deeds were consistent with each other. Although Weir possessed in great measure the ability to make friends and deal diplomatically with others (when he thought it necessary) and to impress others (notably hard-headed bankers) with his own competence, he was not "cooperative" in the usual business sense today; that is, he was not a compromiser willing to water down his views to make them more acceptable, to impress others, or to avoid offending.

One strange quirk in Weir's nature was an extraordinary devotion to the book *David Copperfield.* He once said he had read it a hundred times and would continue to reread it. He kept a copy at each of his five homes and a supply to give away. Did he see in Copperfield's early hardships a parallel with his own early life? Was he warned by the example of Micawber against shiftlessness? Or was there a streak of nineteenth-century sentimentality in him that was warmed by Dickens' occasional mawkishness? Or did Dickens provide him with an escape from the everyday material world?

It is impossible to say. But this strange love for a single book seems to be one way in which he differed from the classic type of entrepreneur—the single-minded innovator and risk taker who concentrates almost entirely on business. His other choices of reading matter were very wide. He preferred the lasting to the ephemeral: books on world affairs, biographies, and history, though he also read detective stories. He read extremely fast and had an extraordinarily retentive memory.

MECHANICS OF SUCCESS

The methods Weir utilized in achieving his success may be summed up under a few headings:

A lifetime plan. Once Weir decided to quit U.S. Steel, he clearly established the goal of building one of the largest integrated steel companies in the country. The Clarksburg tin-plate mill was a stopgap to contribute the necessary funds. He deliberately planned the location of Weirton to make possible an integrated company.

In making, disseminating, and checking on his plans, Weir did not use forms, charts, high-powered machines, and pyrotechnical presentations so dear to the organization man. He focused his mind on the basic questions separating the primary from the secondary, or "details," as he put it. He would draw on his experience and memory, his travels and personal visits and interviews, and use one or at most a few outstanding fact finders. In this way he would assemble something like 85 per cent of the facts obtainable and apply his penetrating analysis to the essentials, conceive the plan, tell his associates about it, and follow it up himself.

Flexibility. Though Weir held tenaciously to his basic objective, he was unusually flexible in the ways in which he sought his ends. Consistency was not a trait he sought to display. He would change his policy violently if he could thereby serve the end, as when he changed his pricing drastically at the outset of the Great Depression and reverted from bulk selling to hand-to-mouth peddling during the great automobile slump. He also rapidly reversed his wage policies when economic conditions changed or when an increase became necessary to ensure that no international union gained a foothold in his mills.

His internal company organization was highly flexible. It was motivated by high rewards, emphasis on the survival of the fittest, and a degree of independence for subordinate managers unusual in industry. He placed no emphasis on formal organization or formal development of individuals. (The latter omission may have been somewhat unwise since at one point the company hastily had to hire executives from other steel companies.)

Conformity in objectives, nonconformity in reaching them. Weir always accepted the basic values of the society in which he grew up. His main objective was frankly the accumulation of wealth, plus independence and freedom to maneuver. He was unorthodox only in his methods of reaching his goals, and that probably because no orthodox ways were open to him.

The fact that he was willing to act differently from competition was his chief strength. If everyone had cut prices when he did, there would hardly have been a larger volume for all. But because he was willing to run away from the crowd, he profited. Similarly, because no one else had thought to move steel mills away from Pittsburgh, he gained advantages of location. He utilized "the power of being a positive stinker" by doing things that were distinctly "not done" in the industry.

Ruthless execution of plans. Weir's long-range goal was broken down into annual rates of increase in what he considered to be the major measures of growth. Assets, investment in plant and equipment were to grow by more or less steady increments regardless of general steel contractions. And expenses for wages and salaries and maintenance were not to get out of line. Through "responsibility accounting" he held each executive rigidly accountable for results both quantitatively and qualitatively. He enforced a Draconian adherence to his plans, even in the depths of depression, on himself as well as on his associates. Financing through bank loans, he said, "keeps us working harder."

Personal inspection and hard work. Though he allowed his executives more freedom than other top managers often do, he did not separate himself entirely from the details of the business. He kept in touch by frequent telephone calls and visits to the various locations. And to avoid corruption from success, Weir liked to quote Einstein: "The only way to escape personal corruption of praise is to go on working. One is tempted to stop and listen to it. The only thing is to turn away and go on working. Work. There is nothing else."

An egalitarian top structure. Weir was deeply conscious of the need for a small oligarchy that could discuss all matters freely. He paid salaries equal to his to the top men, believing they made equal contributions to the company, and preferred to have a group of outstanding top men rather than the biddable nonentities many of the corporate founders surround themselves with.

If much of Weir's later nonconformity turned into rebellion, it may in fact be explained by his clinging to the value structure and goals of his youth when those of his society, and increasingly those of many of his competitors, were changing. As Weir was fond of saying, "There was much that was good in the good old days." It was this that brought Weir into conflict with the New Deal and with many of his business friends (e.g., U.S. Steel and later Ford, after the latter's recognition of CIO unions and the grant of the union shop). Not even Walter Teagle, late president of Standard Oil Company of New Jersey, was able to ease his continued disagreement with the labor boards of the Roosevelt administration (Hugh Johnson threatened to jail him, and his interviews with FDR were mostly cat-and-mouse games).

When Weir had won his battles in a formal way, he became less negative regarding the changing value structure of his time and turned to what might be called constructive nonconformity in the last part of his life. During World War II he fully cooperated in the American war effort, even to the extent of undertaking some seemingly impossible jobs—for example, the rolling of brass on large steel equipment.

THE LATER YEARS

After World War II Weir became convinced that complete refusal to accept the changing values of his society was fruitless and frustrating. Consequently, he actively tried to help shape the values and to persuade others to do the same and to support their beliefs by political action. His basic belief in freedom of economic opportunity and freedom of action did not change appreciably. He still attempted to reduce the scope of governmental intervention. But here, unlike the large majority of businessmen, he attempted to strike at the heart of the government's base for intervention, namely, what he considered to be the excessive amount of international tension and armament. If it could be reduced, then a greater area of freedom for economic and political action would be assured. It was the negative action by governments all over the world that he tried to counter by being positive.

Weir liked to quote Lord Attlee's observation on how to make progress on big, seemingly unresolvable issues: "When the logs are jammed in the river, one must begin by extricating one or two, in the hope that thereby the whole mess might move." And beyond that Weir felt—again unlike many businessmen—that he and his confreres should participate in politics to help legislate a type of government intervention which provides for opportunity or at least does not hinder it.

Toward this end, he wrote annually several papers and speeches, reviving the art of pamphleteering and carrying it to a high level of effectiveness. The Weir tracts were requested by hundreds of thousands of write-ins to the company, even though there was hardly any newspaper or other publicity. As involved in what he considered to be the big international issues as he was in his own affairs, he attempted to be supremely rational in an irrational world. Writing with persuasiveness and forcefulness, he anticipated Ambassador Kennan and Senator Fulbright by almost a decade in his proposals which were designed to halt rising military budgets and the abysmal decline of professional diplomacy, to promote rising living standards and the good life. To this Weir devoted the last ten years of his life. It was the one issue he had not resolved at his death.

5

Centralization versus Decentralization: The Reorganization of the Westinghouse Electric Corporation, 1935–1939[1]

> My intention being to write something of use to those who understand, it appears to me more proper to go to the real truth of the matter than to its imagination; and many have imagined republics and principalities which have never been seen or known to exist in reality; for how we live is so far removed from how we ought to live, that he who abandons what is done for what ought to be done will rather learn to bring about his own ruin than his preservation.
>
> MACHIAVELLI, *The Prince*

[1] This study was carried on intermittently over a period of five years. It was begun at the suggestion of M. W. Cresap, Jr., president of Westinghouse Electric Corporation, and carried out under the general supervision of E. M. Elkin, at that time general tax counsel of Westinghouse. The actual work was done in cooperation with L. E. Kust, at that time of Cravath, Swain and Moore and now general tax counsel of Westinghouse, and H. Forman of the

The great organizers whose work has been analyzed so far enjoyed two major advantages. First, their companies were, at least to some extent, owner-managed, which meant that results were facilitated because they were linked closely and strongly to personal rewards. Second, operations were already partially decentralized, principally because the companies had been put together, in whole or in part, by a series of acquisitions.

The great organizer of this chapter, A. W. Robertson, chief executive of the Westinghouse Electric Corporation in the 1930's, was confronted by a more difficult situation. There were no major ownership holdings to provide special incentives, and the central direction of the company, begun by George Westinghouse, had at no time been appreciably relaxed. Where the other great organizers of this book had to devise methods of coordination and control for decentralized operations, Robertson had both to split apart tightly centralized groups and to ensure coordination and control; for in the 1930's it had become clear that tight centralization was a major cause of difficulty.

NATURE OF THE REORGANIZATION

The radical reorganization of the management structure was begun in 1935, and was well under way by 1936, but was not actually complete until 1939. Essentially, this reorganization involved the splitting of a very large administrative unit into a number of smaller units.

---

company's tax counsel staff. Both helped at every stage of the studies, and without their assistance and advice and the access they provided to numerous original sources, the work could not have been accomplished. I have drawn extensively on original data (accounting and statistical) and memoranda given me by the accounting and budget departments of Westinghouse. I am deeply grateful to the following for supplying first-hand information on various aspects of the reorganization: A. W. Robertson, then chairman of the board; Ralph Kelly, then vice president; M. W. Smith, then vice president; Frank D. Newbury, then economist; A. H. Phelps, then vice president; T. C. Philips, then works manager; and R. S. Shave, then of the budget department. However, the author alone is responsible for the accuracy of the facts and their interpretation.

Before the reorganization, all major decision making—and much that was minor—as well as all basic financial and cost knowledge were concentrated in a small group of top executives. Most important of this "headquarters group" were the chairman of the board, who was also the chief executive; the president, or second in command; and the four vice presidents, in charge of manufacturing, sales, engineering, and finance.

Each of the four vice presidents had direct authority over his function in the "field," that is, in each of the individual product units or plants. Hence each of the plants had several "bosses." A major consequence was a multiplicity of relationships and a lack of clear-cut responsibility for operation of the plants anywhere except at the very top.

This type of highly centralized organization is often characteristic of companies as long as they are still directed by their founders, and sometimes during the time of the founders' immediate successors. A great deal depends on the extraordinary ability of the founder, who has grown up with the business and often possesses a tremendous knowledge of it. He is able to make many decisions on the basis of experience; and in other cases his instinctive judgment serves him well.

Westinghouse probably had been more highly centralized than its major competitor, the General Electric Company, ever since it had started manufacturing direct-current incandescent lighting apparatus in 1884. This was so partly because it was much smaller and partly because George Westinghouse was an owner-manager rather than a hired executive like Coffin of GE. He was intensely interested in all the details of the business, both administrative and technical.[2]

But the genius manager frequently cannot pass on his basic abilities or his acquired knowledge, and the kind of opportunities he seized are not likely to recur. His associates may be familiar with his methods, but they seldom possess the ability to operate as

[2] Harold C. Passer, "The Development of Large-scale Organization, Electrical Manufacturing around 1900," *Journal of Economic History*, Fall, 1952, pp. 389–392.

he did. In any case they are probably near retirement age themselves.

Hence the successors of the Caesar-manager must introduce "systematized management" if the company is to maintain its position. Since there is seldom any one person in the organization who possesses a complete knowledge of the details comparable with the founder's, his successors must let others participate in responsibility and authority; in other words, they must introduce some form of decentralization. And since the company can no longer rely on the founder's inspired hunches, it must utilize a systematic approach to management, through organization, human relations techniques, managerial economics, and so on. Finally, the successors must devise a method of measuring the results of managerial efforts in order to determine how well the decentralized authority is being exercised.

In addition to the passing of the founder and his associates, a major cause of reorganization is an increase in the size of the enterprise. For the economies or gains of increasing size, after a certain point is reached, may be offset by diminishing returns from the management factor, since even a genius can no longer keep an eye on all the activities. As companies grow, problems of coordination increase. More time is required to communicate decisions to all concerned, to receive reports from the multiple production and sales units, and to handle the increasingly interrelated and growing span of control. Control efforts, which are generally haphazard ("management by exception"), become more difficult as the area of control increases and the "master's eye" is no longer omnipresent. Planning, interpretation, paper work, and direction become more involved; more mistakes are made. And as the company grows over the years, the impact and complexity of the outside forces and the outside "publics" increase. Failure to systematize management (and to provide aid for overburdened managers) may lead to a relative and even absolute decline of profits and market position.

There was no ready-made solution to the organization problems of the Westinghouse Electric Corporation in the mid-1930's. The books on management organization generally advocated Taylor's "functional structure," postulating a series of experts exercising diffused specialized responsibility for a series of line operations. This was precisely the situation at Westinghouse at the time. Consultants in management usually had little experience in top-management organization. And the large corporations had rarely tackled the problems with much success. General Motors Corporation and the Du Pont Company were exceptions, but for both the task had been to pull together a series of separate acquisitions rather than to break up a tight centralized organization. Furthermore, the Westinghouse product range was more complex than that of General Motors and even than that of Du Pont.

Considering the magnitude of the problem and the lack of known experience, the Westinghouse Electric Corporation was faced with a gigantic task in evolving and carrying out a workable plan of reorganization. Roughly, it fell into three parts.

Decentralization of Operations

In the decentralization, the many different plant operations were grouped together, on the basis of like products, into six major product divisions, four major product companies, and one international company, all reporting to an executive vice president. The manager of each division and separate company was given greater responsibility and authority and could run his unit partly as though it were a separate business, subject only to the overriding policies and controls of headquarters.

This basic change was recommended in the following words by the Westinghouse Management Advisory Committee on Reorganization set up in 1935:

1. There should be a definite declaration of policy on the part of the Company in favor of the General Manager Plan. The obvious alternative to our present general plan of organization is the single-man control of small company units; or, to state it differently, the General Manager Plan as opposed to the Major Functional Plan.

2. There should be a strong supporting supervising and training group

at headquarters under the leadership of a Vice President. The Vice President of these General Manager plants must assume full responsibility for financial results and must be given corresponding authority. This authority should include the right of approval of all expense-charges made from headquarters or from other plants to his plant.

The Vice President in charge of General Manager Plants would have one or two assistants to see that the available facilities were used by the General Manager. These coordination problems would be solved as they arose.

3. It would be desirable in each plant organized on the General Manager basis that both production and marketing be under the authority of the General Manager. In fact, that plan should be tried first only in those cases where this complete control of the business is possible. In these cases the field salesmen would report to the Plant General Manager.

4. With time and experience, plans can be worked out for those plants (Sharon, for example) where the product must be marketed through the general apparatus-to-industry sales organization. In these cases, the plant would have a small commercial group who would consider the district offices as the Plant's customers. These men would "sell" the plant's products to the general sales organization and would provide any service that would economically increase the sales of the product.

The basic nature of the change is illustrated on Chart 6, published at the time of reorganization. Separate and identifiable field operations (divisions and plants) were established and given far-reaching responsibilities with the necessary authority.

The upper part of the chart, Figure A, shows the original "functional" organization; the lower part, Figure B, the new organization. On the lower chart the district offices are self-contained and not subject to operating control *from any other function* (as in Figure A) and the separate factory units are self-contained to a large extent. In both cases, the relationship to the head office is mutually advisory, but both sales offices and factory units must operate within the broad framework of over-all company policy.

The new organization appears in more detailed form in Chart 7. This shows the revised organization as it appeared in November, 1936. There are separate field operations, large enough for economical operation but small enough for personal supervision.

A
COMPANY ORGANIZED ACCORDING TO LINE FUNCTIONS

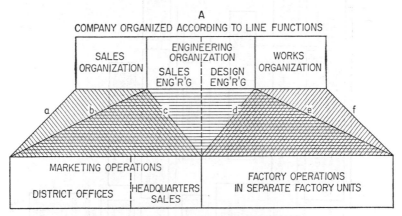

LINES a-c, b-e, AND d-f INDICATE FIELDS OF RESPONSIBILITY.
CROSS-HATCHING INDICATES OVERLAPPING FIELDS OF RESPONSIBILITY AND
AUTHORITY.

B
COMPANY ORGANIZED ACCORDING TO COMPANY OPERATIONS

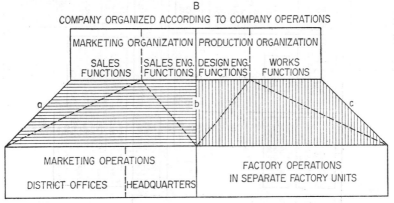

LINES a-b AND b-c INDICATE DIVISION OF DIRECT RESPONSIBILITY.
CROSS-HATCHING INDICATES SAME DIVISION OF AUTHORITY OVER OPERATIONS
(NO OVER-LAPPING

NOTE THAT BOTH CHARTS CONSIST OF SAME LINES (EXCEPT CROSS-HATCHING).
BOTH ORGANIZATIONS HAVE SAME ELEMENTS (WITH SAME POTENTIAL
CAPABILITIES) ARE ARRANGED DIFFERENTLY.

CHART 6. COMPARATIVE ORGANIZATION, FUNCTIONAL VERSUS DIVISIONAL

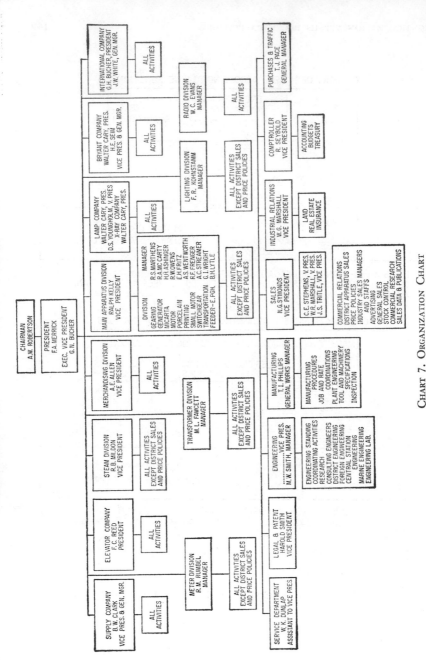

CHART 7. ORGANIZATION CHART

Establishment of a "Functional" Headquarters Staff

The second major change brought about by the reorganization was a change in the assignments of the heads of the basic management functions. These headquarters men ceased to be line commanders directing the various production units and became a "staff" group, exercising "indirect" rather than "direct" authority. This made possible "unity of command," or only one boss or superior for each executive. Thus the vice president for manufacturing at headquarters no longer directed production; his function was to help the divisions improve manufacturing procedures, to coordinate jobs and rates, to set up tool and machinery specifications, and to provide some inspection. Similarly, headquarters engineering and sales became staff functions. Other staff functions, such as industrial relations, were added also; still others were thoroughly revised, for example, purchasing. All together, these changes meant a considerable expansion of the headquarters staff.

Establishment of Central Controls

The reorganization involved considerable delegation of responsibility and authority from top management to the field, but it also necessitated considerable expansion of the staff at headquarters. The chief executive had to be kept informed of the way in which the delegated powers were being exercised, so that he could move quickly to reward success or to discover and correct failure. This meant that a number of highly skilled specialists had to be added to the central group to devise and administer systems of control.

Westinghouse was, in fact, among the first in American industry to adopt the control system known as "flexible budgeting." Under this plan, variable cost standards were established for all controllable operations, changing as volume changed. In this way the manager of each operating unit could be held responsible for any major variation from standard.

It is clear from even this brief description that the Westinghouse reorganization of the middle and late 30's was of major proportions and caused substantial changes in management. Its conception was on a grand scale. We must now turn to consider its execution and impact on the corporation's earning capacity.

IMPACT OF THE REORGANIZATION

The impact of a reorganization can be analyzed in terms of the experience of Westinghouse, which has proved fairly typical of that of other large corporations that have undertaken similar changes since. The impact can be divided into three stages:

1. *The immediate impact.* This is a brief period in which the immediate gains realized from the reorganization outweigh the extra cost. In the case of Westinghouse, this period was approximately a year (1935–1936).

2. *The short-run impact.* This is a period during the second and third years of reorganization when the extra expenses mount and tend to outweigh the gains. For Westinghouse this was roughly eighteen months: 1937 and a part of 1938.

3. *The long-run impact.* Eventually the gains from reorganization begin to outweigh the cost again, and this continues until factors other than organization intervene. Westinghouse entered this period in 1938.

Detailed evidence will be given for each of these observations. The changes during these three periods are described in this section, and the next shows the effect on the pattern of employment and on profits.

Immediate Impact of the Reorganization

A number of major advantages were immediately achieved by the decentralization of operations:

1. *The number of decisions going to the top management was greatly reduced.* By the very nature of the old organization many decisions had to go right to the top, frequently in considerable detail. This resulted in delays and mistakes, in poor relationships and lower profits. For example:

Before the reorganization there were four executives in the Gearing Division reporting directly to East Pittsburgh, each one to a different superior. The works manager, T. C. Philips (later vice president in charge of manufacturing), reported to the general works manager; the engineering manager to the vice president in charge of engineering; the division sales manager to the vice president in charge of sales; and the works executive in charge of stock control to a member of the general works manager's staff.

"There were more executives in my plant not working for me than there were working for me," Mr. Philips said. He added that before making decisions at the Gearing Division, on personnel, equipment, design, sales, and so on, he had to "ask a jury of about a dozen men." On an engineering problem, for example, he had to deal with a number of different engineering departments, such as control, switchgear, circuit breaker, motor and power, and these were located at other plants, chiefly at East Pittsburgh. After the reorganization, Philips himself made most of these decisions.

2. *Orders and information were transmitted more quickly.*[3] Before the reorganization the flow of communication had become increasingly slower and more faulty with the lengthening of the lines and the increase in the amount of information to be conveyed. As a result, selling was delayed and ineffective. There was ineffective communication between manufacturing and selling, and hence at times a good deal of "overselling" to move inventories. There was poor coordination between the plants and the salesmen, which resulted in many complaints, high repair bills, and mounting dissatisfaction among the customers. The engineers could not get the sales department to move fast enough on new products, because "you had to go all the way up the engineering ladder and then all the way down again on the sales ladder." A considerable number of technicians had to be kept on the works payroll merely to make investigations and rectify mistakes. As *Fortune* described the state of communication before the reorganization:

It was a stubborn company that Mr. [A. W.] Robertson [Chairman of the Board] had on his hands at the beginning of the depression. Bulky as a hippopotamus, with its directing brain handling everything from East

---

[3] See *Fortune,* February, 1938, p. 55.

Pittsburgh, the company could not always tell its manufacturing extremities in Mansfield, Ohio, and Chicopee Falls, Massachusetts, the correct thing to do. Nor could it be counted on properly to interpret the stimuli it received from these extremities. Westinghouse engineers would perfect something—say, the grid-glow tube, which stimulated the development of photoelectric cells and electric eyes—and the Westinghouse sales promotors would often miss the train to market with the product. The company was slow in styling; its goods were trustworthy but incorrigibly humdrum in appearance.

These were symptoms, big and little, of a central administrative heaviness. Robertson . . . began to decentralize the organization, placing the engineering and manufacturing autonomy and responsibility for profits with the various plant divisions. . . . Selling, which had more or less been taken for granted, was reorganized under N. G. Symonds, with the consumers' goods and lamp sales department kept distinct from the heavy stuff.[4]

3. *Responsibility and authority were clarified.* As long as a company is small enough for the individual managers to know all their subordinates personally, a functional centralized organization works well. Even in larger companies that produce only a few products or leave a great deal of freedom to their subsidiaries and have merely a few simple controls, a functional system may work satisfactorily. But in the Westinghouse case the company had grown to such an extent that the heads of the individual functions were no longer acquainted with many of the people through whom they exercised command and influence and through whom they had to get the work done. There had also been a great growth in the number of products. Yet the company continued to be highly centralized and controlled. In this way the chiefs of a number of functions impinged on individual executives. Subject to the orders from sales, manufacturing, engineering and control, each executive had two masters or more.

The impact of multiple commands is shown in a different form on Chart 8. Column A shows a breakdown of the company's sales dollar in the early 1930's (before the reorganization) according to profit, administration, engineering research, marketing, production

---

[4] *Ibid.*, pp. 55 and 57.

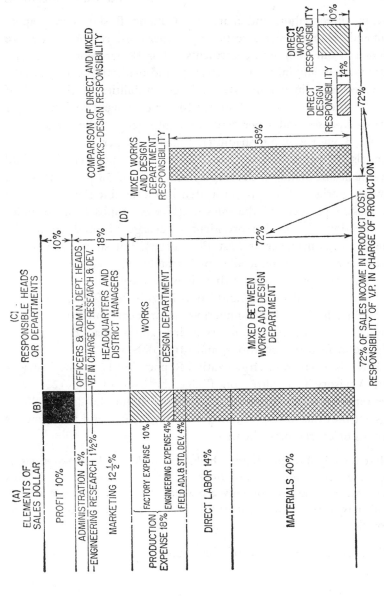

CHART 8. BREAKDOWN OF WESTINGHOUSE SALES DOLLAR ACCORDING TO RESPONSIBILITY (EARLY 1930s)

expense, direct labor, and materials. Column B shows in graphic form and column C states verbally whether these responsibilities are assigned to one or more departments. Thus 18 per cent of the sales dollar went to administrative, research, and marketing expenses (the white rectangle in column B), and responsibilities of the head of these functions conflicted. Another 10 per cent went to factory (or works) expenses, and 4 per cent went into design (the rectangle in column B with a single shading). Finally, 40 per cent went into materials, 14 per cent into direct labor, and 4 per cent into field adjustment and standard development, a total of 58 per cent mixed between works and design (indicated in the double-shaded column B). This 58 per cent of the sales dollar was supposed to be under the direction of the vice president in charge of production (the general works manager at East Pittsburgh), but since he was also at the works that produced approximately one-half the value of the company's production at that time, he frequently mixed up his function of policy making and control with interference in operations. In addition, the engineering department had control over design, both standard and nonstandard, and so had the right to interfere in factory operations, and often did.

Chart 8 is taken from Organization Report No. 17 by the Management Advisory Committee on Budgetary Control, June 22, 1934. This report reaches significant conclusions about the drawbacks of the system of mixed responsibility described above and recommends methods of overcoming them:

Here is a mixed responsibility which, even under the best conditions of cooperation, slows up cost reductions and other actions. If over-all costs or expenses are increased by only a few cents on the sales dollar because of this mixed responsibility, it is a serious matter because of its effects on profits.

To illustrate the nature of this mixed responsibility the report stated:

Design engineers specify quantity of material per unit of product and the number and extent of machining and other direct labor operations, but the Works, also, have direct responsibilities for the cost of material and the cost of labor. Such questions as minimum wall thickness of castings, rigidity of parts for handling and machining, the influence of number of sizes of standard parts or standard units on lower costs because of increased activity of individual parts, all necessitate continuous contact of manufacturing engineers with design engineers during the design of the product. The prevailing opinion in the Works that products cost too much because they are designed too closely, i.e., with insufficient material, illustrates the mixed responsibility for product costs.

The cumbersome committees that are set up under our present organization for cost reduction work are evidence of the mixed responsibilities of design engineering and manufacturing, and of the difficulties that would be experienced if it were attempted to recognize departmental responsibility for material and direct labor expenditures in a complete budget.

For these reasons the following Committee recommendations were fully accepted in the reorganization:

The Company's organization structure must, if the proper degree of control is to be maintained, parallel the breakdown of the sales dollar. Budgets must be prepared for each department of the organization in accordance with the limitations set by the master sales dollar.

The Committee has been guided by the principle that the ultimate aim of Company operations is to produce profits; that to produce profits its operations must at all times be under control, and that the Company's organization must be such as to permit such a control.

Your Committee believes it is impossible to make a similar definite alignment of Company income and departmental responsibilities based on the present company organization.

4. *Executive morale was improved by the reorganization.* The functional, centralized type of organization affected executive morale adversely when the company became large. The ability of many competent executives was not used; their freedom of expression was inhibited. With so much power concentrated in the top echelon at the head office, there was little original work left for even the heads of the plants to do. There were apparent or actual contradictions in orders. Initiative was reduced, and the division managers tended more and more to "let Pittsburgh take care of it." There would be no credit if independent field action were successful, and there

would be blame if it were not. There was much friction among executives because of the overlapping of authority. It was difficult to develop "all-round" executives for top management work. Promotional channels were not clear and sometimes completely blocked. Many of these morale blocks were eliminated by the reorganization.

5. *Objectives became clear and consistent.* Before the reorganization, contradictory objectives were sometimes pushed because there was inadequate coordination among the major functions of management. For example, the natural tendency of the manufacturing people to concentrate on as large an output as possible was reinforced by the bonus system for factory managers. But this frequently led to a disregard of quality and profit considerations. Sometimes excessive inventories were piled up, resulting in heavy storage costs, obsolescence, and decline of asset values. Consummation of successful research in new products was sometimes frustrated in the end by conflicting design orders and unimaginative selling. Increasingly, the objectives of the different management functions had become sectional and divergent. Through the use of a central coordinating staff and central controls, corporate objectives were shifted from maximizing output to maximizing profits; inventories were controlled; and research was more successfully coordinated with product development and sale.

6. *There was better coordination between functions, e.g., manufacturing and sales.* The final conclusion of the management advisory committee was that the reduction in the company's earning power and the increase in unit costs before reorganization were due to a significant extent to the shortcomings of the functional centralized organization. This conclusion was strengthened by the committee's emphatic recommendation that a radical change be made in the organization structure.

The committee cited many examples and a great deal of evidence in support of its contention. A situation reported to the author by A. W. Robertson will illustrate the type of material presented.

Mr. Robertson first saw the need for reorganization, he said, when reports of defective turbines began to reach him. Among these was a claim for $1 million from the Brooklyn Edison Company. On investigation, it was found that one of the major handicaps to efficient production at the South Philadelphia plant (the producer of the turbines) was the need for continuous checking of decisions with the functional heads in Pittsburgh. This caused delays, misunderstandings, conflicts, and mistakes. All engineering designs had to be checked with headquarters; the solution of major manufacturing problems was delayed; and selling had become very ineffective since the plant had hardly any control over it and the turbines were neglected in favor of other products that were considered to be "easier handling."

We may therefore tentatively conclude that the early impact of reorganization laid the basis for an increase in earning capacity because more decisions could be made by those who were closest to the problems and results were more readily traceable to individuals.

Short-Run Impact of the Reorganization

In the short run, roughly during the second and third years of reorganization, the increases in efficiency continued but were outweighed by increased administrative expenses, and this was a continuing and interacting process for some time. Divisional and plant management assumed new and increased responsibilities and therefore required more personnel, especially more staff people, and the decentralized operations meant that more coordination and control were required of headquarters. For example:

Manufacturing. Works managers got over-all authority in the plants, which meant that they needed larger staffs to help them handle such new or expanded functions as:

Production planning and policy making

Work on material and plant projects

Improvements in manufacturing processes

Plant extensions

Product improvement

Coordination of similar products manufactured in more than
  one unit

Transfers of manufacturing parts between units
Production planning and scheduling
Quality control

At headquarters a manufacturing staff was organized to assist the divisions in increasing the efficiency of their operations. Staff men there assembled information on the best and most up-to-date manufacturing techniques and disseminated it to the divisions, received reports on operation, and suggested changes and improvements. Staff members traveled to the various divisions to consult the divisional executives and check on their work; to appraise and, if necessary, to replace personnel; to help divisions plan changes, improvements, and expansion of facilities and improvements in organzation.

Some fifteen or twenty people were added to the personal staff of the vice president in charge of manufacturing (first called "general works manager") in consequence. They worked on basic improvements in quality control, rolling and heat treatment, inventory control, manufacturing training, and coordinated manufacturing activities with those of other major functions.

Sales. Divisional sales groups were set up under the division managers and made responsible for divisional sales volume and prices of products within limits set by general headquarters policies. In consequence, new marketing functions had to be carried on at divisional levels:

Elementary-level sales forecasting at a number of locations.

Advertising programs and greater participation in determining central advertising policies.

Preparation of proposals and bids for the district sales managers.

Sales Service. Groups were added to take care of special problems and customers' questions. Thus the transformer division added ten to twelve order service specialists; the lighting division added three men; the small motor division four to five.

The effect on the divisions can perhaps best be shown by a case example; that of the South Philadelphia Steam Division.

Before the reorganization, South Philadelphia operations were directed by Pittsburgh headquarters, which had fairly complete control over sales as well as over production and engineering. But headquarters thinking was dominated largely by electrical engineering and electrical products, and the same was true of the district sales offices, since they were responsible to sales executives at headquarters. And neither headquarters nor district sales offices were really familiar with turbine sales problems.

With the advent of decentralization, the division had to develop its own selling techniques, indoctrinate the personnel operating from the district offices, and finally compete successfully with the electrical salesmen in the district offices and gain customer acceptance. It took a number of years to build up really effective selling since the South Philadelphia representatives had to be trained from scratch and total training time for a turbine salesman may be anywhere from three to five years. (He has to know mechanical design, thermodynamics, and power-plant practices. He must be able to advise the customer, sell him on the best specifications and most economical use, and work with him over a period of time.)

Engineering. Each division set up its own engineering department or expanded the existing one. Many set up their own laboratories and their own tool and welding centers. This made local development and testing possible and meant considerable saving of time and better results.

One example of the expansion necessary is the changes made in the Generator Division:

1. A drafting group was added, subdivided into turbine generator and motor units.

2. Design facilities were set up.

3. The electrical section was divided into electrical and mechanical departments.

4. The engineering manager assumed more responsibility for the basic business functions of the division, as well as more responsibility for production, delivery, and quality.

The steam division invested a considerable sum of money to study the shortcomings of Westinghouse turbines, making an exhaustive analysis of turbines built in the period of the 20's in order to find the causes of customer complaints. And as in the case of the sales training, it took a long time for the full benefits to become effective since the manufacturing cycle for a steam turbine is from twelve to twenty-four months. The division also set up a new research department, an engineering development group, and a standards group and added other engineering personnel.

At headquarters, too, the engineering function was elaborated in order to provide highly specialized counseling service to the plants and divisions and permit interchange of information on improved practices between divisions. Since the divisions, even with their new laboratories, did not have adequate facilities for research on such problems as circuit breakers, nitron, insulation developments, plastics, electronics, and so on, great expansion of headquarters research was necessary. This eventually paid off through the development of many more new products, but this again took time. Other expansion took place in industrial engineering and the development of engineering standards, and a department was established to recruit and train students and plan student training at headquarters and the divisions.

Purchasing. Plants were assigned increased purchasing functions, such as the preparation of purchasing standards and specifications and the maintenance of ledger records in order that headquarters might check on the expanded field activities. Furthermore, purchase requisitions had to be filled out for all orders over $500 and sent to headquarters for central allocation in order to make possible quantity discounts, quality advantages, and the gains of reciprocity. Thus the plants required additional purchasing personnel.

A bigger change, however, occurred in the purchasing department at headquarters. Andrew H. Phelps, who became vice president in charge of purchasing about Apr. 1, 1938, described the changes in his department as follows:

When I assumed my present task I found an organization old, set, lazy, unwilling to try new ideas, and quite impossible from a progressive operating point of view. Purchasing before that time had been a function of certain men who had grown up in the service—perhaps starting as office boys—without technical training, without extensive ability, and without a lot of other things that we had to have in order to build an organization to expend over a million dollars a day. So I came back with a determination to expand this organization and to pull into it young technically trained men who would go somewhere in our company and show us the way to accomplish big things in purchasing. Within the year before the war started, I had gathered in over 200 such men, many of them from technical schools, colleges, and business schools. Many came from Harvard Business School. Within another year we drew in 200 more men. Before Dec. 7, 1941, we had taken nearly 1,000 men into our purchasing organization for our different plants. These men brought something to the functioning of purchasing at Westinghouse.[5]

As this new staff was acquired, the purchasing function was centralized as directed by the company president's Letter No. 130: "To coordinate the activities of the local purchasing agents to serve best the interests of the Divisions and over-all Company."

The purchasing staff at headquarters acquired or expanded the following functions:

1. *Personnel.* A staff of ten assistants was acquired to aid in hiring and firing, salary administration, transfers and promotions, training and supervision of personnel in the plants.

2. *Reciprocity system.* A complete ledger record on reciprocity was set up, listing orders from about 10,000 to 15,000 customers. Thus orders could be rotated among customers, and small companies were not overlooked.

3. *Checking of purchase requisitions* on orders of $500 or over sent by plants and divisions.

Traffic. Traffic staffs at the plants were increased by some 5 to 15 per cent so that shipments might be expedited and more modern methods installed.

Industrial Relations. In most plant locations and district offices one or sometimes several men were added to relieve the local manager of his industrial relations problems, partly because the company was anxious to confine its collective bargaining negotiations to a local pattern. In addition, some plants acquired experts

[5] Andrew H. Phelps, "Salesman in a New Day," address given to the Worcester Sales Executive Club, Worcester, Mass., and address before the Purchasing Agents Association of Buffalo, N.Y., May 12, 1948.

on grievances, safety, training, wage and salary administration. (Since the industrial relations function is so intimately concerned with the problem of people, its "localization" added greatly to its effectiveness.)

A headquarters industrial relations department was established also, in May, 1937. Its functions were to handle union contracts, union organization, central employment, wage and salary administration, social insurance, accident prevention, and training. This department was used as a court of final appeal, especially on grievances and basic industrial relations policy. New staff was needed also for extensive training and improvement of selection techniques, both designed to improve managerial competence.

In so far as collective bargaining was concerned, the expansion was largely due to the rise of unions and the need for uniform administration and legal interpretation of the Wagner Act. But the department's nonunion functions, essentially personnel functions, were considerably expanded at this time in line with the company's policy of providing more staff counsel in the field of human relations. This may have contributed to an improvement in morale and relationships among employees and managers, and so have contributed indirectly to greater profitability.

Public Relations. In 1937 the public relations function was added at headquarters to coordinate the company's and the plants' contacts with the public through the press and other media. In this way a foundation was laid for improvement of the corporation's relations with its various publics, and in addition there was better product acceptance.

Accounting and Control. Before the reorganization, district and plant accounting consisted merely of checking suppliers' invoices and sending them to headquarters for payment, making up the payroll, billing shipments, keeping machine-tool records, and providing cost estimates. In the years of reorganization, the following functions were added:

1. Preparation of the "No. 5 operating statement," giving the details of factory expense control and information on expenditures "before the fact." For the first time operating executives got data

on "controllable costs" that they could influence, and they did improve them.

2. Breaking down of distribution costs so that each division had data on sales billed and types of goods sold. This led to a more effective control and reduction of distribution costs.

3. Internal auditing to furnish useful and timely accounting information to the works manager.

4. Systems and procedures suggestions and improvement.

The reorganization of the company into distinct entities making and selling different products made it possible to install a budget-control system and to control each unit, as well as the company as a whole, on a profit-and-loss basis with an allowance for changes in business activity. The organization of the company now paralleled the breakdown of a "master sales dollar," and when the expenditures differed from this master pattern, central management could take action immediately.

With, and in part because of, these controls, new functions were added at headquarters:

1. A budget department, headed by a budget director, was established to prepare budgets for each department and division of the company and to watch performance against budget.

2. The central-control function expanded in the areas of corporate accounting, social insurance, and government accounting and undertook the study of cyclical fluctuations.

3. The headquarters staff had to coordinate divisional accounting —general ledger, accounts receivable, claims and royalty accounting, tabulating, and payroll accounting to make possible realistic comparison of results.

4. A systems and procedures section was established to control and formalize reporting on data and functions to streamline paper work.

5. A clearinghouse was established for the processing of interunit documents. Thus the repetitive documents were regularly scheduled, closely watched, and rigidly maintained. Each month, strictly on schedule, the results of all transactions were sent to headquarters in "pegboard" form. There they were consolidated and used in the

preparation of the over-all financial statements of the corporation. In this way accounting data became more timely and more useful. *No Quick Change.* All these changes took considerable time, and it took time also to change attitudes within the company. Even if people accept change outwardly, they may resent it consciously or unconsciously and can do much to hold it up by passive resistance or underutilization of their reserve capacity. Some were opposed to the particular change because it did not improve their status sufficiently or worsened it; others—many of them older employees— were instinctively opposed to any change at all.

Even many of the headquarters executives found it difficult to change. Because they were located at East Pittsburgh, they continued to direct operations there and the decision-making powers of the local management did not change appreciably. Eventually it was found necessary to move headquarters to a separate and distant office building in the city of Pittsburgh itself in 1937, and after this it became possible to shift headquarters work from centralized control to indirect staff services. The heads of the various functions gradually ceased to make operating decisions and devoted themselves to advice and consultation. In so doing they helped the divisional operating units to function more profitably.

And there were other reasons why the changes were necessarily slow in coming:

1. At the time Westinghouse reorganized there was *no generally known experience* available to the company. Literature on "decentralization," "headquarters staff," and "centralized controls," if any great amount of it existed at the time, was not known to the company. The reorganizers had to proceed on the basis of trial and error, and so their efforts may be characterized as pioneering. Thus the process of reorganization had to be carried on step by step, plant by plant, function by function, while the company learned through experience. The size, number, and complexity of the problems, and the weight of tradition, made careful testing and difficult coordination necessary.

2. There was a shortage of men experienced in reorganization procedures.

3. Executives who could assume the increased responsibilities were also not too plentiful, and selecting them and training them took time. It also took time to convince executives who had had little or no authority in the past that the authority now given was genuine. The chief executive had to convince them of this, provide examples and incentives, permit mistakes to be made occasionally. Executives who were given greater power were simultaneously given two or three years to show that they could learn to use it properly before they were discarded as failures or moved to other positions.

4. Reorganization meant tearing apart groups, teams, and collections of people who had worked together for many years. Elton Mayo, Fritz Roethlisberger, William Foote Whyte, and other students of human relations have convincingly shown that the breakup of an established working group may be very damaging to morale (often quite unintentionally so) and that it takes a long time to reestablish spontaneous cooperation.

5. There was no simple and common pattern for the many plants. Some, like the plant at Mansfield, had to be started again from scratch; some, like the South Philadelphia plant, made million-dollar products, while others, like Bridgeport, produced items costing less than 10 cents; some had to be physically moved.

7. Some executives now became too independent, did not consult with others sufficiently, and could no longer be adequately controlled. Some of the young men in the purchasing department, for example, were too cocksure and trusted too much to "science" and calculating machines of all kinds.

8. Where uniformity was necessary—in wage scales, for example, or capital expenditures—it was difficult to achieve. Decisions tended to vary among plants and divisions.

9. For a time the divisional and plant executives were ignorant of the value of the specialist advice available to them and did not use it adequately. The best and highest-priced talent in many fields was assembled at headquarters, but some of the men in the divisions considered it a waste of time to consult the headquarters staff, and it took a long time to disabuse them of this idea. Others spent a great deal of time, money, and effort checking and rechecking

with headquarters on the proper exercise of their responsibility. Some specific examples will show why the increase in profitability took considerable time:

1. In 1936 both the staff and the capacity of the Motor Division were expanded, production was standardized, and an assembly line planned. It was estimated that 60 per cent of the motor orders could be standardized, and some deviation was allowed on the remainder. Actually, subsequent orders showed a complete reversal of these percentages: a total of 70 per cent of them were off-standard. Because of this and the organization difficulties, the motor line did not get into full production until the war, and only then were the benefits of the investment in staff and plant realized.

2. At the Trafford plant the system of production was reorganized and the accounting system thoroughly overhauled. The changes were not fully effective until 1942–1943.

3. The South Philadelphia plant required several major reorganizations in staff personnel before the organization ran smoothly. Finally, a team of young men which had been created and trained over the years was able to handle the war orders—the jet engines, the atomic materials—which required great imagination and a flexible organization.

4. There were major moving and reorganization expenses in a number of plants, and it took time to recoup them.

Ultimate Impact

The third and last phase of reorganization is the long-run impact —the effect evident after the major changes have been completed and the people within the organization have adjusted to them. This is the period when the disturbances of the shakedown tend to have subsided and the costs of reorganization have stopped growing but the benefits continue to accrue.

Westinghouse realized many of the benefits of the immediate and short-run period in greater measure in the long run—that is, after three or four years.

Managers of the administrative units had learned to take responsibility and were able to exploit their proximity to the problems to the full and provide constructive solutions. They no longer needed to communicate details to headquarters, but were able to take full advantage of the accumulating knowledge of the central staff. Responsibility for controllable costs was clearly defined, which meant that managers had an incentive to use the money allotted to them wisely.

At the top management level, the time formerly devoted to decision making was sharply reduced and top management was able to devote more time to the development of new profit-making ideas and their implementation, to the personal inspection of subordinates' work, and to improving relationships with the company's outside "publics," especially labor and government.

Ultimately, this made possible a much speedier and more successful adaptation to market changes. Westinghouse sales declined less rapidly than those of General Electric in periods of downturn. Through the flexible budgets, Westinghouse seemed able to adjust costs more quickly. The staff specialists at headquarters won acceptance and played an increasing part in raising profitability. At the local level, community relations improved.

Finally, there was a general improvement in management; the inadequate were retired or weeded out or placed in positions that corresponded more nearly to their abilities. Most important of all, the decentralized management system made possible the development of a larger supply of managerial talent, which was a major factor in the increased profitability, continuity and expansion of the company.

CAN A REORGANIZATION BE QUANTIFIED?

The shift from centralized to decentralized organization at Westinghouse and its effects have so far been described only in qualitative terms. But qualitative evidence often lacks a certain degree of conclusiveness.

Could this type of information receive further support? Can the process and the result be quantified? Can we ascertain the changes in administrative expenses—total and components—resulting from the reorganization? Can we, perhaps, even ascertain the approximate impact of the reorganization on profits?

An attempt has been made to do so. The data used and the results obtained are, needless to say, not perfect. Nor can it be said that the changes indicated are solely due to the reorganization since a great many variables affect costs and profits.

However, an attempt has been made to eliminate as many of these variables as possible by examining cost and profit figures for Westinghouse in relation to those of its principal competitor, General Electric, and the industry as a whole.

It is hoped that the statistical methods employed will be of some help to others by making possible somewhat more accurate predictions of the cost of an organization change, particularly the costly and hazardous process of shifting from a centralized to a decentralized structure. In addition, the figures are intended to strengthen the evidence provided by the qualitative study, even though it is not possible to prove a case entirely beyond doubt.

Below is a summary of the evidence provided by a statistical study, and the data on employment and administrative costs are given in more extended, though still condensed, form for lack of space, in Appendix B on pages 227 ff.

Extent of the Reorganization

The first question naturally asked about a reorganization is evidence that it took place on a large-enough scale materially to affect the operations of the company.

Quantitative evidence of this, in the case of Westinghouse, is provided by the figures on administrative personnel, both numbers and costs.

It would be expected that as a result of the decentralization local operations would require additional staff in order to meet new responsibilities, and that headquarters staff would also have to be enlarged to aid the decentralized operations, to coordinate them, and to provide accounting controls. But as the organizational relationships were finally adjusted, some decrease in staff and administrative expense might be expected.

Even a considerable increase in staff and administrative expense at Westinghouse over the years in question might not afford much evidence of a radical reorganization unless the rise was greater than those in comparable or competitive companies, since the increase might be merely indicative of a general trend.

Taking 1935, the year in which the reorganization began, as 100, we find:

1. Divisional administrative personnel rose from 4,323 people (100) in 1935 to more than 7,000 in 1939 (160.4). The increase in the central administrative and technical staff was very small: from 3,540 in 1935 (100) to 3,651 in 1939 (103.1), but there was a considerable shift among the different categories that provides evidence of decentralization. For example, the sales staff dropped immediately, by almost 400 people, indicating the shift of the actual sales function from headquarters to the field; but the administrative staff rose by one-third over the four years, and the increase occurred mainly in accounting and engineering.

2. Comparison between Westinghouse and the electrical apparatus industry from 1935 to 1939 shows that the ratio of administrative and technical employees to production employees rose at Westinghouse at a time when it was decreasing in the rest of the industry. (Since the period 1935 to 1939 was a period of rising industrial activity, for the most part, a decrease in the ratio might have been expected.)

3. Further confirmation of the occurrence of the reorganization and its nature is obtained from comparative studies of administrative and manufacturing costs. Total selling, general and administrative expense rose by $10 million, or nearly 50 per cent, at Westinghouse between 1935 and 1939. The reverse was true for the General Electric Company and for a representative sector of American manufacturing. For both the latter, manufacturing expense increased to a greater degree than administrative expense.

The ratio of administrative and technical employees at Westinghouse reached a peak in July, 1938, and thereafter began to decline. By October, 1939, when the manufacturing expansion was in full swing and the reorganization was generally completed, the ratio of administrative employees to production employees fell below the January, 1938, ratio and remained there.

Effect on Profitability

Major company reorganizations are prompted by a variety of situations, yet they generally have one major common objective, improvement of "future profitability," that is, an increase in revenue that will more than offset the costs incurred.

A first approach to the question, "Does a reorganization pay off?" therefore would be to examine the profits and financial position before and after the reorganization.

But the "before and after" performance of a reorganized company is not sufficient evidence that the reorganization has produced this result. It is necessary to eliminate, so far as possible, the factors of change that are unrelated to the organization structure. One of these, of course, is the change in the state of the economy, and a second test would be to consider the relationship between Westinghouse operations and the economy as a whole. But this, too, is far from conclusive, since some industries may prosper more than others or lag behind the economy.

Perhaps the most nearly conclusive (though not entirely so) approach is a comparison of results with those obtained by the company's major competitors and the industry as a whole. If Westinghouse's position relative to the entire electrical supplies industry and its major competitor (General Electric) improved noticeably after the changes in structure, there is strong indication that the reorganization paid off.

Specific quantitative measures used in these three approaches might be as follows:

1. In the first approach, increased asset turnover or a reduction in the amount of assets per dollar of sales and greater profit per dollar of sales

2. In the second approach, an improvement in the company's performance relative to the economy as a whole or a relatively smaller downswing in a period of decline than the company had experienced in similar periods in the past

3. In the third approach, a greater percentage share of the electrical supplies or equipment market or, in the event of a downswing in the market, a relatively smaller decline for Westinghouse than for competitors or the industry as a whole

The Westinghouse Electric Corporation appears to have met all these tests successfully, though there may be differences of opinion

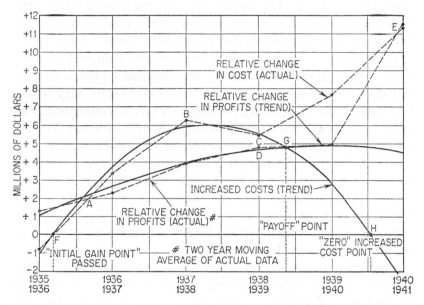

CHART 9. TIMING PATTERN—NET GAINS OR LOSSES OF THE WESTINGHOUSE REORGANIZATION, 1935–1941

as regards the *degree* of success. It may also be noted that after the conclusion of the reorganization the Westinghouse Electric Corporation appeared to grow faster in sales than any other billion-dollar corporation.

For reasons of space, the detailed statistical studies are omitted here,[6] but one example of the improvement in Westinghouse performance is shown in Chart 9. This is the result of a very elaborate comparison of Westinghouse experience with that of its major competitor, General Electric:

[6] These may be obtained from the author.

1. A comparison of the relationship of Westinghouse and GE for a period of years before the reorganization, in terms of sales, expenses, and profits. A high degree of correlation was revealed.

2. A projection of the pre-reorganization relationships of the two companies into the reorganization period 1935 to 1939.

3. Ascertaining of the actual relationships of the two companies from 1935 to 1939. (The comparisons were not extended beyond 1939 because defense contracts so changed the product mix of the two companies that meaningful comparisons became impossible.)

The upper broken line on the chart represents additional administrative expense; the lower broken line additional profits, that is, administrative expenses and profits over and above what they would have been if the pre-1935 relationship with GE had continued. The unbroken lines show the trends of administrative expenses over the same period as a two-year moving average of actual data.

The area to the right of point C shows what happened afterwards. While relative costs were, for a while, still higher than relative profits, the latter started rising at a much faster rate than the former until, at point E, relative profits exceeded relative costs. This represents the period of the long-run impact, when the gains from reorganization began to be realized.

Since many of the data in this latter period were influenced by the impact of the defense program, which drastically changed the product mix of the two companies, the trends of the data for the earlier years were extrapolated to determine what would probably have happened had not World War II occurred. The trends indicate that relative costs would have fallen below the 0 line at point H, that is, below their level at the time the reorganization began, while relative profits would have remained at a much higher level. The area bounded by the solid lines to the right of point G represents the probable long-term impact of the reorganization under normal circumstances, assuming, of course, that GE did not reorganize too.

It thus seems that Westinghouse's performance improved as a result of the reorganization and that the actual data probably understate the true extent of the improvement.

6

To Whom
Is Management Accountable?

> I submit that it is only by trial and error, by insistent scrutiny and by readiness to re-examine presently accredited conclusions that we have risen, so far as we have risen, from our brutish ancestors; and I believe that in our loyalty to these habits lies our only chance not merely of progress but even of survival.
>
> JUDGE LEARNED HAND

The great organizers described in this book were almost all men who held substantial investments in the companies they organized or reorganized, and their own interests corresponded closely with those of the stockholders.

But now that the Supreme Court has made it clear that management must beware of the type of "incipiency" (potential monopoly) it discerned in the GM–Du Pont relationship,[1] danger of another

---

[1] *United States of America v. E. I. du Pont de Nemours and Company, General Motors Corporation, et al.,* 353 U.S. 586 (1957). The majority opinion

type of incipiency may have been increased: disintegration of the economic and legal basis for management's existence through the euthanasia of the owners for whom it is supposed to act.

In perhaps one-third of the 200 largest corporations (which control approximately 50 per cent of all manufacturing assets) there are today no owners, in the sense of beneficial owners, who hold enough shares to exercise direct influence on management. In the other two-thirds, however, ownership has not yet been completely diffused, and there is still a measure of control by the actual risk takers. True, the owners or families of owners who control so large a proportion of the shares as to be able to control the board of directors are a rare phenomenon in this group of companies. They are confined to perhaps 10 per cent of them, among which are the Ford Motor Company, W. R. Grace and Company, and the Sun Oil Company. But in many cases an owner, especially one representing several others, may hold a large enough number of shares to obtain a seat on the board of directors and exercise some, though not a controlling, interest. Examples are the five Du Pont directors on the General Motors board, the Mellon directors on the Gulf Oil board, and the Block directors at Inland Steel. Such partial proprietors are represented on the boards of somewhat more than half the 200 largest corporations, and the percentage is quite likely higher in the case of the smaller enterprises, especially those founded more recently.

The partial proprietors are the remaining legitimate representatives of the owners, for since they hold a substantial amount of shares themselves, their interests tend to be those of the owners rather than of the managers.

The fact of the potential and actual conflict of interest between owners and managers is what lends the issue of corporate control

---

was written by Mr. Justice Brennan, with Chief Justice Warren and Justices Black and Douglas concurring. Mr. Justice Burton dissented, with Mr. Justice Frankfurter joining. Justices Clark, Harlan, and Whittaker took no part in the decision. See, however, the opinion of the trial judge, Walter J. LaBuy of the U.S. District Court for the Northern District of Illinois, Eastern Division, 126 F. Supp. 235 (1954).

its importance as a problem area. While our folklore and textbook economic theory assume an identity of interest, not even management spokesmen pretend this to be the case, as will be shown later in pages dealing with the image that management in many large corporations now holds of itself as a mediator among owners, employees, government, consumers, and the general public.

And the trend is toward increasing power by internal managers and the lessening or elimination of their accountability. The partial proprietors are disappearing and may well become as extinct as the dinosaur. Estate taxes are the principal cause of their extinction, or at least of the transfer of their wealth and power to foundation executives. The breaking up of large estates among a number of heirs also tends to reduce their influence.

And even if the potential influence remains, it is doubtful to what extent it will be exercised by a second or third generation. For there appears to be almost a pattern of American inheritance: the richer the estate, the more likely are the heirs to be interested in or fitted for anything but the business. Unless very careful thought is given to continuing the "dynasty," as in the case of the du Ponts and the Mellons (which stand out as exceptional in continuing family influence in large American corporations), founders' families are not likely to be a continuing influence. (Another exception that might be mentioned is the Milbank family, as shown by their sudden ouster of the president of Commercial Solvents after a quiet and effective gathering of opposition proxies.[2])

In many cases the "corporate dinosaurs" who are inevitably passing from the scene are not training successors. They feel that the world, as it now is, no longer provides room for them or for others like them. Pressed for a solution to the problem of replacement, one of them—aged 85—quoted Tennyson:

> Twilight and evening bell,
>   And after that the dark!
> And may there be no sadness of farewell
>   When I embark.

[2] *Fortune*, May, 1959, pp. 134–137, 168–172.

"You ask me what can be done now," he said. "My name is Simpson, not Sampson. I am not my brother's keeper."

It is probable, then, that the corporate dinosaurs are unable, by and large, to provide their own successors, much less multiply themselves. It is only in new industries with great wealth potential and individual opportunity that they are likely to arise: among Texas oil millionaires, the great corporate or individual aluminum proprietors, the rising owners of electronics and research enterprises, and Americans who build new business empires abroad. But their activities are likely to be merely a marginal part of our economy.

One remaining substitute for individual partial proprietors has been through an increase in company partial proprietorship through the purchase of full or partial control in other companies acquired by investment of company funds, and it is this that has probably been rendered less likely by the General Motors decision.

The precise nature of the role of the corporate partial proprietor tends to vary considerably, and quite often the power residual in the shareholdings of one company in another remains completely passive. The holding management may be too much occupied with its own problems or believe profoundly in the principle of letting sleeping dogs lie or fear the legal consequences of intervention.

Under a second type of relationship, the activities of the company holding the shares are quite unrelated to those of the "held" company. Hence no contributions may be possible except after long exposure. This is particularly so when technical problems dominate.

Because of a quirk in the tax laws, this type of relationship is becoming more common. When one company has suffered considerable losses over a number of years and has cash available or treasury stock of some value, it may acquire profitable companies and subsequent to the merger pay no tax on their profits for a number of years. Hence such loss companies which have either ready cash or book values greater than their stock prices are a favorite target for outsiders. If internal management lets a company go to the verge of bankruptcy and there is any hope left, such outsiders may be able to take over control, combine the company with other profitable ones, and reorganize it. But examples of this are few in number and confined mostly to companies where relatively few shares have been outstanding.

One such illustration is the old Philadelphia and Reading Anthracite Coal and Iron Company,[3] into which wealthy outsiders first forced their way. ("You have to force your way on boards. No one goes out and invites you," said one of them, Percival E. Jackson.) They bought up other profitable companies and at the same time reorganized the parent company, with very successful results. As Thomas F. Hyland, the largest single shareholder in Philadelphia and Reading, became concerned with the decline of his company and the mounting losses, he decided he ought to act:

I was not a widow or an orphan who had had my stock for years and watched it go to hell, but I sympathized with them. The widows and orphans never fight, but I was willing to. I bought at a bargain, and I wanted to get something out of it. The other large stockholders weren't doing anything. Some insurance companies held stock because they had been bondholders. They didn't try and get good management. They didn't go to the management and say: "Your inventory position is preposterous; your costs are out of line." They just sold out.[4]

Under a third type of relationship, the company holding shares may be in the same kind of business as the firm on whose board its representatives sit (this might be called a horizontal relationship), or it may be engaged in an earlier or later stage of production (which might be called a "vertical" relationship), making possible the use of the product of one company by the other.

An example of the horizontal relationship is provided by the watch industry. The Benrus Watch Company acquired a minority interest in the Hamilton Watch Company large enough to enable it to obtain minority representation on the Hamilton board of directors. However, the United States court concerned was readily persuaded to enjoin a voting of the Benrus holdings, since it was

[3] Carl Rieser, "The Egghead, the Upstart and Old P & R," *Fortune*, August, 1959, pp. 84–88, 188–194.
[4] *Ibid.*, p. 88.

assumed that an interlocking directorate would influence competitive behavior.[5] For similar reasons the merger between the Bethlehem and Youngstown steel companies was disallowed and similar arrangements in steel, oil, and other industries are being questioned by the Department of Justice. Thus a horizontal relationship between the corporate partial proprietor and the company in which it holds a minority interest is presumably illegal if the relationship is likely to influence competitive behavior. There may be cases where such a relationship has no Sherman or Clayton Act implications and might entail no public disadvantage, and substantial private advantage, but this type of relationship is not likely to increase.

The vertical type of relationship, therefore, has held the greatest promise for corporate partial proprietorships, the situation in which the partial proprietors of one company have a partial proprietorship in another and there is a supplier relationship between the two corporations. This was the situation in the GM–Du Pont case:

The primary issue and the one against which the Supreme Court decided the case—a single issue—was whether Du Pont's commanding position as GM's supplier of automotive finishes ... was achieved on ... merit alone, or because of its acquisition of GM's stock, and the consequent close intercompany relationship ... with the resultant likelihood, at the time of the suit, of the creation of a monopoly in a line of commerce.[6]

Said the Court majority:

Section 7 [of the Clayton Act] is designed to arrest in its incipiency not only the lessening of competition from the acquisition by one corporation ... stock of a competing corporation, but also to arrest in their incipiency restraints or monopolies in a relevant market. ... *The section is violated whether or not actual restraints, or monopolies, or the substantial lessening of competition have occurred or are intended.*" (Italics added.)

Many students of monopoly and of management are likely to find the minority opinion of the Supreme Court more persuasive than the majority opinion. The Du Pont Company and its counsel presented a very strong case indeed, and one that was sustained by

[5] Irston R. Barnes, *Georgetown Law Journal,* Summer, 1958, p. 598.
[6] *Ibid.,* p. 564.

Judge Walter J. LaBuy of the Federal District Court in Chicago. But all this is now irrelevant in the light of the final ruling. Now even a threat to investigate by the Department of Justice's Antitrust Division or from the Federal Trade Commission may lead to the abandonment or silencing of corporate partial proprietorship.

Thus a number of forces are tending to eliminate the partial proprietor, whether individual or corporate. Unless a substitute is found, results could be serious for individual companies and for the free-enterprise system itself; for if the link between ownership and control is entirely dissolved, management has no real basis for its position.

The theoretical and actual foundations of the free-enterprise system are two: First, it ensures efficiency because the inefficient company will soon be driven out of existence by competition. Second, there is the so-called "golden rule of private ownership": "Where the risk lies, there lies the control"; that is, those who risk their capital in business ventures should have the power to control the use that is made of it and hire and fire those who merely act as managers. And the second concept reinforces the first, since those who stand to gain or lose most heavily have the greatest incentive to keep the enterprise efficient and profitable.

Thus, even though management might be tempted to relax and cruise along in comfortable inefficiency, the owners, if they are rational and can exercise their powers, are expected to press for results at least equal to those of the best comparable companies and to replace the management that is unable or unwilling to ensure that such results are obtained.

At the present time, conditions for some of the larger companies, while still competitive to some extent, are not competitive enough to enforce a high degree of efficiency. Because of their very size, power over price and product, and independence of the capital market—or because competitors have an eye on the Department of Justice and want to keep the "weak sisters" in business—some managements have a very large margin for error.

The decline of ownership influence is likely to be greatest in these corporations, since it is the large companies in which ownership is likely to be most diffused and unable to exercise any power.

So the two automatic controls can no longer prevent the rise and perpetuation of less than fully efficient corporations and managements, both of which appear to be self-perpetuating.

This spreading state of affairs is rousing critics the world over. Some of them have presented seemingly devastating cases against the large corporations and the devices by which their managements seem to perpetuate themselves. One of the most cogent and caustic of these critics is Professor Ben W. Lewis, who arrives at the prediction that

the years ahead will see a great increase in conscious, collective, governmental controls and of governmental enterprise, and that bigness will be a major focal point of the development. This development will reflect a growing, intensified concern over the private possession of economic power so vast that even its possessors are frightened by the implications of their holdings.

Our giant firms are sitting like fat, delectable ducks, virtually inviting the government to open fire with something more effective than anti-trust. The invitation will be accepted.[7]

Professor Lewis is mainly concerned with the softening of the competitive atmosphere surrounding some large corporations. When those same corporations are governed by managements that are completely divorced from ownership and are accountable to no one but themselves, their position becomes even more vulnerable.

The solution might take the form of stricter regulation by government agencies, or even of "public directors" appointed by the government to membership on the boards of leading companies, a prospect that is not so remote as it might seem since it has been seriously proposed in the past.

A specific portent of the shape of things to come is the appointment by the New York State Legislature of a Joint Legislative Committee to Study the Revision of Corporation Laws, under the chairmanship of Senator Frank S. McCullough. The Senate's majority leader Walter J. Mahoney has drawn legislative attention to the

[7] "Open Season on Bigness," *Harvard Business Review*, May–June, 1959, p. 112.

stockholder struggle at the New York Trust Company. There the six management representatives who were elected to the board of directors owned only 1,430 shares, or 0.5 per cent of those outstanding. On the other hand, 1,000 stockholders owned 256,000 shares, or almost 25 per cent of those outstanding. The latter were denied board representation partly in order to exclude questioning of management's long holdout against mergers. It should also be noted that the new Commissioner of the California Division of Corporations, John Sobiesky, is attempting to enforce cumulative voting in California corporations, holding: "This office views with disfavor any voting procedure which denies representation on boards of directors for holders of substantial minority interests. Such an iron curtain against minority representation promotes inefficiency and waste in management and makes it more difficult for inefficient management to be exposed or removed."

It has also been suggested that the Securities and Exchange Commission might constitute a kind of independent review should no other exist. Thus the provisions of the Investment Company Act of 1940 and the Securities and Exchange Act of 1940 might be extended. The SEC might be empowered to express an opinion if requested to do so by management or by the holders of a certain percentage of any class of a corporation's securities on any controversy between stockholders and management made subject to a vote at a stockholders' meeting. (A similar, though more liberal, provision exists in the India Companies Act.)

The more radical idea of government-appointed directors has arisen at various times, following a wave of popular emotion. In World War I, there was Wilson's emotional appeal for a "world made safe for democracy," and afterwards there was some sentiment for application of this concept to business enterprise, and the "industrial democracy" suggested took the form of the Plumb Plan for the nationalization of the railroads and "joint consultation," under which workers' representatives were to sit on boards of directors. The latter plan grew to fruition in post–World War II Germany, where it is called "codetermination." Under this plan union representatives sit on the boards of directors of coal and steel companies. (Fortunately for the companies, the union representatives became more management-minded than management itself.)

The Great Depression revived criticism of the business system in the United States, and the demand arose, supported by President Roosevelt, for publicly appointed directors to enforce what were then conceived to be the public responsibilities of businessmen. One of the proposals was that the senior judges of the United States district courts assume places on the boards of prominent corporations, a proposal that was quashed only because it was pointed out that these director-judges might have to sit in judgment on themselves.

While business recovery silenced the agitation, the advent of a strongly "liberal" Congress and a powerful labor movement, coupled with the growing criticism of business evidenced by the literature, could cause the specter of government-appointed directors to rise again, perhaps using the slogan of "a people's capitalism" as a front. The rumor may not be true, but it is said that some Congressmen have gone so far as to threaten the possibility of board memberships for themselves, with the ultimate aim of mobilizing the power of the United States to protect foreign investments!

Some observers are looking to the labor unions and their large internal and pension funds to capture giant corporations for the cause of "public" representation—or special representation, as in the case of Dave Beck's support of Sewell Avery at Montgomery Ward. (Avery then readily granted the union shop, against which he had fought all his life.)

It would appear, then, that many influential people, including some politicians, are taking notice of the declining accountability of corporations. Some of them may be waiting to rush in where angels fear to tread.

Rightly or wrongly, the large corporation has been charged with some measure of responsibility for the inflation of recent years. This appears to be precisely the kind of issue that may sooner or later force public representation into the top echelon of corporate decision making. Already executives of the steel, auto, and other industries have been required to devote a considerable part of their time and energies to defending their price policies in Washington.

Unhappily, the solution that seems obvious to many of the critics of management's present lack of accountability appears to beg the question. For our experience with governmental agencies charged with metering business is not such as to inspire confidence in their metering ability. Merely recalling the record of a number of alphabetical agencies already engaged in this task is enough to cause doubt of their devotion to the public interest where it is opposed to the special interests of the industries and companies with which they soon tend to identify themselves. The temptation of "feet under a mahogany table not to kick" is often too strong to overcome.

Thus attention is returned to the case for independent review, even though it is still an uphill fight. The basic thesis of this chapter is that only through the organization of some form of independent review can management avoid the major hazards to its own position, which are likely to be moral and economic as well as legal. Devising some means of providing that review will be a major problem for the great organizers of the future.

CONSEQUENCES OF ABSENCE OF ACCOUNTABILITY

If we neglect for a moment the possibility of checks exercised by forces other than ownership and competition and consider that management in most large companies eventually reaches a position where, to all intents and purposes, its power over the organization is beyond review, there are likely to be consequences of the utmost seriousness in both the moral and economic spheres that will encourage the demand for government control.

Moral Consequences

The essence of the moral issue is, of course, the potentiality of abuse of unchecked power. Mr. Justice Stone, in a series of opinions, clearly recognized that "there is no place in a democracy for the exercise of irresponsible power. Where it exists it must be broken up or directed to the public good. Those who have power, in the words of the Constitution, 'have to answer in another place' for their acts. If there is no other place in which to answer, the power itself must be denied." [8]

This observation is, of course, drawn from Lord Acton's brilliant and well-known observation that "power tends to corrupt and absolute power tends to corrupt absolutely." Plato's discussion of the same problem presents the same conclusion.[9]

Individuals in management, as elsewhere, can be trusted to act in individual circumstances in accordance with highest ethical and altruistic standards despite the absence of sanctions of any kind. But can the same necessarily be said of managers in general in all conceivable circumstances, any more than it can be said of any other large and diversified group of human beings? As one of the foremost champions of the free-enterprise system, the late Henry C. Simons, pointed out, no producer group can be trusted with unchecked power because the only use of power is its abuse.[10]

Even in the case of malpractice for which legal penalties exist— ordinary misappropriations of funds, for example, or conspiracy with gangster leaders of unions against employees—restraint is less likely to be exercised if management is absolute. If management is not

[8] Walton H. Hamilton, "Legal Tolerance and Economic Power," *Georgetown Law Journal*, vol. 46, no. 4, p. 563.

[9] "Athenian Stranger: Nothing can be clearer than the observation which I am about to make.

"Megillus: What is it?

"Athenian Stranger: That if anyone gives too great a power to anything, too large a vessel to sail, too much good for the body, too much authority to the mind, and does not observe the mean, everything is overthrown. And, the wantonness of excess runs in the one case to disorders and in the other to injustice, which is the child of excess. I mean to say, my dear friends, that there is no soul of man ... who will be able to sustain the temptation of arbitrary power—no one who will not, under such circumstances become filled with folly, that worst of diseases, and be hated by his nearest and dearest friends...." Plato, *Laws* III.

Other great students of human nature have made similar observations; cf. Shakespeare's conclusion, "Take but degree away and hark what discord follows," *Troilus and Cressida*.

[10] "Monopoly power must be abused. It has no use save abuse." Henry C. Simons, "Some Reflections on Syndicalism," *The Journal of Political Economy*, March–December, 1944, p. 6.

accountable to anyone, it is all too easy for it to conceal the truth until the depredations may have gone very far indeed.

And what of perfectly legal, though unethical, conduct—for example, unreasonably high bonuses and other benefits for top managers to the detriment of stockholders' income and equity? [11] Here the moral issue is one of degree, and the possibility that otherwise ethical men will be tempted into something less than a completely fair division of returns may be great. And this temptation may be the greater because the standards of relationship between management and shareholders tend to become increasingly impersonal; management neither knows nor sees the people it may hurt. Thus when a man's obligations are both to another party (whom he does not know and which cannot reach him) and to himself, he may almost unconsciously favor himself.

An example may illustrate the type of abuse that is likely to occur. One of our largest corporations recently reduced the option price on shares available to key employees by a large percentage following a year of unprecedentedly heavy losses (which occurred after the planning chief had forecast several hundred million dollars profit). Management defended this reduction as necessary to "hold on to key executives," who, of course, included those who made the decision. Yet it would scarcely have harmed the company if the management *had* left, for financial results and competitive position had been deteriorating for several years. Thus management rewarded itself for bad performance. The stock-price concessions were themselves a tacit admission that prospects for the company were not too bright. As Robert Tilove observes in his study *Pension Funds and Economic Freedom*,[12] "if management dictates what management is to receive, it is inevitable that eventually the question ceases to be incentive and becomes an assertion of management's power to take what it alone considers warranted."

Another moral hazard is that the top man or group may fall prey

[11] See, for example, the findings of David Roberts in very extensive studies of top-executive compensation, carefully checked for statistical validity, that this varies, not with profitability, but with the size of companies. "New Facts about Executive Compensation," *Management Review*, July, 1955, pp. 473ff.

[12] The Fund for the Republic, New York, 1959, p. 82.

to the delusion of infallibility, for the man who has no equals, only subordinates, is almost bound to be touched by it to some extent. This tends to defeat individual development of those down the line and to induce conformity even in small matters. Already business is under attack for this, and the attacks are finding a responsive audience, as the popularity of the book *The Organization Man* shows.

Thus men may be made to act, not necessarily in the interests of the business, but in the interests of the superior who can demand and enforce conformity. They are made to fit into the arbitrary boxes on the organization charts. The result may well be to invite the services of highly paid apple polishers and to discourage men of merit.

The final aspect of the moral problem of an unchecked management is that it may tend to be prosecutor, judge, jury, hangman, all at once, again with no power of appeal by its victims. It calls to mind the case of the prisoner in Franz Kafka's *The Trial* who was arrested without knowing the charges against him, tried, condemned to death, and hanged, still ignorant of what it was all about. Would this analogy be too far-fetched in the case of an executive who lost his job without cause or one who was manipulated to do things he did not understand and would not want to do if he did understand them?

Economic Consequences

Fundamental business decisions relating to major expansions or contractions, new products, financing, the selection and promotion of key personnel—these are essentially matters of judgment which cannot be solved wholly on the basis of figures or technical data alone. There are always intangibles that cannot be quantified.

Since no one person can ever have full knowledge of all the intangibles involved, a chief executive is more likely to make the economically correct decision if he checks with others who are not wholly dependent on him and can state their views freely on the basis of the issues and their unique personal knowledge, rather than on the basis of the personalities involved.

In addition, the very fact that there will be a review by persons not dependent on him will make the chief executive more disposed to reach the best decision possible. Knowing that he may be called to account, the chief executive is more likely to think out his proposals carefully and to judge them more by the extent to which they will further the company goals than by what they will do to further his personal goals. As an example, during the recent recession, a number of large corporations floated additional bond issues, superimposed at higher rates on other lower-rate issues, even though substantial overcapacity already existed. No one benefited except those who were put in charge of the idle plants.

An outside check may provide positive as well as negative incentives, quite aside from financial rewards. For while there is little real satisfaction in self-praise, the recognition and respect of a group of qualified independents can be very satisfying.

Further, such an independent review makes it less likely that personal goals will be at variance with company goals. In its absence the importance of an executive in his own eyes may well depend on the size of the activities he manages—the volume of sales, the magnitude of his staff and budget, the impressiveness of the company's buildings and his own executive suite, and other perquisites and status symbols.

There seems, in fact, to have been a greater number of instances in recent years in which companies have apparently expanded largely for expansion's sake, acquiring new divisions and subsidiaries that actually resulted in a drain on their resources. Some of these have had to be disposed of later at a loss.

Undue expansion of capacity in existing divisions has been another recent manifestation of the same tendency. In the durable-goods industries there have been a number of cases in which the forecasts of industry sales and company share of market were based on what the chief executive wanted to see happen rather than on what the facts seemed to justify. The resulting overexpansion of capacity and budgets eventually produced severe losses and panicky expense cutting. Because their chief executives were so occupied a few years ago with keeping up with "the corporate Joneses," many durable-goods companies are now faced with the continuing problem of adjusting supply to demand.

The unchecked or free-wheeling executive is also subject to heavy temptation to exemplify the workings of Parkinson's law by increasing administrative expense beyond a reasonable point, for the more "assistants to" and staff advisers he has, the more important he seems to be.

Increased administrative expenses may, of course, often be justified. Staff people may contribute as much to profitability as line people. For example, a tax counsel may produce a major saving, or a safety expert prevent costly accidents. But much of the administrative expense incurred in recent years seems to have been for services so new or so intangible that it is hard to measure their real contribution. Certainly there appears to be a wide margin between some of the amounts often lumped into administrative expense and the potential gain from the expenditures. Money spent for entertainment, for example, is sometimes far in excess of actual need. And what follies are perpetrated in the name of "good will"! How many companies really know the over-all return from their advertising outlay or are really trying to gauge it?

In an increasing number of companies administrative expense is greater than operating expense, and in most it is tending to rise both absolutely and relatively. For example, the detailed studies of Seymour Melman [13] appear to indicate that the ratio of administrative expense in industry was 22.2 per cent of production expense in 1947, as compared with 13 per cent in 1909, and still continues to rise. And recently it has been stated on high authority that the recent halt in the increase of United States productivity is principally due to the rise in administrative expense,[14] an indication that the consequences may be serious not only from the viewpoint of stockholders, but from that of the economy as a whole.

[13] "The Rise of Administrative Overhead in the Manufacturing Industries of the United States, 1899–1947," *Oxford Economic Papers,* January, 1951, p. 66, and his *Dynamic Factors in Industrial Productivity,* Basil Blackwell, Oxford, 1956, pp. 73–94.

[14] Board of Governors, Federal Reserve Board, quoted in *Fortune,* April, 1958.

It is quite possible, in the absence of an independent check, and in a climate in which the chief executive has assumed the mantle of infallibility, for companies to misinform their stockholders and the general public for some time, and even for the chief executives to deceive themselves. This is partly due to the imprecise methods of measuring managerial performance. The very nature of accounting data makes them less conclusive, the shorter the period of time considered. The vagaries produced by differing rates of depreciation, by varying degrees of maintenance, by changes in the basis of inventory valuation, and by the transfer of certain unusual gains or losses directly to the income statement or surplus, as well as by the postponement of capital expenditures in times of declining profits, are too well known to require elaboration.

Again the accumulated past resources of a corporation (accumulated, that is, by merit or by virtue of market or product power) may be drawn upon and wasted away over a long period of time by a management that does not care and does not have to care. For the corporation appears to survive, if not as long as a poorly run political institution, at least long enough to maintain the present management with high pay and no concern for what may happen after its passing. Thus it happens that rising demand for the industry's product or results of some stroke of luck are attributed to management's own efforts. But if things turn out badly, then the same management claims it had nothing to do with the poor results (however well competitors may have done)—it is "just one of those things." As far as sales go, management feels that, "the Lord giveth and the Lord taketh away."

Again management inefficiencies may be hidden by excluding foreign competition, by an "administered price structure," or by a partial monopoly situation created by patents or the barrier of the high capital investment needed to enter the industry. Or a company may continue to earn high profits because of the resources or market established by a previous outstanding chief executive on whose contributions a successor management still cruises without making contributions of its own and which it may use as a means of masking its own shortcomings. All these human failings *need* not occur, but in the absence of a check there is a possibility that they may occur. Partial proprietors have, at least, a very strong motivation to prevent abuses of this kind. Their actual contributions are difficult to *prove* in all cases, but a qualitative study, detailed in Appendix A on pp. 239 ff. of some of the contributions made in companies where they provided a constructive check on internal management indicates that, at its best, partial proprietorship may do a great deal to advance the economic welfare of the company.

In this qualitative study interviews were conducted with a number of partial proprietors who took an active part in the decisions of the directors. Our sample included several of the substantial minority stockholders in the company regarded by many as one of the most economically successful manufacturing organizations, General Motors, with special reference to the years 1921 to 1929, when there is little doubt about the competitive nature of the industry. GM was, in fact, battling for survival during much of that time.

The second set of interviews was with a number of mining companies—copper, zinc, lead, and coal—largely because the managements interviewed mostly welcomed the check and attributed some outstanding advantages to it. The third group interviewed were outspoken trustees for property holders—bankers, lawyers, professional directors who felt free to speak their mind and who had the conviction to act accordingly.

The detailed contributions of these partial proprietors who were interviewed are recorded in Appendix A on pp. 239 ff. under the following headings:

1. The provision of business acumen (technical knowledge, management techniques, adapted management skills, catalytic contributions)

2. Furthering executive talent and its effective exercise

3. Providing an opportunity for freedom of discussion of basic issues

4. The development of basic and original concepts of organization

5. The provision of continuing board membership of outstanding quality

6. Appraisal of results accomplished

In addition to the qualitative contributions of the partial proprietors, a study of their quantitative contributions was attempted. Appendix B on pp. 261 ff. analyzes profits as a percentage of sales and investment of the 200 largest corporations listed by *Fortune* for 1956 and 1957. Results showed that concerns under partial proprietary control (officers, directors, associates, and large stockholders holding more than 10 per cent, but less than 50 per cent, of the common stock) have had better records of performance generally than those under complete internal management control or complete proprietary control. At least the evidence appears to be conclusive enough to warrant stating that this proposition was *not* disproved.

Now to return to the Du Pont case. The basic issues were (1) whether the 23 per cent of GM stock held by the Du Pont Company resulted in control (i.e., a company with sales of approximately $2 billion per annum controlling a company with sales of approximately $10 billion per annum); and (2) whether the mere existence of capacity to influence purchasing power was contrary to the provisions of the Clayton Act.

From a purely legal point of view it was difficult to argue that a 23 per cent stock interest in a company as widely held as General Motors is not control. In the last twenty years many a company holding considerably less than 23 per cent of a utility has been divested of those holdings because of a legislative fiat that 10 per cent ownership of a company makes it a controlled subsidiary.[15] There is also the common judgment by the courts that "much less than a majority of stock is frequently sufficient for purposes of control." All the arguments advanced by Du Pont were disposed of by a unanimous Supreme Court decision more than a decade ago in the *North American Case* in which the stockholdings in two of the controlled companies were 17.7 and 19.2 per cent.[16]

[15] Public Utility Holding Act of 1935, 49 State 807, 15 U.S.C. 79 (b) (a) (8) 1952.

[16] See William McGovern in the Summer, 1958, issue of the *Georgetown Law Journal*, pp. 658ff.

Du Pont could very well have asked what profit it would have gained by forcing a couple of million of dollars of annual paint sales on GM when it had to consider the much larger potential loss resulting from any antitrust action. The Du Pont Company might also argue that "incipiency" was not recognized by the Supreme Court in some of its reviews of verdicts of lower courts against the leaders of the United States Communist Party, though the analogy could perhaps not be successfully sustained.

Certainly, among many of the non–Du Pont partial proprietors interviewed for this study, there was a strong feeling that Du Pont did in fact control GM and that the company had been fortunate to enjoy this association for so many years without interference. There was an equally strong feeling that the Du Ponts should have met the charge of incipient control squarely rather than have denied it altogether. The defendants in the Du Pont case might, however, reply that admission and defense of control would have been gratuitous, as it might not have been germane to the legal issues involved, but would have required a resort to economics rather than to law. But then the composition of the Supreme Court which they faced was perhaps open to economic reasoning and even more so to the argument for "rebuttal power" through an independent review provided by the Du Ponts. While the latter were understandably "gun-shy," an independent study might have shown that they actually did make substantial substantive contributions to the improved utilization of the subscribed capital to GM on behalf of *all* the stockholders and in line with their legal obligations as owners and trustees for the owners. The great success of GM, both absolutely and in comparison with other automobile companies especially (some of which fared extraordinarily badly without the contributions of partial proprietors), might have provided the basis for a very strong case, possibly before the Supreme Court, and surely before the forum of public opinion and the judgment of history. The preservation of freedom of speech within GM management— possibly not paralleled in some of the other automobile companies in the United States, either because this proprietary check was wholly absent (as at Chrysler after its founder's death) or was completely neglected at times by its ownership (for the latter part of Henry Ford, Sr.'s, life)—might also have been cited. Quite possibly the contribution to freedom of speech might even have had a powerful influence on some of the majority members of the Supreme Court, who are much imbued with the importance of this heritage. Thus hindsight appears to indicate that the Du Ponts apparently based their defense largely on grounds on which they could not hope to win in the light of the prevailing majority of the Supreme Court and quite possibly that of the community at large (having regard to the difficulties encountered in passing legislation which would soften the tax blow of the divestiture of Du Pont).

THE ALTERNATIVE CHECKS

In the light of potential and actual failings of unchecked managements, the question may well be raised as to the checks that may exist in the absence of any restraint from heavy competition or the partial proprietors. Many of those who have hailed "the managerial revolution" and many of the unchecked managements believe that workable restraints do exist and that they are adequate to enforce proper conduct, namely, the rise of professionalism and social responsibility among managers.

Professionalism of Management

Often cited as a check imposed by management upon itself is its growing professionalism. As professionals, it is argued, managers will be increasingly interested in doing a good job of management in all its phases. In fact, the very freedom from pressure by the owners will enable the internal managers to shape their conduct more nearly in accordance with the standards demanded by their profession.

The efficacy of this check depends on the nature and status of professional management. Professionalism requires a body of knowledge which can be taught and which applies with at least some degree of universality. To say that management is a profession implies that the application of this knowledge will produce predictable results, that managers will conform to standards and meter themselves by the results.

In support of professional claims it has been said that there are certain "management skills"—planning, organizing, controlling and so on—that are equally applicable to any organization—business, military, religious, governmental—and that the man who possesses them is able to manage any type of operation with equal success, just as a doctor may cure a patient with whom he has had no previous acquaintance.

Actually, there has been little transfer of management skills from one sphere of administrative activity to another, say, from medical to business administration.[17] What there has been has not always been successful. Where the transfer has been accomplished with apparently successful results, these results may have been due to factors other than knowledge of management skills, such as sufficiently long exposure to innate and technical requirements of the organization, an extraordinarily versatile personality, or a fortunate combination of circumstances. Immediate or short-run transfers are not denied, but they appear to be sufficiently rare to cast doubt on the existence of professionalism.

There appears to be even relatively little transfer of general managers from one industry to another or even from one function to another.[18] It seems to be almost impossible to transfer in or out of some industries, or even in or out of some companies, and often for very good reasons. The knowledge required to fill a management position satisfactorily is not only managerial; also required in most cases is familiarity with technical matters, products, personalities, and tradition, knowledge that can be acquired only through long and painstaking experience in the actual situation.

An analysis of the common qualities of leaders, based on a large number of leadership studies, found, in fact, that the one

[17] See Chapter 1.

[18] For lack of executive mobility see the following studies: "Fortune's Nine-hundred," *Fortune*, November, 1952, pp. 132; David Roberts, "New Facts about Executive Compensation," *Management Review*, July, 1955; Gladys Palmer, *Labor Mobility in Six Cities, 1940–1950*, Social Science Research Council, New York, 1954.

quality possessed by all was excellence in the technical specialties with which they were concerned.[19]

Frequently the *sine qua non* in the selection of the head of an enterprise is technical knowledge. For example, the top men in many oil companies are geologists by training simply because the principal way of making real money, until recently at least, has been through finding more oil. Usually, also, knowledge of a specific more or less technical management function is required— production, marketing, accounting—and the selection of the top man is likely to depend largely on the area in which the company's most important problems happen to lie at the moment.

The last can be illustrated by a brief account of the changes of top leadership at General Motors. The first head of the corporation was W. C. Durant, who may be said to have invented the idea on which the corporation was based—a car for every purse. The concept required the acquisition of a great deal of capital for the purchase of different automobile companies, and Durant was a superb promoter and money raiser. After two years a management consolidation was necessary and C. W. Nash took Durant's place, introducing the beginnings of staff services. But in 1916, when a new period of acquisition was required, Durant came back again. Four years later overexpansion, coupled with a recession, brought GM to the verge of bankruptcy. So P. S. du Pont, who with others had performed a similar lifesaving operation at E. I. du Pont de Nemours, became president of GM in 1920, until in 1923 he turned over the company to Alfred P. Sloan, Jr., and a group of associates who pioneered engineering, accounting, and marketing techniques. When the time came to select Sloan's successor, in 1947, the company's main problems were union and governmental relations. C. E. Wilson, who was considered especially competent in these fields, was chosen. Five years later, after the first postwar demand for cars had been satisfied, marketing and styling problems came to the fore again, and H. C. Curtice, whose main contributions appeared to lie in the merchandising field, became president. Finally, the 1958 declining auto market appeared un-

[19] J. A. C. Brown, *Social Psychology of Industry*, Penguin Books, 1954, p. 221.

likely to permit expansion immediately no matter how persuasive the marketing effort, and this gave prominence to the need for cost reduction. In addition, the Supreme Court's antitrust decision in the GM–Du Pont case appeared to accent the financial problems because of the probable need to dispose of the Du Pont financial holdings. Hence a financial man, F. C. Donner, became chief executive.

Obviously, many of these managers supplemented their technical ability with the so-called "management skills" and with leadership ability as well. But it is equally obvious that intensive experience in the phases of the business in which it was most important that the managerial skills and leadership qualities be exercised was also a ruling factor in their selection.

The "managerial skills" and "leadership qualities" supposed to be universally applicable are as yet ill-defined. And so are the "principles of management" that have been laid down by various writers. In the field of management it is rarely possible to predict with certainty—as it is in the physical sciences—that certain steps will inevitably produce certain results. And the other sciences —the social sciences—on which management must draw for aid are, in their managerial applications, "soft" sciences, in which there are few hard-and-fast rules.

Hence, since management is not universal but needs to be buttressed by specific technical knowledge in order to be effectively exercised, since results of managerial efforts are not really predictable on the basis of principles, there appear to be no managerial standards as such by which a manager can meter himself (except in a subjective or inexact sense). Hence professionalism, even if it were embraced, does not as yet provide a check that could take the place of the partial proprietors.

These reflections on the state of management as a profession are not intended as a criticism of those who are working to develop management as a science. There is a small but growing body of knowledge in the field with which every manager needs at least nodding acquaintance. It must be pointed out, however, that while many of the past and current studies have been valuable in providing bricks and mortar, "the house of management" has not yet been built; not even the foundations have been laid.

The lack of a real science of management is, of course, not surprising when we reflect that the study of management is at best only about half a century old and that the other sciences took centuries to attain their present state of fairly exact knowledge, often under easier circumstances and conditions than exist in the large subjective area with which management has to struggle. There is no reason for the serious students of management or its practitioners to be ashamed of the state of the managerial art and the beginnings of its scientific efforts; but they should make clear when and why they are scientists, artists, or just plain mystics; and that there are as yet really no professional standards that can control management conduct and make other checks unnecessary.

Social Responsibility of Management

Many of those who hold the view that management is a profession have also, as a concomitant, espoused the idea that the manager's responsibility is not entirely, or even primarily, to the stockholders who pay his handsome wages. Rather, they hold, his job is to allocate the returns of the enterprise among all the groups whose interests may be affected by corporate activities: stockholders, employees, customers, government, suppliers, members of the communities in which plants and offices are located. Management's job, in this view, is to reconcile the interests of these groups where possible; or where there is a conflict of interest, to dispense even-handed justice.

Those who regard the management job in this way are also of the opinion that managers are fast developing a sense of "social responsibility" which acts as a check on their conduct, as potent or even more potent than any check the owners could exert.

For instance, Gerard Swope, for many years outstanding as the president of General Electric, "agrees that directors and stockholders provide no practicable curbs on management. . . . Management today does define its own responsibilities. It depends on the personal factor of the president in each case. It depends on whether he is selfish and narrow or broad and has a sense of stewardship." [20]

Two questions may be asked of the promoters of this concept by those who are interested either in social welfare or the survival of the free-enterprise system. First, is it possible to rely entirely on the manager's sense of social responsibility to provide an adequate check on him? Second, is it desirable to give managers broad responsibility for allocating resources among the various publics of the company, desirable, that is, either from the standpoint of the economy as a whole or the standpoint of management itself?

In the allocation of the company's returns, some portion, of course, is reserved to the manager himself—his salary, bonuses, and various perquisites. Now it would seem contrary to all notions of equity (as well as corporate law) that an arbiter should also be a party at interest. To put any man into such a position is to subject him to many of the moral hazards discussed earlier, the more so because the issues are not clear-cut. There is no general agreement, for example, on the socially equitable size of a "fair" wage, a "fair" return to stockholders, a "fair" salary to a manager. There is no scientific way of determining any of these figures. Precisely for this reason an independent check tends at least to reduce arbitrariness. There is no question of the good faith of many of those who attempt to act in the name of social responsibility, but it would seem to require "a scientific saint" to live up to it.

And if managers abandon their traditional roles as profit maximizers in favor of the role of an arbiter whose main job is to keep things running smoothly, what becomes of the dynamism of the American economy? If "smoothness" and the reconciliation of conflict are the principal aims of the former profit makers who will be really interested in developing new methods and machinery, and so raising the standard of living? And if the varying social responsibilities cannot in fact be reconciled—maximum growth, full employment, stable or declining price levels, rapidly rising money wages, an expanding arms and international economy—might not "smoothness" become a substitute for thinking and courage? Again,

[20] David Loth, *Swope of GE,* Simon and Schuster, Inc., New York, 1958, p. 129.

there is no doubt that many companies are taking account of the prevailing standards of safety, stability of employment, old-age needs, local community requirements in education, hospitals, recreation, etc. But these are not particularly new; and while their scope has been expanding, it is usually only a small part of what is considered quite correctly a cost of doing business. It is a far step from these practices to those of the top executive who spends a great deal of company money and much of his own time arbitrating a large part of our national income. For if the manager arrogates to himself such authority over so many different segments of the economy, he is, in effect, setting himself up as a monarch rather than as the representative of one of the parties at interest (the owners) in the continuing struggle among the various countervailing powers.

If the manager really should function in this way, all the various parties at interest as well as the general public may well begin to ask some voice in selecting him, since it is contrary to all democratic tradition for those who make the rules and hold the scales of justice for the country as a whole not to be accountable in some way to the general public.

Thus the more managements achieve independence from the stockholders, the less legal basis there would appear to be for their power and the more they will become self-perpetuating groups accountable to no one. Such a situation would be bound eventually to lead to massive government intervention. Hence managers might do well to look more critically at the implications of the new role that is being offered them by some writers on management. At first glance it may look attractive, since it exalts the manager, but it may end by destroying both his ability to function and his exaltation.

SUBSTITUTES FOR THE PARTIAL PROPRIETORS

The foregoing considerations do not necessarily mean that all managements have to be subjected to some kind of a check all the time. In some cases, there may well be no need for it. But it is difficult to argue against the presence of a potential check, for if management does a perfect job there will be no need to exercise it, or the check will merely confirm that management performance has been excellent.

If the partial proprietors disappear in many cases, and if control by government is undesirable, what possibilities remain?

Small Stockholders as Partial Proprietors

One potential source of independent review is the "atomized" stockholder, who, like the individual citizen, is said to be able to make his voice heard if only he will "participate in stockholder democracy." However, it is obvious that the more widely the stock of a corporation is held and the more extensive "the people's capitalism," the less powerful the individual stockholders and the less the chance of successful combination among them. This holds true even if "50,000 spending units own two-thirds of the total stock," [21] for each of these spending units holds usually only a small fraction of the shares of any one company. Even though the absolute total of all shares and the proportion of all stock held by small stockholders is significant, it is not so in terms of exercising power unless that power can be organized and galvanized. The small individual stockholder can write a letter to the president of the company; he can speak up at a stockholders' meeting; he can vote his shares against the management if he feels dissatisfied. And it is true that occasionally the small individual stockholder may succeed in becoming "the still small voice of management's conscience." But the small stockholder has no power of doing so unless the conscience is already there. Quite often his letter is not answered or answered only if it is "constructive." He may speak at a meeting, but again there may be no answer. He may vote "no," but there may be no alternative to the official proposals backed by a large number of proxies automatically voted in management's favor. And the small stockholders' "representatives" on the board of directors find the usual overwhelming endorsement of manage-

[21] Victor Perlo, "People's Capitalism and Stock Ownership," *American Economic Review*, June, 1958, pp. 345–346.

ment's proposals by the stockholders a comfortable set of blinders; so they will not have to be bothered by even pinpricks of conscience. Hence it would appear to be false flattery to say to the individual stockholder: "You may own only a few shares, yet without you there is no home in the country, no company plane, no corporation-owned limousine at his [the president's] disposal. ... You are a mighty important man and you are becoming more powerful every day." [22] The author of this statement forgets to mention that he became powerful at the Penn-Texas Company only after organizing a group of wealthy backers holding enough shares to give him representation on the board of directors and ultimately to oust the president and assume his position. Even an outspoken and hard-working individual stockholder like John Gilbert may make at best the impression of a gadfly. As one of the corporate dinosaurs put it, "If the stockholder is dissatisfied, he has two choices—either he can sell his stock or he can jump into the river."

Thus the small individual stockholders' position does not appear to have changed much since they were described by Adam Smith in his *Wealth of Nations* in 1776 as "people who, having invested in a joint stock company, neither did nor could take much further interest in its affairs except to welcome the dividends paid to them." It would seem that many shareholders have acquired something more closely resembling the attitude or incentive of bondholders. While most are willing to commit their money, they are unwilling to give of their time or their brains to the corporation.

Small owners, of course, have their representatives in the supposedly controlling body of the corporation, the board of directors. But though the stockholders elect, they usually do not select the board of directors. And the directors do not always act as fiduciary trustees for the owners; in quite a few cases it is actually difficult for them to do so. For while, theoretically, the stockholders control the corporation, the internal management controls its affairs.

The representatives of the owners in many companies are nothing more than "inside boards" made up of active members of management. There may be individuals who can properly play the dual

[22] David Karr, *Fight for Control*, Ballantine Books, New York, 1956, pp 1–2.

role of member of management and representative of the owners, but it is difficult to see how it is possible for the average manager to split his personality in this way.[23] It may be undesirable for him to do so in any case: some transactions, deals, or practices inside the "management family" had better never be seen by any outsider. So-called "outside boards" with "outside" directors tend to be merely "inside outsiders," that is, men from outside the company chosen by the inside management and possibly beholden to it. Many of them do not have the time or the inclination to represent the stockholders adequately.

Proxy Fights

If the small individual stockholder wants to make his voice heard, he must, as a rule, combine with others. Such temporary combinations usually take the form of a proxy fight, that is, a gathering of the votes of as many shareholders as possible, with the objective of defeating a management resolution or substituting another for it, or of gaining representation for a point of view on the board of directors. Success in the latter case often requires a provision for cumulative voting.[24] In this way the votes for the number of directors eligible can be bunched into the vote for one and thus offer the possibility of minority representation. Cumulative voting can, however, be frustrated by staggering the duration of the terms of office of board members, premeeting discussions among members of the "in group," appointment of majority directors to committees, changes in the number of directors, making decisions without

---

[23] "The independence and the detached point of view are diluted when the Board includes active officers dependent upon the president for promotion and pay." David Loth, quoting Swope, *op. cit.*, p. 60.

[24] For detailed studies see Charles M. Williams, *Cumulative Voting for Directors*, Harvard University Graduate School of Business, Division of Research, Boston, 1951; Charles M. Williams, "Cumulative Voting," *Harvard Business Review*, May–June, 1955, pp. 108–111. It should be noted that cumulative voting exists in less than 40 per cent of the corporations subject to the regulations of the Securities and Exchange Commission, i.e., corporations listed on one of the three exchanges. Many managements oppose cumulative voting because of the possibly disrupting and negative influence of minority directors.

reference to the board or at least without consulting members likely to be opposed, and other devices.[25]

Before 1934 the minority stockholder often found it difficult to make his voice heard. He was dependent on his company's charter and by-laws. With the passage in 1934 of the Federal Securities and Exchange Act, publicly regulated stockholder participation was set in motion (Section 14R). While SEC does not require the use of proxies (though the New York Stock Exchange will have such a requirement for all stocks listed),[26] once solicitation is under way a number of SEC requirements must be met (Regulation X-14). The basic purpose is to protect investors by requiring disclosure to them of certain basic information at the time their proxies are solicited "to enable the average 'prudent' investor to act intelligently upon each separate matter with respect to which his vote or consent is sought." [27]

In this direction the SEC requirements may be summarized as follows: [28]

1. "Full disclosure" of all relevant information in the proxy statement, such as information regarding the nominees for directorships and the names of persons who will directly or indirectly bear the cost of solicitations. Solicitations must not contain misleading statements nor omit material facts. Copies of soliciting material must be submitted to the Commission in advance of release (misrepresentation includes presentation of misleading statistics, implication of guilt by association, and rhetorical leading questions).[29] The

[25] Corporations in Illinois are an exception because they are unable to frustrate cumulative voting by the device of staggering the election of boards of directors. It is possible that the court decisions may spread the safeguard to other states.

[26] *Business Week*, Apr. 11, 1959.

[27] J. Sinclair Armstrong, Commissioner SEC, "Proxy Contests under the Securities and Exchange Commission's Proxy Rules," Chicago, Feb. 9, 1955, SEC Release 4775 (1952), 4979 (1954); "More about the Securities and Exchange Commission's Proxy Rules," Bretton Woods, N.H., 1955; Ralph H. Demmler, "Proxy Contests and the SEC," *The Exchange*, March, 1955, pp. 1–4.

[28] W. G. Bruehl, *The Proxy Battle*, Dartmouth College, Hanover, N.H., 1955.

[29] Address by SEC Commissioner Gadsby in New York, April, 1958.

position of the Commission itself is that of impartial umpire, neither approving nor disapproving the position of any party involved.

2. Allowing any stockholder to take the opportunity of presenting issues to other stockholders through a statement in the proxy not to exceed one hundred words on "a proper subject for action by the security holder."

3. Providing the stockholder with means to bring a given issue to the vote.

These regulations make it possible for dissident stockholders to express their views. The privilege is not, however, used much (so-called "dual solicitations" in "listed" companies do not amount to more than a few per cent of total solicitations, though these are on the increase). The reasons are principally inertia and expense. Insurgents who lose do not receive reimbursement. Perhaps SEC might consider permitting expense reimbursement in proxy fights in which, say, an adequate minority supports the issue and the issue itself is sufficiently relevant and appropriate to be brought to the attention of *all* stockholders without SEC taking a stand for either side.

However, in a large corporation with hundreds of thousands of shareholders, of whom no one holds more than a fraction of 1 per cent of the outstanding shares, a successful proxy fight is a task "so hazardous and expensive as to be of little practical advantage," [30] unless in the rare instance in which the opposition is as financially powerful and adept in public relations as internal management. The proxy fighters usually have to be outsiders who are partial proprietors elsewhere and potentially substantial proprietors in the company which they are attempting to control. Such an outsider must be ambitious, energetic, and persuasive enough to win a place among the "inner ring." One need only list the qualifications required for this kind of insurgent to convey how rare he is. Even so, his arrival on the board of the corporation he is trying to control may not result at all in in-

[30] See the authoritative and excellent study of Percival E. Jackson, *Corporate Management: The Directors and Executives*, The Michie Company, Charlottesville, Va., 1955, p. 115.

dependent review. He may prove to be either a bitter minority of one on a board which he is dividing, or, in command of full power, he may prove to be more dictatorial or even less competent than his predecessors. He may be even more power-hungry and skilled in the techniques of acquiring and holding power. Furthermore, the successful proxy raider may well be a restless man, prone to make a quick killing after power seizure (meanwhile paying himself and his group large sums, running down the plant, and either distributing the cash surplus as dividends or using it to raid other organizations). Rather than have the "son of a wolf" raid the company treasury, most stockholders seem to prefer to keep a management in power that is at least no more than "a sheep in sheep's clothing." That the potential threat of raiders may keep managements on their toes is not denied, but so far few of them have been Robin Hoods who exercised a high-level independent review on behalf of all the stockholders. There have been few who have been able at all to upset internal managements: in the ten-year period from 1943 to 1952 only 10 per cent of the corporations subject to SEC regulations were involved in proxy fights, and some of these were not concerned with the election of directors, and even less with the issue of independent review.

More Independent Directors

One widely discussed organizational substitute is the "public director," a man not appointed by government but independent enough of internal management to provide independent review. Such a man would usually be a person well known to the public in general or to a specific segment of it, who has made a genuine contribution to the public welfare or is considered capable of doing so. Because of his need to maintain his public reputation, it is held, he would continue to be independent and perhaps be able to draw management's attention to the needs of particular segments of the public, or even act as mediator, in addition to making contributions to the organization itself.

The difficulties of making contributions become apparent as soon as we translate the general desiderata into concrete terms.

Historically, the concept of the public director does not augur well for consistent success. First, he was probably thought of originally as an outside financial expert who would help the large corporation utilize its considerable investments in the most profitable manner. This was the origin of the so-called financial "public directors," George Whitney, John M. Hancock, and Sidney Weinberg, to mention three of the most outstanding who were able to bring corporations back to the goal of increasing return on investment and still exercise some of their public responsibilities. Each of these men has occupied many important directorships. Each of them has been a giant in his own right. But the supply of this type of director appears to be too small. The scarcity augurs poorly for the prospect of successors.

The usual financial director, some may claim, is overly interested in the financial success of his own firm and may push decisions which enable him to float new stock or bond issues or to provide short-term loans on which he would earn not only commissions but also substantial capital gains, at least in the short run. It is possible for directors representing underwriting houses to contrive acceptance of financing through new issues by bringing up the matter at five minutes to five, when most members of the board are anxious to catch trains and planes.

An even less well-qualified type of public director is the captive director. He is conceived of as a member of internal management who is particularly well qualified to present the viewpoint of some special company "public." Thus the personnel director is supposed to represent the employees, the financial vice president the financial community, the purchasing agent the suppliers, and the marketing man the customers, etc.

Lewis Brown, the imaginative and able board chairman of Johns-Manville, conceived this idea, but it never came to much because it amounted, practically, to a self-contradiction. True, representatives of suppliers, customers, and financial institutions might be called to the board, but frequently they are interested only in their own specialties, not in the over-all needs of the company. And since they would be dependent on the good will of the management, they might not possess the power of independent review, however great their good will and however substantial their potential contributions. And if the board members were all members of internal management, dependent on the president, they would have no power of independent review at all.

A third type of public director is a management-appointed public figure, such as a university president or dean (sometimes even a professor), a retired general, an ex-diplomat or government official, an outstanding scientist or inventor, a distinguished legal counsel, an economist, or a prominent outside figure in the management movement. Any one of these could make a major contribution to a corporate management by drawing attention to the public impact of a proposed corporate action on, for example, wages and prices, political participation, plant location, and so forth. Such a director could not only communicate a public point of view, as represented in the national or state capital or in his sphere of activity, but could also serve at times as a mediator between the various "publics" making claims on the corporation, reconciling divergent views or anticipating public consequences of corporate action. Worthy projects like hospitals and public educational institutions might receive the appropriate corporate attention, along with other community needs. The increasing impact of international affairs on the life of each of us might find some hearing in the forum of the large corporation. The possibilities are endless and the opportunities for constructive work by the public director great. Yet this type of public director may often lack both the power and the competence necessary for independent review. To some extent the public director would owe his appointment to one or more members of internal management, and "there where your treasure lies, there lies your heart also." Quite unintentionally this may be the situation in which the public director finds himself. At the least, his effectiveness may be impaired by the conflict between his ideals and his newly acquired business interests. And he is likely to lack the business acumen necessary to command the respect of management executives and make effective independent review possible.

Financial Institutions

Our conclusion may have to be that there appears to be only one workable alternative to the replacement of the dinosaurs, the partial proprietors, namely, the institutional investors. These investors—mutual funds, life insurance companies, savings banks and pension funds, as well as individual trusts managed by bankers—have always been an important potential influence. Today they could often be dominant. The percentage of issues listed on the New York Stock Exchange held by institutions has risen from a value of $9.5 billion, or 12.4 per cent, in 1949 to an estimated $30 billion, or 15.3 per cent of the total, at the end of 1957. If the equities of the individual trusts that are institutional are included, the 1958 total comes to about 30 per cent of the value of all issues on the New York Stock Exchange.[31]

Pension funds have risen faster than any other institutional funds. According to the SEC statistician Vito Natrella, they have risen from $5.6 billion in 1950 to $22.0 billion in 1959,[32] or more than half of all institutional holdings, and they are said to rise at an annual rate of $4 billion. By 1965, it is estimated, they will have reached $50 billion, and more if the pension coverage of the work force should rise beyond its present one-fourth. (Some look for a leveling off at around $100 billion.) To this may be added the equity holdings and purchases of educational endowment funds, private foundations, and union treasuries. (Though union funds have not been widely invested in equities, they could be.) Of the 1,500 companies whose shares are listed on the New York Stock Exchange, the institutional investors have large holdings in about 200 "investment grade" issues that are also public favorites.

The fear of inflation, the rising respectability of equities, and the yields (actual and prospective) are, of course, among the major

[31] *London Economist,* Jan. 10, 1959, p. 129, and Robert Tilove, *op. cit.,* p. 38.
[32] Gilbert Burck, "A New Kind of Stock Market," *Fortune,* March, 1959, p. 121; "Private Pension Funds," *Business Week,* Jan. 31, 1959; William B. Neenan, "Pension Funds and the Equity Market," *Labor Law Journal* (Chicago), September, 1956; William B. Neenan, "Review of Institutional Activity in the Equity Market, 1951–1954," *The Journal of Finance,* December, 1957

factors in this fast-rising popularity of equities among institutional investors. American Telephone and Telegraph has put 10 per cent of its $2.6 billion pension funds into common stock and is acting as bellwether; GE, 32 per cent; Bethlehem Steel, 70 per cent; and Sears, 84 per cent.

In some cases, of course, management appoints the trustees, and the stock chosen is that of the company itself, which means a strengthening of management control. But this is not usually the case, and in many cases pension funds are actually forbidden by the terms of their investitures from purchasing "own company" stock.

The opposition of the trusts of all kinds to the use of rebuttal power in their relationship to managements through their stockholdings is extremely strong. In interviews they advanced the following reasons for nonintervention:

1. If you buy shares in a company, you thereby, *ipso facto*, have to be loyal to the management of that company. Otherwise you should not have bought shares in the first place.

2. Trust officers may lack the competence, or the time, to take an active interest in the management of the company with which they deal.

3. Participation, if unsuccessful, can be blamed on the trust officer; if he does not participate, he cannot be blamed. And if he can persuade "the fraternity" to nonintervention, as has happened up till now by and large, then no one can be blamed.

4. Voting against the management raises a danger that "interlopers" and "incompetents" will find an opening. Managements, feeling threatened, may appeal to the public and Congress against "bullies."

5. If the trust officers disapprove of management's policies, they can signify their disapproval by selling the stock.

The principal error in this reasoning is, of course, that management does not have all the right answers in matters of interest to stockholders, and where there is a clear conflict of interest, it is the right and duty of stockholders' representatives to support the interests of their principals.

It may also be asked whether just selling a stock without any attempt to remedy a remediable situation is not actually a counsel of despair. Is this not a perpetuation of the deplorable tendency to refuse to accept the accountability that is inherent in trusteeship?

First, the trustees disenfranchise their numerous and trusting clients without even consulting them.

Second, they act illogically by refusing even to try to improve the price of their shares.

Third, if they simply sell their stock, they are letting others hold the bag and enabling management to point to a shorter holding period and claim that "continuity of control" requires that it be supreme.

Fourth, if the financial institutions hold a substantial block of the shares in a company, say, 50 to 60 per cent, and do not vote their shares at all—and many of them do not—then any marauding group can conceivably gain control with perhaps 5 to 15 per cent of the stock. If they vote blindly for management, their failure as trustees will surely be held against them.

Finally, these trustees may invite government intervention almost by default. The "new tycoons," as they have been called, are new all right, but they are in no way tycoons. If they refuse to take the place of the individual and company minority stockholder directors, the outlook for the stockholder, and in the long run for management, is not favorable. If the trusts do not gradually modify their stubborn opposition to the exercise of rebuttal power, if ingrown managements continue to move into the void left by the dinosaurs, various public authorities may well be tempted to fill the vacuum.

Instinctively, some of the institutional investors have realized their obligations. Gingerly and cautiously, they are beginning to move in and ask questions, and if any kind of managerial sensitivity exists, searching questions and moral suasion can lead to a subtle exercise of rebuttal power. For instance, *Business Week* (January, 1959) describes how analysts for funds call on companies where sizable positions are held or an addition to the portfolio is contemplated and ask some fairly sharp questions about various phases of the company's operations. "For example, one analyst recently asked the officer of one big Connecticut firm why it continued pouring money into a division that was a steady money loser. Apparently the question was asked by analysts from other groups having a position in the company's stock—mutual funds, investment companies and insurance firms. Before long the company got rid of that division."

In some cases, too, trustees have worked hard on the management for years and resigned only when their persuasion got nowhere, as the J. P. Morgan directors did at Montgomery Ward. In still other instances trustees have been forced to take sides in a proxy fight even though they were very reluctant to commit themselves, as the Chase Manhattan Bank was when confronted with a choice between the incumbent management and the insurgents for whose stock the bank was a trustee.

But these things do not happen often enough. Thus a large investment trust with many shares in a well-known company dispatched emissaries to the management when shares began to slide badly. But it held on until the price of the stock dropped substantially and then sold without making an outcry.

Giving the beneficiaries of the funds a voice in the voting of the shares does not seem to provide a workable answer, though it has been attempted in at least one case. Sharp Congressional questioning warned the trustees of the Sears, Roebuck pension trust that the setup would perpetuate management control of the company because Sears directors appointed the trustees (usually company officers) and the trustees in turn always voted the fund's stock for management. Now the 95 per cent of the employees who have vested rights in the pension plan are polled by an independent research organization to find out how they want to vote the fund's Sears stock that is credited to them, and the trustees are then expected to follow these instructions. This raises several difficulties: Who will frame the questions? And will the voters be given a veto power over all major propositions? Will they be provided with an absolutely impartial resumé of the pros and cons? And who will provide it?

So the institutional investors are either going to be thrown back into their original state or expose themselves to the threat of public control. How can they escape from this dilemma?

A National Panel

One way might be through the formation of a nationwide association of institutional investors for the purpose of selecting and appointing their own representatives to the boards of companies in which their combined holdings are large, either absolutely in terms of total dollars or relatively as a proportion of shares of outstanding stock. Each of these institutional directors should have outstanding technical competence and should be completely independent of the internal managements of the companies on whose boards he sits, because he serves on several boards and because he is so well paid that he can afford to be independent. (The expense could presumably be met easily because of the substantial allowance for administrative expenses of institutional funds.) These professonal directors will, of course, not be perfect substitutes for the dinosaurs, but they may have greater power of survival and adaptability to changing circumstances. In this way, companies with an independent review would once again become leaders and pace setters, perhaps forcing the reluctant ones to follow suit, if not to be competitive, then at least for the sake of respectability.

If the legal and moral foundation for the exercise of management power continues to be eroded as the influence of ownership declines and management becomes increasingly beholden to itself alone, is it not likely that management, to forestall public intervention, will increasingly have to buy protection from some of its publics? And buy it with other people's money, at that. There already is growing evidence of this, a posture much akin to that of a gangster outfit. As management comes more and more to dilute its historic *raison d'être* of maximizing profits for its owners in the name of social responsibility, employee welfare, industrial peace, community betterment, supporting higher education, and the like, the question of chief interest that emerges is: On what grounds is the pressure for ever larger donations to each of these causes to be blunted? The contributions to each of them are rising, and it would be interesting to see if they are rising faster than dividend disbursements. If as yet they are not, it seems clear that they soon will be. There is no reason to suppose that such largesse will be distributed where it will do the most good; rather it will go where it will buy the most time. Unless reforms are introduced from within, two developments seem only postponable, not avoidable: time will run out and reforms will be forced into the executive suite from the outside, and among those most insistent on such coercion will be those whose appetites for corporate handouts have outgrown the capacity of corporate giving.

In conclusion, it may perhaps be said that the case for independent review appears to be strong. Admonition to avoid the legal, moral, and economic hazards of evading it, to be more "professional," "more social-minded," is for children, not for corporate executives. Nor will bigness yield to littleness, and there is great doubt whether we should want it to do so.

Thus attention is drawn back to the case for independent review. The proposals advanced in that direction appear to be feasible, and they are likely to be strengthened by experience and maturity. Yet independent review is no easy solution and may be blocked by major obstacles: (1) Few managements can be expected to admit to themselves, much less to their stockholders, that a conflict of interest may exist between them to such an extent as to require a basic reform at the top of the corporation. (2) Managers, like other mature men, are inclined to keep supervision of themselves to an unavoidable minimum. (3) Ingrown managements may tend to view the whole matter as a question of "public relations" and seek to provide the appearance of independent review rather than the actuality.

In spite of the many difficulties of solving the problem of continued independent review, it might be well for those who refuse to face it and its possible solution to bear in mind the pertinent observation of T. S. Eliot in *The Idea of a Christian Society:* [33]

[33] From *The Idea of a Christian Society*, p. 3. Copyright, 1940, by T. S. Eliot. Reprinted by permission of Harcourt, Brace and Company, Inc.

The fact that a problem will certainly take a long time to solve, and that it will demand the attention of many minds for several generations, is no justification for postponing the study. And, in times of emergency, it may prove in the long run that the problems we have postponed or ignored, rather than those we have failed to attack successfully, will return to plague us. Our difficulties of the moment must always be dealt with somehow: but our permanent difficulties are difficulties of every moment.

Appendices to Chapter 5

A. Changes in Employment Patterns *

As was described in Chapter 5, the primary features of the 1935 Westinghouse reorganization were the shift of management and administrative functions from the central office to the newly designated divisional offices, the addition of more staff personnel at headquarters to help the division managers make their operations more profitable, and the provision of central controls. The significance and the extent of the changes wrought by the reorganization can, therefore, be demonstrated in part by an analysis of the employment of administrative and technical personnel as compared with manufacturing employees in the period of the reorganization.

Increase in Staff

As a first step, the record of employment in the headquarters staff will be analyzed. Then the composition of employment in two divisions of the company and the company as a whole will be reviewed. Finally, the employment pattern at Westinghouse will be contrasted with that of the remainder of the electrical industry. The year 1935 was chosen as the base year, the last full year before the reorganization, and the year 1939 as the last year affected exclusively by the reorganization and not yet seriously affected by rearmament.

Headquarters staffs. Though part of the management decision

* The statistical material in this appendix was prepared by Professor Seymour Melman of Columbia University, who has pioneered in the analysis of the relationship between administrative and production expenses (A/P ratios).

making was removed from headquarters and relocated in the several divisions, central-office functions were expanded in the direction described above. This expansion required an increase in personnel that exceeded the number of employees transferred to the divisions. This is disclosed in the data of Table 5–1.

The effect of the decentralization process was most apparent in the size of the sales staff at the central administrative office. During the period 1935 to 1939 the sales staff was reduced from 2,312 to 1,808, a drop of 22 per cent. Over the same period, however, the general administrative functions of the general office were substantially expanded and employment in them rose 35 per cent, from

TABLE 5-1. WESTINGHOUSE: CENTRAL ADMINISTRATIVE AND TECHNICAL STAFF, 1934–1939

Department	1934	1935	1936	1937	1938	1939
	Number employed					
Administration	1,032 *	1,115	1,544	1,502	1,378	1,503
Sales	2,195	2,312	1,927	2,148	1,787	1,808
Engineering	115	113	289	275	316	340
Total	3,342	3,540	3,760	3,925	3,481	3,651
	Index number (1935 = 100)					
Administration	92.5	100	138.5	134.7	123.6	134.8
Sales	94.9	100	83.3	92.9	77.3	78.2
Engineering	101.8	100	255.8	243.4	279.6	300.9
Average	94.4	100	106.2	110.9	98.3	103.1

* Excludes 344 accountants assigned to the several divisions and to district offices, but includes East Pittsburgh works accountants.

Note: In each case the data are annual averages of the original monthly figures.

SOURCE: Westinghouse Electric and Manufacturing Co., Summary of Payrolls (excluding Lamp Division), 1934–1939.

1,115 employees in 1935 to 1,503 in 1939. The development of central engineering functions was even more pronounced. Here the increase from 1935 to 1939 amounted to 201 per cent. The net effect of these developments was a slight increase in the central-office staff over the 1935–1939 period.

Administrative and technical staffs in the divisions. With the type of reorganization described above, it would be expected that management and administrative personnel outside the central office would increase rather sharply. They did. From 1935 to 1939 there was a 60 per cent increase in the divisional [1] administrative and technical personnel. This increase is shown in the second line of Table 5–2. Divisional administrative and technical staffs in-

TABLE 5-2. WESTINGHOUSE: CENTRAL AND DIVISIONAL ADMINISTRATIVE AND TECHNICAL STAFFS, 1934–1939

	1934	1935	1936	1937	1938	1939
Staffs	Number employed					
1. Central administrative and technical	3,342	3,540	3,760	3,925	3,481	3,651
2. Divisional administrative and technical	4,323	4,450	5,443	7,022	7,034	7,138
3. Total administrative and technical	7,665	7,990	9,203	10,947	10,515	10,789
	Index number (1935 = 100)					
1. Central administrative and technical	94.4	100	106.2	110.9	98.3	103.1
2. Divisional administrative and technical	97.1	100	122.3	157.8	158.1	160.4
3. Average administrative and technical	95.9	100	115.2	137.0	131.6	135.0

SOURCE: Westinghouse Electric and Manufacturing Co., Summary of Payrolls (excluding Lamp Division), 1934–1939.

creased from 4,450 employees in 1935 to 7,138 by 1939. The 60 per cent rise from 1935 to 1939 is particularly indicative of the effect of the relocation of administrative and technical functions in the divisions. Moreover, for the firm as a whole, administrative and technical staffs increased by more than 35 per cent from 1935 to 1940.

Staffs of particular divisions. Because of the regrouping and relocation of manufacturing activities that took place during the

[1] The noncentral office administrative and technical personnel are referred to as "divisional," although before the reorganization they were not, of course, divisional, but merely located at the plants.

period of management reorganization, the employment data for all the divisions of the firm, covering the period 1935 to 1939, could not be readily analyzed. It was possible, however, to develop such data for the Lighting Division (Cleveland) and for the Transformer Division (Sharon).

Table 5–3 is an analysis of the administrative, technical, and manu-

TABLE 5-3. WESTINGHOUSE: LIGHTING, ILLUMINATING DIVISION (CLEVELAND):
ADMINISTRATIVE, TECHNICAL, AND MANUFACTURING PERSONNEL, 1934–1939

Department	1934	1935	1936	1937	1938	1939
			Number employed			
1. Administration	49	34	37	55	48	51
2. Sales and clerical			60	66	45	42
3. Total administration (1 + 2)	49	34	97	121	93	93
4. Engineering	21	16	26	34	35	34
5. Total administration and engineering (3 + 4)	· 70	50	123	155	128	127
6. Manufacturing hourly	328	266	316	443	236	346
7. Total employees (5 + 6)	398	316	439	598	364	473
			Index number (1935 = 100)			
1. Administration	144.1	100	108.8	161.8	141.2	150.0
2. Sales and clerical		100.0	110.0	75.0	70.0
3. Total administration (1 + 2)	144.1	100	285.3	355.9	273.5	273.5
4. Engineering	131.2	100	162.5	212.5	218.8	212.5
5. Average administration and engineering (3 + 4)	140.0	100	246.0	310.0	256.0	254.0
6. Manufacturing hourly	123.3	100	118.8	166.5	88.7	130.1
7. Average (5 + 6)	125.9	100	138.9	189.2	115.2	149.7

SOURCE: Westinghouse Electric and Manufacturing Co., Summary of Payrolls (excluding Lamp Division), 1934–1939.

facturing employment in the Lighting Division. The administration group shown in line 5 of Table 5–3 was expanded over this period. The engineering staffs located at this division were also enlarged, though not in the same degree as the general administrative group. There was a considerable increase in the number of sales and clerical personnel, some of whom presumably were transferred from East Pittsburgh. It should be noted, in this respect, that after 1937 the number of these employees dropped sharply, possibly indicating that reorganization was, even at that early date, improving efficiency. The division's total administrative and technical group grew from 50 employees in 1935 to 127 by 1939, an increase of 154 per cent. The trend of hourly manufacturing employment in this division contrasts with the administrative and technical staff development. From 1935 to 1939, the number of hourly employees increased by 30 per cent, while the administrative and technical group rose by 154 per cent. In the single year 1935–1936, total administrative and technical personnel increased by 146 per cent, while the manufacturing hourly employees increased by 19 per cent. The unique pattern of growth of administrative and technical staffs is consistent with the expanded range of managerial and technical functions allocated to this division in the reorganization.[2]

In the Transformer Division (Sharon) the growth of hourly manufacturing employment was somewhat greater than the increase in administrative and technical staffs. The former rose by 96 per cent from 1935 to 1939, as compared with an 80.5 per cent increase in the latter (Table 5–4). As compared with other firms in the electrical apparatus industry, this growth was still unusual, however.

The experience of this division also differed from that of the Lighting Division with respect to the changes from 1935 to 1936. In the Transformer Division, hourly manufacturing employees increased by 47 per cent between 1935 and 1936, as compared with a 26 per cent rise in administrative and technical staffs. It may be inferred from these observations that there was no uniform experience among the divisions of the firm with respect to the magnitude

---

[2] Even though administrative employment in the Lighting Division rose faster than manufacturing employment over the period as a whole, there were two instances in which the reverse occurred. In the 1937 upswing, manufacturing employment increased 40 per cent over 1936, while administrative employment rose by only 26 per cent. In 1939, manufacturing employment was 47 per cent greater than in 1938, while administrative employment fell by about 1 per cent. The more than doubling of administrative and engineering personnel that occurred between 1935 and 1936 probably made possible the comparatively small advance between 1936 and 1937, and by 1939 increased efficiency made it possible for the administrative staff to handle the increase in the number of hourly paid workers without any increase—in fact, with a small decrease—in its own numbers. A similar pattern occurred in those years in the Transformer Division and in the company as a whole.

and timing of changes in composition of employment because of management reorganization. This is in keeping with the fact that the management reorganization was a process carried out over several years following 1935.

TABLE 5-4. WESTINGHOUSE: TRANSFORMER DIVISION (SHARON): ADMINISTRATIVE, TECHNICAL, AND MANUFACTURING PERSONNEL, 1934–1939

Department	1934	1935	1936	1937	1938	1939
	Number employed					
1. Administration	178	180	187	263	260	259
2. Sales and clerical			37	47	54	61
3. Total administration (1 + 2)	178	180	224	310	314	320
4. Engineering	135	138	176	291	237	254
5. Total administration and engineering (3 + 4)	313	318	400	601	551	574
6. Manufacturing hourly	801	1,102	1,622	2,746	1,525	2,162
7. Total employees	1,114	1,420	2,022	3,347	2,076	2,736
	Index number (1935 = 100)					
1. Administration	98.9	100.0	103.9	146.1	144.4	143.9
2. Sales and clerical		100.0	127.0	146.0	164.9	
3. Total administration (1 + 2)	98.9	100.0	124.4	172.2	174.4	177.8
4. Engineering	97.8	100.0	127.5	210.9	171.7	184.0
5. Total administration and engineering (3 + 4)	98.4	100.0	125.8	198.0	173.3	180.5
6. Manufacturing hourly	72.7	100.0	147.2	249.2	138.4	196.2
7. Total employees	78.4	100.0	142.4	235.7	146.2	192.7

Total Employment

The changes in employment patterns in the corporation as a whole may be directly examined through an analysis of aggregate employment data of the company (Table 5–5). These data are cast in categories that are comparable with those used for showing employment changes in the Transformer and the Lighting Divisions.

From 1935 to 1939 total employment in the Westinghouse Electric Corporation increased from 27,061 to 31,366, a rise of 16 per cent. Hourly manufacturing employees increased by 8 per cent, as disclosed in line 9 of Table 5–5. The 8 per cent increase in hourly manufacturing employees over this period, however, was substantially exceeded by the rise in total administrative and technical personnel, shown in line 8 of Table 5–5. This group increased by 35 per cent over the period 1935 to 1939. Within this class of em-

TABLE 5-5. WESTINGHOUSE: EMPLOYMENT IN ADMINISTRATIVE, TECHNICAL, AND MANUFACTURING OCCUPATIONS, 1934–1939

Department	1934	1935	1936	1937	1938	1939
	Number employed					
1. Engineering	1,799	1,753	1,979	2,413	2,211	2,417
2. Sales	2,195	2,312	2,374	2,657	2,639	2,551
3. Administration	1,340	1,352	956	1,115	1,148	1,100
4. Order service and general clerical			448	538	451	451
5. General			260	358	313	476
6. Total (1 + 2 + 3 + 4 + 5)	5,334	5,417	6,017	7,081	6,762	6,995
7. Manufacturing salaried	2,331	2,573	3,186	3,866	3,753	3,794
8. Total administration and technical (6 + 7)	7,665	7,990	9,203	10,947	10,515	10,789
9. Manufacturing hourly employees	18,671	19,071	22,535	29,876	17,131	20,577
10. Total employees	26,336	27,061	31,738	40,823	27,646	31,366
	Index number (1935 = 100.0)					
1. Engineering	102.6	100.0	112.9	137.6	126.1	137.9
2. Sales	94.9	100.0	102.7	114.9	114.1	110.3
3. Administration	99.1	100.0	70.7	82.5	84.9	81.4
4. Order service and general clerical			100.0	120.0	100.7	100.7
5. General			100.0	137.7	120.4	183.1
6. Total (1 + 2 + 3 + 4 + 5)	98.5	100.0	111.1	130.7	124.8	129.1
7. Manufacturing salaried	90.6	100.0	123.8	150.3	145.9	147.4
8. Total administration and technical (6 + 7)	95.9	100.0	115.2	137.0	131.6	135.0
9. Manufacturing hourly employees	97.9	100.0	118.2	156.6	89.8	107.9
10. Total employees	97.3	100.0	117.3	150.8	102.2	115.9

SOURCE: Westinghouse Electric and Manufacturing Co., Summary of Payrolls (excluding Lamp Division), 1934–1939.

ployees, the largest increase was registered by the manufacturing salaried group, which includes the management staffs of the various divisions. The 47 per cent increase in the size of this group from 1935 to 1939 is in keeping with the enlarged scope of managerial control at the division level. Furthermore, it was the manufacturing salaried group, appearing in line 7 of Table 5–5, that registered the largest degree of increase of all groups shown here from 1935 to 1936. The 29 per cent enlargement of total divisional managerial staffs is consistent with the reorganization process, as to both character and timing.

Employment at Westinghouse versus Employment in the Industry

The character of employment trends in the Westinghouse Corporation during the period 1935 to 1939 is disclosed by a comparison of the composition of Westinghouse employment with that of the remainder of the electrical apparatus industry. For the years 1935, 1937, and 1939, the data of the Census of Manufactures disclose salaried personnel and wage-earner employment in the electrical apparatus industry—"wage earners" being defined primarily as hourly production workers. The salaried group of employees of the Census of Manufactures includes administrative and technical staffs.

Accordingly, the data shown in Table 5–5 for total administrative and technical employees at Westinghouse correspond to the salaried employees category of the Census of Manufactures. Similarly, the manufacturing hourly employees group at Westinghouse should correspond to the wage-earner category of the Census. In order to compare Westinghouse with the remainder of the industry, we subtracted the Westinghouse employment from the total employment reported for the industry in each year. These data are shown in Table 5–6.

At Westinghouse the administrative group as a whole increased from 7,990 in 1935 to 10,789 in 1939, a rise of 35 per cent. During the same period, the production wage-earner group rose by only 8 per cent. For each census year, Table 5–6 shows the ratio of administrative to production employees, that is, the number of administrative and technical employees per hundred wage earners. This ratio rose from 41.9 to 52.4 at Westinghouse from 1935 to 1939.

In contrast to the Westinghouse record, the ratio decreased in the remainder of the industry, in keeping with the short-term trend from low to high levels of industrial activity. During such periods manufacturing employees, on the average, increased to a greater degree than did administrative and technical staffs.

Westinghouse had a reverse pattern. During the same period, there was a relatively sharp growth in the proportion of administrative

TABLE 5-6. ADMINISTRATIVE AND PRODUCTION PERSONNEL IN WESTINGHOUSE AND IN THE ELECTRICAL APPARATUS INDUSTRY, 1935–1939

Department	Index number (1935 = 100)					
	1935	1937	1939	1935	1937	1939
	Westinghouse					
Administration (A)	7,990	10,947	10,789	100	137	135
Production (P)	19,071	29,876	20,577	100	157	108
A/P, per cent	41.9	36.6	52.4	100	87	125
	The electrical apparatus industry minus Westinghouse data					
Administration (A)	35,872	49,440	47,379	100	138	132
Production (P)	160,570	227,784	257,143	100	142	160
A/P, per cent	22.3	21.7	18.4	100	97	83

Note: The contrast appearing in Table 5-6 may be somewhat of an overstatement of the comparison in A/P ratios at given times, because of an element of incomparability which is known to be present in the reported industry employment data of the Census of Manufactures. The Census Bureau has not been able to make reliable counts of central-office staffs in the manufacturing industries for inclusion in the various industry reports. The data for these employees are, however, completely included in our Westinghouse employment figures. Experience with these problems leads to the conclusion that even if complete counts of central-office employment were included in the electrical apparatus industry data, the effect would not appreciably alter the differences in changes over time between Westinghouse and the remainder of the industry. For these differences in rates of change are large. If the central-office employees are completely included for the remainder of the industry, it would lessen the differences in A/P ratios at each given time.

SOURCE: U.S. Census of Manufactures; Westinghouse Employment Data.

to production employees.[3] This increase is traceable to the reorganization process, which involved an expansion of administrative and technical functions, and therefore staffs, at both the divisional and central-office levels.

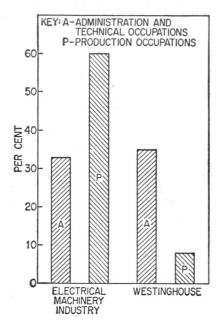

CHART 10. CHANGES IN LABOR FORCE
IN ADMINISTRATION AND IN PRODUCTION,
1935–1939

The special development at Westinghouse is depicted in Chart 10, whose vertical bars measure the percentage increase in administrative and production staffs for Westinghouse as compared with the remainder of the industry.

During the period of management reorganization from 1935 through 1940, the administrative and technical staffs of the West-

[3] In the period 1935 through 1937, the proportion at Westinghouse fell much more sharply than in the rest of the industry. This may have been due to the already high proportion existing in Westinghouse in 1935. Under such circumstances a slight improvement can have a far greater effect than in a company with a smaller proportion of administrative employees.

inghouse Company grew both in absolute size and in relation to the direct manufacturing staffs. This rise in administrative and technical personnel occurred at all levels of the company.

This was the special pattern of Westinghouse employment during the years 1935 through 1939. It can thus be seen that the reorganization was carried out, so far as shifts and increases in administrative personnel are concerned, on a massive scale, which underscores its far-reaching significance.

B. ADMINISTRATIVE AND MANUFACTURING COSTS

In order to disclose both the absolute and the relative growth of the cost of administrative and technical engineering activities, it is necessary to segregate selling, general, and administrative expense from the manufacturing expense (cost of sales). Selling, general, and administrative expense may be analyzed in relation to both cost of sales and to net sales as indicators of the manufacturing activity of the company.

These categories of cost and sales have been developed for the Westinghouse Corporation and for the firm most comparable with it, the General Electric Company. In addition, it was possible to prepare comparable data for 892 manufacturing companies representing a wide range of industrial experience. These data are of importance to an appreciation of the special experience of the Westinghouse Corporation over the period 1935 through 1940.

The reports of the Westinghouse Corporation to the U.S. Securities and Exchange Commission provided the basic data utilized for these analyses. The reported data were corrected for completeness through an examination of Westinghouse costs as supplied by its budget department. These records disclosed that several classes of conventionally defined administrative expenses had been grouped, during the period reviewed, within the class of factory expenses and therefore appear in the aggregate accounts as part of the cost of sales. These extra administrative outlays included:

1. Additional compensation to selling and administrative employees

2. Additional compensation to engineering and manufacturing salaried employees

3. Purchasing department costs
4. Accounting costs at works
5. District accounting costs
6. Customer consultation and sales engineering

The amounts included in these costs are shown in Table 5–7.

TABLE 5-7. WESTINGHOUSE: SELLING, GENERAL, AND ADMINISTRATIVE EXPENSE
CHARGED TO COST OF SALES, 1936–1939

Expense	1936	1937	1938	1939
1. Additional compensation to selling and administration salaried employees	$ 769,997	$1,869,013	$ 344,207	$ 664,485
2. Additional compensation to engineering and manufacturing salaried employees	914,897	2,369,111	412,293	873,675
3. Purchasing dept. costs	193,026	276,000	255,200	282,000
4. Accounting costs at works	583,061	1,015,900	888,900	970,300
5. Accounting costs, district	109,989	155,167	152,037	152,067
6. Customer, consulting, and sales engineering	668,022	669,762	749,427	828,295
7. Total	3,238,992	6,354,953	2,802,064	3,770,822
8. Selling, general, and administration expense as reported to SEC (in thousands)	23,790	30,402	26,249	27,494
9. Total correction (7) as percentage of reported amount (8)	13.61	20.90	10.67	13.72

They varied from 8.3 per cent of reported selling, general, and administrative expense in 1934 to 20.9 per cent of reported selling, general, and administrative expense in 1937. The sums involved here were removed from the cost of sales category and added to the appropriate class of selling, general, and administrative expense. This classification of outlays is consistent with general accounting practice.

Administrative expense, cost of sales, and net sales for Westinghouse appear in Table 5–8.

From 1935 to 1940, selling, general, and administrative expense increased by 87 per cent. Manufacturing expense rose by only 83 per cent over the same years. Line 5 of Table 5–8 reflects this

TABLE 5-8. WESTINGHOUSE: SELLING, GENERAL, AND ADMINISTRATIVE EXPENSE, COST OF SALES, AND NET SALES 1934–1941

Category	1934	1935	1936	1937	1938	1939	1940	1941
					($ thousands)			
1. Selling, general, and administration expense (A)	21,021	21,108	27,029	36,757	29,051	31,265	39,471	40,222
2. Cost of sales (CS)	70,267	87,362	103,067	137,109	114,805	121,693	160,248	249,103
3. Net sales (NS)	92,159	122,589	154,469	206,348	157,953	175,071	239,431	369,094
4. A/NS, per cent	22.8	17.2	17.5	17.8	18.4	17.9	16.5	10.8
5. A/CS, per cent	29.9	24.2	26.2	26.8	25.3	25.7	24.6	16.1
				Index number (1935 = 100)				
6. Selling, General, and administration expense (A)	99.6	100	123.0509	174.1377	137.6302	148.1192	187.0	189.6
7. Cost of sales (CS)	80.4	100	117.9769	156.9435	131.4129	139.2974	183.4	285.1
8. Net sales (NS)	75.2	100	126.0	168.3	128.8	142.8	195.3	301.1
9. $\dfrac{\text{Index (A)}}{\text{Index (NS)}}$	132.4	100	101.6	103.4	106.8	103.7	95.8	63.0
10. $\dfrac{\text{Index (A)}}{\text{Index (CS)}}$	123.9	100	103.5389	110.9556	104.7311	106.3331	102.0	66.5

pattern in the form of the number of dollars spent on administrative expense per $100 expended for manufacturing purposes. Thus in 1935 the ratio of administrative expense was 24.2. By 1940 it amounted to 24.6.

The unusual character of this development is suggested by the 95 per cent rise in net sales that occurred from 1935 to 1940. Administrative and allied costs are typically semifixed charges that do not show the same flexibility in relation to net sales as manufacturing costs, taken as a whole. During the 1935–1940 period of business expansion, the most typical pattern in American manufacturing was for both net sales and manufacturing costs to rise faster than administrative costs. The reverse was true for Westinghouse.

In order to reveal the relative growth of administrative as compared with manufacturing expenses, we divided the index of administration (line 10) by the index of cost of sales from 1935 through 1940. The effect of this division is as follows. If both categories of expense increase in the same degree from year to year, the effect of dividing the indices would be to leave the result at 100. If the numerator of this ratio, administrative expense, increases in a greater degree than the denominator, the result is a figure greater than 100; similarly, if the denominator, manufacturing expense, should increase in greater degree than the numerator, the result would be less than 100.

From 1935 through 1939, administrative expense was clearly increasing in greater degree than production expense. By 1940, however, there was the beginning of a marked decrease in the relative growth of administrative costs as compared with production costs, as disclosed in the declining value of this ratio. The full force of the relatively less growth in administrative expense appeared by 1941. During that year, for the first time since 1935, the growth of production cost substantially exceeded the growth of administrative cost.

The pattern in Westinghouse costs in relation to sales is graphically disclosed in the chart of Westinghouse costs and sales (Chart 11).

The vertical axis of this chart shows expense in millions. Thereby selling, general, and administrative expense and cost of sales are plotted against net sales of the X axis. Passing through the origin is the "break-even" line (*A*), which is drawn at a 45-degree angle. At all points on this line expenses are equal to net sales. The slope of this line, which is equal to 1, can be used as a measure of performance. If another cost-sale line has a steeper slope, then expenses are rising faster than sales, indicating a lessening of profit

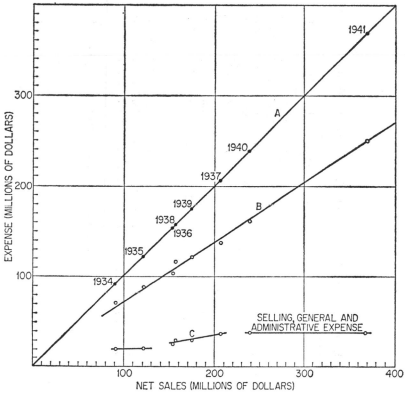

CHART 11. WESTINGHOUSE MAJOR EXPENSE CLASSES AND NET SALES, 1934–1941

margins. A line with a flatter slope indicates the opposite. Both the cost of sales line (*B*) and the selling, general, and administrative expense line (*C*) on the chart have slopes of less than 1.

A contrasting pattern is disclosed here. Cost of sales varied in a rather orderly manner in relation to net sales over the entire period 1934 to 1941. Administrative expense, on the other hand, was virtu-

TABLE 5-9. WESTINGHOUSE: EMPLOYMENT IN ADMINISTRATIVE, TECHNICAL, AND MANUFACTURING OCCUPATIONS, 1938

Department	Jan.	Feb.	Mar.	Apr.	May	June	July	Aug.	Sept.	Oct.	Nov.	Dec.
1. Engineering	2,406	2,331	2,273	2,235	2,211	2,173	2,177	2,171	2,184	2,141	2,115	2,119
2. Sales	2,717	2,723	2,747	2,735	2,713	2,625	2,595	2,577	2,578	2,562	2,545	2,552
3. Administration	1,170	1,174	1,153	1,155	1,151	1,146	1,142	1,146	1,126	1,123	1,127	1,148
4. E (1, 2, 3)	6,293	6,228	6,173	6,125	6,075	5,944	5,914	5,894	5,888	5,826	5,787	5,819
5. Manufacturing salaries	4,095	3,963	3,891	3,827	3,770	3,719	3,659	3,657	3,657	3,589	3,608	3,605
6. Order service and general clerical	474	452	455	449	459	447	449	441	479	456	422	434
7. General	423	410	352	334	294	284	279	273	265	274	281	291
8. E (4, 5, 6, 7) = total administrative and technical	11,285	11,053	10,871	10,735	10,598	10,394	10,301	10,265	10,289	10,145	10,098	10,149
9. Manufacturing hourly	21,931	17,634	17,793	17,084	16,658	15,930	15,500	16,240	15,733	17,359	16,500	17,213
10. Total	33,216	28,687	28,664	27,819	27,255	26,324	25,801	26,505	26,022	27,504	26,598	27,362

SOURCE: Westinghouse Electric and Manufacturing Co., Summary of Payrolls (excluding Lamp Division), 1938.

TABLE 5-10. WESTINGHOUSE: EMPLOYMENT IN ADMINISTRATIVE, TECHNICAL, AND MANUFACTURING OCCUPATIONS, 1938

| Department | Index number (January = 100) | | | | | | | | | | | |
	Jan.	Feb.	Mar.	Apr.	May	June	July	Aug.	Sept.	Oct.	Nov.	Dec.
1. Engineering	100	96.9	94.5	92.9	91.9	90.3	90.5	90.2	90.8	89.0	87.9	88.1
2. Sales	100	100.2	101.1	100.7	99.8	96.6	95.5	94.8	94.9	94.3	93.7	93.9
3. Administration	100	100.3	98.5	98.7	98.4	97.9	97.6	97.9	96.2	96.0	96.3	98.1
4. E (1, 2, 3)	100	99.0	98.1	97.3	96.5	94.5	94.0	93.6	93.6	92.6	92.0	92.5
5. Manufacturing salaried	100	96.8	95.0	93.5	92.1	90.8	89.4	89.3	89.3	87.6	88.1	88.0
6. Order service and general clerical	100	95.4	96.0	94.7	96.8	94.3	94.7	93.0	101.0	96.2	89.0	91.6
7. General	100	96.9	83.2	79.0	69.5	67.1	66.0	64.5	62.6	64.8	66.4	68.8
8. E (4, 5, 6) = total administrative and technical	100	97.9	96.3	95.1	93.9	92.1	91.3	91.0	91.2	89.9	89.5	89.9
9. Manufacturing hourly	100	80.4	81.1	77.9	76.0	72.6	70.7	74.0	71.7	79.2	75.2	78.5
10. Total	100	86.4	86.3	83.8	82.0	79.2	77.7	79.8	78.3	82.8	80.1	82.4

SOURCE: Westinghouse Electric and Manufacturing Co., Summary of Payrolls (excluding Lamp Division), 1938.

TABLE 5-11. WESTINGHOUSE: EMPLOYMENT IN ADMINISTRATIVE, TECHNICAL, AND MANUFACTURING OPERATIONS, 1939

Department	Jan.	Feb.	Mar.	Apr.	May	June	July	Aug.	Sept.	Oct.	Nov.	Dec.
1. Engineering	2,203	2,248	2,311	2,333	2,338	2,428	2,469	2,485	2,492	2,503	2,584	2,612
2. Sales	2,506	2,513	2,514	2,544	2,561	2,579	2,567	2,590	2,581	2,559	2,535	2,568
3. Administration	1,075	1,084	1,109	1,103	1,108	1,111	1,106	1,108	1,095	1,094	1,104	1,102
4. Total (1 + 2 + 3)	5,784	5,845	5,934	5,980	6,007	6,118	6,142	6,183	6,168	6,156	6,223	6,282
5. Manufacturing salaried	3,727	3,712	3,713	3,714	3,765	3,776	3,769	3,791	3,807	3,833	3,917	3,999
6. Order service and general clerical	449	447	449	450	452	454	454	453	445	448	452	457
7. General	319	326	382	393	468	499	529	553	608	589	542	498
8. Total administration and technical (4 + 5 + 6 + 7)	10,279	10,330	10,478	10,537	10,692	10,847	10,849	10,980	11,028	11,026	11,134	11,236
9. Manufacturing hourly	17,489	18,380	20,059	20,272	20,156	19,764	19,867	20,576	19,939	22,137	23,020	25,273
10. Total	27,768	28,710	30,537	30,809	30,848	30,611	30,761	31,556	30,967	33,163	34,154	36,509

SOURCE: Westinghouse Electric and Manufacturing Co., Summary of Payrolls (excluding Lamp Division), 1939.

ally unchanged during 1934 and 1935. From 1936 to 1939, however, there was a sharp increase in the relative magnitude of these costs as disclosed by the upward sloping line fitted to the plotted points of these years. From 1940 to 1941 this growth pattern had leveled off, as indicated by the substantially lesser slope of the trend line connecting the administrative expense of these two years.

Thus, while the relation of manufacturing costs to net sales was relatively homogeneous over this period, the pattern of administrative expense displayed sharp changes. The different behavior of these two elements of cost in relation to net sales is consistent with the rise of administrative and technical personnel disclosed in other tables.

The relative decline of administrative costs began some time in 1938 and continued beyond the end of 1939. In order to discover some of the details of this development, an analysis was made of the structure of employment in the Westinghouse Company on a monthly basis for 1938 and 1939. Tables 5–9 to 5–11 show the number of employees in each of the main occupational groups, on a monthly basis for 1938 and 1939. The crucial categories are those for the total administrative and technical employees and for the hourly manufacturing employees.

The development of these two classes of employees is shown in Tables 5–9 and 5–11. Lines 8 and 9 in the tables show the monthly number of each of the crucial categories of employees for 1938 and 1939.

In order to discover the relative development of the two main employee groups, the monthly percentage changes for each were computed for 1938 and 1939. For this purpose, January, 1938, is used as the base period (100). The various lines on Table 5–10 show these changes for each class of employees. During most of the period the administrative and technical group did not vary by more than 10 per cent of the base number. The hourly manufacturing group varied by as much as 30 per cent.

The critical aspect of the development is shown in line 6 of Table 5–12, for this compares the percentage changes in the two employee groups by dividing the index of administrative and technical staffs by the index of manufacturing hourly employment. When the former increases more, or decreases in a lesser degree than the latter, the ratio rises. When the reverse occurs, the ratio falls.

TABLE 5-12. WESTINGHOUSE: THE RATIO OF ADMINISTRATIVE AND TECHNICAL TO MANUFACTURING HOURLY EMPLOYEES, 1938–1939

Department	Jan.	Feb.	Mar.	Apr.	May	June	July	Aug.	Sept.	Oct.	Nov.	Dec.
						Number employed						
1. Total Administration and technical												
1938	11,285	11,053	10,871	10,735	10,598	10,394	10,301	10,265	10,289	10,145	10,098	10,149
1939	10,279	10,330	10,478	10,537	10,692	10,847	10,894	10,980	11,028	11,026	11,134	11,236
2. Manufacturing hourly												
1938	21,931	17,634	17,793	17,084	16,658	15,930	15,500	16,240	15,733	17,359	16,500	17,213
1939	17,489	18,380	20,059	20,272	20,156	19,764	19,867	20,576	19,939	22,137	23,020	25,273
3. Total administration and technical per 100 manufacturing hourly												
1938	51.46	62.68	61.10	62.84	63.62	65.25	66.46	63.21	65.40	58.44	61.20	58.96
1939	58.77	56.20	52.24	51.98	53.05	54.88	54.83	53.36	55.31	49.81	48.37	44.46
					Index Number (January, 1938 = 100)							
4. Total administration and technical												
1938	100.0	97.9	96.3	95.1	93.9	92.1	91.3	91.0	91.2	89.9	89.5	89.9
1939	91.1	91.5	92.8	93.4	94.7	96.1	96.5	97.3	97.7	97.7	98.7	99.6
5. Manufacturing hourly												
1938	100.0	80.4	81.1	77.9	76.0	72.6	70.7	74.0	71.7	79.2	75.2	78.5
1939	79.7	83.8	91.5	92.4	91.9	90.1	90.6	93.8	90.9	100.9	105.0	115.2
6. Ratio: administration and technical to manufacturing hourly (4:5)												
1938	100.0	121.8	118.7	122.1	123.6	126.8	129.1	122.8	127.1	113.6	118.9	114.6
1939	114.2	109.2	101.5	101.0	103.1	106.6	106.5	103.7	107.5	96.8	94.0	86.4

SOURCE: Westinghouse Electric and Manufacturing Co., Summary of Payrolls (excluding Lamp Division), 1938, 1939.

This ratio increased during 1938 and began to decline in the latter part of the year. By October, 1939, however, the ratio moved below 100, reflecting substantial additions to the hourly manufacturing group, with small increases in the administrative and technical class of employees. These developments in the relative growths of administrative as compared with hourly manufacturing employees are shown graphically in Chart 12.

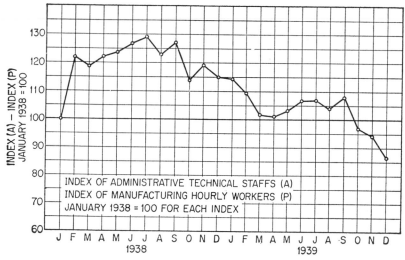

CHART 12. WESTINGHOUSE: CHANGES IN COMPOSITION OF EMPLOYMENT

The 100 value on the vertical axis of Chart 12 represents the relation of administrative to manufacturing employees as of January, 1938. For each month thereafter the plotted points represent the comparative degrees of change in each employee group as compared with the base period (January, 1938).

When viewed on a monthly basis during 1939, the relative growth of administrative and technical employees declined while the direct production force was being enlarged. As a result, the curve measuring the relative growths of these employee groups dipped below the January, 1938, level. During the whole of 1939 hourly manufacturing employees increased 44 per cent, while administrative and technical staff rose by only 9 per cent. The effect of this employment trend appeared in the cost data of the Westinghouse Company for 1940 as a downturn in the index of administrative costs as compared with the index of cost of sales (line 10 of Table 5–8).

After 1939 the annual outlay for administrative functions diminished as compared with that for production functions. This result is clear from the data on Westinghouse cost (Table 5–8, line 10).

Appendices to Chapter 6

A. Illustrations of the Proprietary Check

This appendix summarizes specific and outstanding experience of partial-proprietary contributions to successful management. It is based largely on interviews with past and present directors of General Motors and on the detailed correspondence between directors and management of GM, as put into the record by General Motors, Du Pont, and the Department of Justice in the GM–Du Pont anti-trust trial. The contributions of partial proprietors to General Motors management relate principally to the years 1921 to 1929. In addition, contributions from other partial proprietors in the mining industry, as given in interviews, are mentioned. A summary of some of the outstanding contributions of these partial proprietors to their management follows.

Business Acumen

Partial proprietors have contributed substantial, highly specialized, and rare technical knowledge, especially when the directors representing them were executives or directors of another corporation. For example, Newmont Mining Corp., which has substantial holdings in a number of mining concerns, provides considerable technical contributions, directly through its directorial representation and indirectly through its own staff of experts, which supplement the technicians employed by the companies of which it is a partial proprietor. Similarly, retired employees on the GM board still provide a background of technical knowledge against which the judg-

ments of the internal management can be checked, though this contribution becomes less important as the passing years diminish their
acquaintance with the technical problems. Parenthetically, it may
also be observed that lack of knowledge of specific technical conditions and peculiarities may be a distinct handicap for a director
and often reduces the usefulness of the so-called professional director. Because of his experience with other companies, his judgment and recommendations may be in continuous conflict with the
"common sense" of the industry or company.

A second type of technical contribution can stem from outstanding knowledge of a management technique. This is most obviously
so in the area of finance. Bank, trust, or insurance directors representing considerable holdings can supplement the financial acumen
of the internal management. The same may hold true for suppliers
or customer-directors with substantial holdings. But there is the
danger in both cases of substantial technical blindspots and domina-
tion of personal interests over those of the company which they are
to serve; e.g., representatives of financial interest may recommend
short-term financing through bank loans when self-financing would
appear to be more in the corporation's interests, or the issue of
additional equity *not* in the interests of the rest of the owners.
At GM, however, the banker-directors in the early twenties were
a major factor in paving the way toward public acceptance of
the auto industry.

The third type of business acumen provided by partial proprietors
is that gained through over-all management experience in a number
of other outstanding companies, provided this experience becomes
increasingly transferable and is adapted. To a limited extent, this
may hold in regard to the so-called management skills—planning
and forecasting, organizing and staffing, and controlling—accumulated over a number of years, provided there is capacity for
adaptation. The du Ponts provided this for GM by insisting on
first-class product performance, and in this way they laid a basis
for the great development and position of the auto industry in the
United States economy. Or the directors representing the financial
interests, from the banks and financial institutions, might aid by reports on special developments in their fields, of interest to and im-
pinging on the motor industry.

Finally, there is the type of business acumen which in essence is a combination of intangible qualities such as an inquiring mind and the ability to ask searching questions, the ability to discern the forest for the trees, a long-term view that can balance the stress internal management may lay on putting out fires because it is overwhelmed by what might be called "immediacy."

An outsider, simply because he is an outsider and not too close to the problems, if he possesses good business experience *and* the power to be heard, may often suggest new ideas, or new combinations of old ones; and he may also serve as a *catalyst*, stimulating new contributions from the management itself.

A series of illustrations may document these points.

The business acumen of partial proprietors may be of a very high order, as can be gathered by a quick review of some of GM's substantial minority stockholders. The Du Pont directors representing the investment of the Du Pont Company in GM have included the following men:

Pierre S. du Pont, who made major contributions by arranging the "rescue" operation of GM. The great respect in which he was held by the financial community made the job of refinancing the company possible, and his experience in reorganizing and rescuing Du Pont eighteen years earlier was of great help to GM, as were his judgment and his ability to choose men and his knowledge of organization.

Lammot du Pont, who was able to contribute largely to group management and forward planning by drawing on his simultaneous experience at Du Pont.

Irénée du Pont, who provided stimulus to innovation and new products.

Walter S. Carpenter, Jr., who supplied thoroughness and wisdom he had acquired at Du Pont.

Donaldson Brown, who adapted the pricing and marketing methods and controls that he had first developed at Du Pont.

John J. Raskob, an idea man and promoter.

Argus B. Echols, who contributed from his great financial experience.

Lammot du Pont Copeland, a brilliant financial mind, able to act quickly and directly.

Of the substantial minority stockholder directors created by GM itself and now retired, the following may be mentioned:

Alfred P. Sloan, Jr., whose contributions lay principally in general management and sales. He served as a balance wheel for du Ponts, operators and bankers.

C. F. Kettering, who contributed long-range product planning and technical inventions.

C. S. Mott, who represented the stockholding point of view.

J. L. Pratt, who possessed great technical knowledge, fairness, and a strong sense of justice.

C. E. Wilson, a Roman patrician for honesty and uprightness in labor and public relations and articulate in discussing them.

Furthering Executive Talent and Its Effective Exercise

Partial proprietors may contribute to the development of executive talent mainly, of course, through their relationship to the company president. The partial proprietor can be a sounding board or a counselor, especially to presidents who cannot discuss certain of their problems with their own subordinates and have no one else to turn to. As one of them expressed his situation, "I am a lonely wanderer on the wrong side of the fence doing a job on which I cannot consult anyone." Many presidents have a number of favorite directors to consult on different topics, and it is the possibility of assurance, reassurance, or supplementation that can be of such great help. Alfred Sloan remarked on the wisdom of Walter Carpenter, "to whose counsel I often defer," on the value of visits to George Whitney at J. P. Morgan to consult on a difference of views with subordinates, and on "the irreplaceable contributions of the Du Pont directors" and the guidance of Pierre S. du Pont.

Specific contributions to the furtherance of managerial talent were most frequently made through membership on the GM salary and bonus committees on the board. Here the vital decisions on promotion and special rewards can be made without personal involvement.

Equity in the compensation of individuals and in recognition of outstanding performance is, of course, in part at least, always a matter of judgment. There must be *interpretation* of factual data relating to performance, and the opinion of supervisors must also be taken into account. Directors can provide help in the evaluations partly by careful study and comparisons, partly by informal association with the men concerned; and because they are partial proprietors, they possess a strong incentive to link reward with effort. Certainly one is impressed by the amount of time and conscientious effort put forth by the substantial minority stockholders at General Motors, as these were described by the late E. F. Johnson, for many years on the GM bonus and salary committee and himself an outstanding example of probity and competence.

In addition to providing financial reward, much can be done to further the development of internal managers. There is a large volume of correspondence between the top executives of GM and principal stockholders attesting to the conscientiousness of both. Thus the Du Pont directors were much concerned that potential successors to top management should have "met a payroll" and demonstrated profit-making capacity in operations, that they should be acceptable to the rest of the groups and be relieved of operating responsibility while serving on top committees. The Du Pont directors were concerned that financial affairs be directed by men with more than sheer financial technical ability. They wanted to ensure coordination of financial policy with top policy and objectives.

Hence a good deal of discussion was devoted to the training of the successors of the Du Pont directors who were retiring or overburdened. It was suggested that Henry Belin du Pont get acquainted with GM's personnel through membership on the salary and bonus committees. At one time Alfred Sloan was asked "to force the assumption of extra responsibility on other members of the Executive Committee so as to develop a better supply of timber for the presidency and chairmanship."

In the choice of a new chief executive to represent the owners in the daily affairs of the business, the partial proprietor can draw on his knowledge of inside management, gained through service on committees, and possibly on alternatives from outside. Certainly his presence on the board ensures that candidates will have to pass scrutiny.

Then, when the new chief has been chosen, the partial proprietors can aid him in the hard task of establishing his authority and intervene if he continually fails to meet the objectives set. That failure is, in fact, almost the only event that almost always leads to the intervention of major stockholder-directors. Usually one or two directors will take the initiative and attempt to rouse the others. This may lead either to speedy agreement or to a power struggle, such as the spectacular battle at Kress between the trustee-directors and the principal shareholder-director Rush H. Kress, in which the latter finally threw in the title after a decisive vote. Another example is the Equitable Life Assurance Company fight to get rid of the president and a second dismissal within the year of the new president who "did not work out."

Freedom of Discussion

Partial proprietors possess the power to be independent. At least they command it potentially because they are usually well enough off financially and have enough status elsewhere to be independent of their directorship. They are, therefore, free to speak their opinions since disagreement, loss of friendship, and even loss of their seats on the board of directors do not basically threaten their economic existence. Nor, since their stake is essentially a financial one, are they necessarily bound by personal consideration. Friendship is not necessarily a bar to free expression, and much can be forgiven a man of economic status.

Of course affluence itself can render a man negligent of a director's responsibilities. Any concern he feels may appear unimportant in terms of the total relationship involved. The idea of "letting sleeping dogs lie" is powerful indeed. The consequences of free expression—where it takes the form of criticism—may well be ostracism from the good fellowship of the board and the disapproval of the club. Unconsciously at least, each director is aware of the risks, which may be summed up in the words of Pope Gregory VII, "I have loved justice and I hated iniquity; therefore I die in exile."

Few GM executives, however, suffered any penalty for independence. Freedom of discussion on basic management problems was probably a major factor in the company's success.

It contributed more to a better total plan and improved execution than one-man decisions could have. It prevented the frequent and sometimes disastrous errors that occur when one man grows to believe himself infallible. It brought about a better acceptance of decisions. And above all, it made it attractive for top thinkers and doers to continue their participation.

This atmosphere of free discussion, as it often does, had its origin in a tradition which had been carried down through succeeding generations. It arose, in its articulated form at least, from the correspondence of the founder of the Du Pont Company, Eleuthère Irénée du Pont, and Thomas Jefferson. The latter's counsel became deeply ingrained in the minds of many of the succeeding executives: "The human character, we believe, requires in general constant and immediate control to prevent its being biased from right by seduction of self-love."

This was the basic attitude of Pierre S. du Pont when he took over the presidency of General Motors in 1920, and it was strengthened by the fact that a contrary attitude had almost spelled disaster for General Motors. P. S. du Pont's predecessor, W. C. Durant, had brought General Motors almost to the brink of bankruptcy, and a contributing cause of the difficulty was his tendency at times not to listen to anyone's advice. Thus his decisions were usually either brilliant *or* disastrous.

The bankruptcy was all but completed under the new regime, when Kettering's plan for a copper-cooled engine was strongly pushed to acceptance by P. S. du Pont and some of his associates against the protests of the engineers. The du Ponts felt that this might save General Motors and help restore its competitive position vis-à-vis Ford. Both they and Kettering had the best intentions. They were willing to spend up to $100 million on the new engine, even though some of the engineers protested so strongly as to suffer nervous breakdowns. The engineers were overruled, but their protests did have the effect of slowing down the expenditures. The experience after the initial outlay showed that the engineers were right: the engine did not perform as expected, a committee chaired by the engineer Hunt found. Instead, Hunt and his associates pressed for an improvement of existing models when inventories were worked down far enough. These better cars were in such an improved position by 1923 that they contributed greatly to the betterment of GM's financial and competitive position. (Then it was Kettering who had the nervous breakdown.) While the full story still needs to be told, this conclusion held. The du Ponts learned the lesson: never again did they force a major investment or policy change over factual opposition.

Subsequently P. S. du Pont established the atmosphere that permitted free discussion. He used the board meetings, and especially the board committees, to inform the directors of changes contemplated, the bases and reasons why, and invited their views and opinions. And to ensure against rubber-stamping, he chose as directors men who could afford to be independent, either because of independent wealth or because of their public reputation.

Sloan and his associates set up the organizational mechanism of formal committees and informal discussions to resolve major issues. The very atmosphere of free interchange on the GM board and the many times when opinions on the resolution of basic problems were sought made it possible for Sloan to act in the same way with his associates. This was most prominently demonstrated in Sloan's relationships to his principal colleagues with whom he checked his major proposals and whom he expected to respond freely. And Sloan asked others to do the same. In a letter to Raskob of Feb. 13, 1926, he urged:

"I hope in the discussion that you will see fit to ask John Pratt to enter same. He has some information and a viewpoint which I am sure will be helpful. Mr. John Thomas Smith has some ideas which I think should be brought into the picture."

Sloan himself went far in carrying freedom of discussion down the ranks of management, and he used some interesting methods to do so. In discussing proposals with individual executives he would listen and then ask searching questions before even indicating his own point of view. And he might well take a subordinate's side against a superior in order to learn the former's real opinion. For example, the proposal that production be adapted to dealers' sales as fast as possible rather than overload the dealers was agreed upon by Sloan and Brown. But in subsequent meetings with the division managers, Sloan took the other side, to be sure to hear all opposing arguments; if they were not overwhelming, he intended to move for adoption of the new policy. His subordinates, in turn, were expected to carry this down the line. As Walter Carpenter tells it:

P. S. du Pont's complete support of Sloan's method of persuasion and "sell" rather than command made it possible to do many things that could not have been done in any other way.... Sloan might sit and argue his point for hours. Then he would sit back and say: "Maybe I am wrong and we shouldn't do as I think." And he would bear no grudge subsequently even though his opinion did not prevail.

And C. E. Wilson comments similarly that he held Sloan in great regard and affection; that he could frankly call Sloan's attention to any facts Sloan had overlooked, and that Sloan would avoid dogmatism when he lacked the facts.

Freedom of discussion probably flourished most under P. S. du Pont. That was partly because his presidency coincided with the "storm-and-stress period" of GM, when most things were in a ferment, when the principals had to establish themselves, when they were in their youth and did not have to defend ancient ramparts, and when the world in general was favorable to genuine democracy, not only in political affairs, but also in human relationships. Pierre rarely structured a board meeting, but left it free for individual contribution.

The tradition of free discussion was carried on by Pierre's successor as GM chairman, Lammot du Pont. He not only let himself be persuaded, but was even overruled, since his vote counted no more than those of his colleagues despite the influence of his position and his stockholdings. Yet he could disagree and be stubborn to an extraordinary degree (he was forever writing letters, bringing up a new idea or questioning an old practice). Lammot could usually be persuaded only by stubborn facts. (As one of the first automobile owners in Wilmington, he used to drive full speed regardless of obstacles. One autumn day, driving as usual through heaps of leaves, he became hopelessly stuck by bricks hidden under the leaves.)

The impact of this atmosphere of free discussion on one of GM's principal officers and the advantages are well described by Donaldson Brown.

With my associates on the financial staff, I recognized that we would not secure effective control of financial policies by arbitrary edict. You can't cram basic policy down the throats of those who must be depended upon to carry them out and expect good results. Everyone concerned in the organization must be brought to understand and to accept, in spirit, the validity of the policies imposed.

Moreover, sound policies cannot be formulated without the cooperation and assistance of personnel all the way up and down the line. There must be, in fact, a "two-way flow" in managerial human relations. The downward flow begins with authority at the top level of management, and continues down through all echelons of management, each responsible within the limits of assigned jurisdiction for administering established company policy. The upward flow consists of questions, facts and opinions arising out of actual experience in all phases of the business. These are vital to the sound determination of policy, and must be allowed to exert proper pressure in policy formulation.

This kind of two-way flow is essential for the simple reason that in a big, complex industrial combination it is impossible for top management to lay down policy in terms sufficiently explicit to eliminate the need for the broad exercise of judgment by employees who must execute policy. In a small enterprise, where one man can keep his finger on every detail of the business, the situation is quite different. Large industrial units can achieve the same end result only by the kind of broad coordinated policy control.

There is another reason why this two-way flow of ideas and information is indispensable to modern business. Everything in the field of industrial management depends upon and revolves around human impulses and human relations. Participation in the formulation of policy, and in its execution, plays an important part in developing the self-reliance and potentialities of the individual.

Even if it were possible, in the name of efficiency, to eliminate the need for individual initiative through cut-and-dried directives from an infallible superior, that would be a wrong course to follow. The effect upon the character and the spirit of the human beings involved would be tragic. In our human frailty, we need encouragement, an occasional pat on the back, the solid satisfaction of individual accomplishment and proper recognition of a job well done. . . . I cannot emphasize too strongly the part that this has played in the development of GM to its present position.

The early meetings of the GM board of directors and the informal discussions and correspondence between directors and inside management under the presidency and chairmanship of P. S. du Pont (1920 to 1928) were thus especially effective in laying the basis of a free discussion among these men that was rich in frank interchange.

The organization plan worked out by Sloan and his associates was discussed in the first post-reorganization meetings of the board and received approval without much modification. But some members of the board were still greatly concerned about the soundness of their investment and urged that thorough appraisals be made.

Among these was J. P. Morgan & Co., which had put considerable sums of money into GM (on the recommendation of Raskob), for once without an investigation. Some of the directors' concern led to the establishment of an inventory committee under the chairmanship of John L. Pratt, which began its work by extricating GM from its heavy commitments for supplies and later from the established purchasing standards. This stimulated the insistence of the Du Pont directors and some of the ex–Du Pont executives on the need for central coordination and controls, the organization of the coordinating committee, and the development of financial signals. There were many debates on these matters.

But of course the directors with financial holdings were most concerned with putting GM on a permanently competitive basis. Toward this end a technological breakthrough might be decisive. Hence various directors brought forward all kinds of suggestions.

Irénée du Pont was particularly insistent on his "pet products" and pushed for the use of tetraethyllead, a gasoline antiknock compound. Sloan said he wanted to make users of tetraethyllead standardize the blending of the compound with gasoline. The material, made by E. I. du Pont de Nemours & Co., was distributed by Ethyl Gasoline Corporation, owned half by General Motors and half by Standard Oil Company of New Jersey. Irénée du Pont thought the compound should be sold "like so much coal," and the oil industry should do as it pleased in blending.

On Mar. 29, 1926, the General Motors chief put his argument to Irénée du Pont in this manner:

> In your letter of March 27 you say that it is not your idea to permit people to sell ethyl gas without having a sufficient amount of tetraethyl lead in it to make an antiknock. Now it is exactly for that reason, in which I thoroughly agree with you, that I have been thinking, rightly or wrongly, that we should establish a standard gas as sure as anything possibly can be, considering all the bootleggers and gyps and everything else there is in the oil business. If you sold the material to Tom, Dick and Harry without adopting a standard you would get just the result that you say you would not permit and it was solely for that reason that I think we have got to protect the trade name.

Irénée du Pont replied that he was fearful that Sloan's plan would delay expansion of the ethyl business and said that under his plan the oil companies would sell ethyl gas under their own trade-marks, which would get a "black eye" if they failed to measure up.

On June 22, 1927, Irénée du Pont renewed the argument, urging an "about-face" on grounds somewhat similar to those previously advanced. Sloan summed up his arguments in a seven-page letter. Irénée du Pont replied, "I am not convinced by your letter." He added, "The facts are we are still dribbling along at the rate of 100,000 or 150,000 pounds a month. Two years ago we thought we would be making ten times that amount by now."

Sloan came back with another letter saying that the reputation of the product had to be protected, and several days later he sent still another, which made the point that "we are raising the compression of our engines and to do so we must have a standard of fuel to go by." Sloan concluded: "I regret very much that you do not agree with us on this point, but I know you want us to state exactly how we feel because that is the only way we can get anywhere, and I would appreciate it very much, if you would carefully analyze this letter and give me your ideas why and where I am wrong. I will continually keep in mind the question as to whether we are right on the questioned issue."

Irénée du Pont then apparently gave up, saying, "I shall stop complaining of the situation because I feel that Chrysler's move on the high compression head is going to force the sale of antiknock fuel to a point where we will be bound to merchandise in larger quantities."

Sloan's disputes with Lammot du Pont in 1927 were over the latter's contention that it would be a "very grave error" for Ethyl Gasoline Corporation to get into the manufacture of tetraethyllead, at that time supplied to the company by the Du Pont Company. Ethyl, however, went into the manufacturing business.

Around the same time, Lammot du Pont attempted to dissuade Sloan from continuing some types of GM's chemical research, especially as it related to rubber research. He felt that GM's chemical department was not well organized for the task and did not have the personnel to be successful. Sloan pointed to some previous chemical research whereby some unknown material was injected into the gasoline to increase the compression and produce a fuel of antiknock qualities. "My experience—perhaps yours is different —indicates that it does not always follow that discoveries along any of these lines come from those sources where they would be most expected." The expenditure was less than one one-hundredth of total GM sales, and Sloan offered to bring the matter before the executive committee for debate, concluding with an important observation bearing on freedom of research and morale:

I have found when any of our people are desirous of tackling an unusual job, that provided the expense is not too great, we usually learn something of value either on the subject or in some other way and it is good in many ways, from a psychological standpoint. I know of many instances where certain of our people become greatly interested in a certain idea, the value of which perhaps they overestimate. If they are prevented from developing these ideas, in a way, it has a reactionary influence. On the contrary, if they are encouraged, even if it results in some cost to the corporation, it has a beneficial influence on the entire picture.

And Sloan strongly defended the principal proponents of synthetic rubber, Kettering and Midgley, for outstanding results accomplished in previous years.

Lammot du Pont was finally convinced and replied: "I appreciate fully what you say as to the desirability of allowing good minds who are extremely interested in important investigations to have a little more than the normal amount of rope. We do it also and I believe it tends to keep up enthusiasm and interest of all concerned."

A few months before Lammot du Pont suddenly changed his manner of addressing Sloan from "Dear Alfred" to "Dear Mr. Sloan." He reported that Du Pont's paint department had been "considerably upset because of the difficulty in getting accurate information as to the probable requirements of the various GM units for Duco." He complained that after pressure for deliveries the month before, there were suddenly cancellations "right and left" and we "cannot make out what it all means." Sloan replied that the burden of inventory adjustment was thrown in part on the suppliers. "We take the position that it is their duty to cooperate with us and, naturally, the Du Pont Company is no exception to the rule."

In answer to "Dear Alfred," Lammot explained he did not make himself clear and had not intended to intimate that Du Pont "would attempt to dictate to General Motors." What was of concern was "what is anticipated as a possibility is never as much of a shock as that which has been thought of as an impossibility." Actually Du Pont's paint department made the mistake (so common among politicians and historians) of believing that the current year would be the same as the last year. This is clearly evident from Lammot's conclusions that "a little knowledge is worse than none. This, however, is only true when the possessor of that 'little knowledge' thinks he knows it all." Sloan finally consented to furnish the GM production schedules to Du Pont in order to cut costs of supply by reducing fluctuations between demand and supply. This followed the precedent of the dealer ten-day reports as a help toward an equilibrium in the supply and demand for cars.

Space prohibits analyzing further examples of the free-swinging discussion and debate that prevailed. Other instances might be quoted from debates on annual model changes, dealer policies and relationships, the bonus plans, export policies (distribution of American cars produced in the United States or abroad), etc. It was a matter of give and take, with the large stockholder-directors making suggestions and needling. Yet the insiders held their own, challenging the directors on many occasions. As Irénée du Pont put it on another occasion, "I have sometimes disagreed with the majority on matters of policy, yet at the same time I have always felt that all of you were using the utmost of intelligence and that perhaps I was on such occasions the one 'unruly juror'."

Unfortunately, the era of directorial response and challenge became less vigorous after 1928 when John J. Raskob accepted the chairmanship of the Democratic National Committee without consulting the GM board or management. He was backed by P. S. du Pont. Sloan felt that, however good the intention (the abolition of Prohibition), with roughly half of GM's potential customers Republicans, the new political ties of GM's finance committee chairman might be detrimental. He was supported by Lammot (while Irénée stayed neutral) and carried the board. In the subsequent vote, P. S. du Pont resigned as chairman of the board and Raskob as chairman of the finance committee, never to return to these positions. Coleman du Pont, former President of Du Pont and later a United States senator, supported Raskob. In a letter in which he apologized for his poor handwriting "having gone democratic," he commended political participation of executives and felt the company should support it. The du Ponts later supported Raskob in his attempt to sell his GM holdings over some objections from GM's internal management. Sloan, however, won on the political issue, as he later won out on the question of the full-time return of some other executives who had left GM for government jobs.

It would lead too far to review the various subjects of discussion and debate on the GM board. Suffice it to say that debate continued, that it was helpful, and that Sloan himself even approved it though it led to his being overruled at least three times by the board in the last five years of his chief executiveship. He felt that it strengthened his performance and kept him from presenting foolish ideas. No doubt it was a major factor in attracting and holding outstanding management talent, in developing it, and in giving it real opportunity.

Organization

The theory and method of dividing work in a large corporation to avoid diminishing return from the scarcest of all factors of production, management, is a subject of much discussion among partial proprietors and internal managements, wherever there is any constructive relationship at all. So it was with GM's management and its substantial minority stockholder-directors. The exchange of ideas began before the demise of Durant, largely between those at Du Pont who had been commissioned to rethink that company's basic organization and Alfred Sloan. The Du Pont subcommittee on organization set up toward the end of World War I consisted of two men, Donaldson Brown and H. G. Haskell, whose "views were undoubtedly a reflection of Mr. Barksdale's [one of Du Pont's pioneers in systematic management] management concepts." The third man, Pickard, "came around to sharing our judgment that a decentralized form of organization was most suitable, with both authority and accompanying responsibility delegated down the line." Sloan came to know of these views through the visits and interchange of views with Du Pont directors and executives. He told the author that he discussed them in detail with Harry Haskell on a trip to France in the spring of 1920. Undoubtedly, therefore, GM's organization plans of 1920–1921 benefited from some of the ideas of the Du Pont directors.

Certainly there was a good deal of parallelism between the organization bases and structures of Du Pont and General Motors. The

Du Pont contributions appear to have been very considerable, if only because of the influence of the two Du Pont memoranda on organization in 1919.

Especially important were the contributions of substantial minority stockholder-directors through their membership on the executive committee of GM. Similar participation may occur in other corporations.

Broadly speaking, and without going into the specific details, the involvements of the members of the executive committee at GM were as follows:

First, a thorough acquaintance with the characteristics of the business, its organization, the power of the different executives, and nature of the coordinative process. This knowledge was obtained from frequent briefings by internal management and from statistical reports.

Second, establishment of concrete policy as a guide line for departmental policy. This, of course, has been done in numerous areas of corporate activities.

Third, guidance on basic problems on which no policy of precedent existed. Policies were formulated as problems arose, great care being taken to avoid interference in administration and to assign authority commensurate with the delegated duty. Where the distinction between policy and administration could not be drawn, the executive board might assume the responsibility for direct action in administrative matters, provided it avoided doing so whenever possible. When it did assume responsibility, it explained the reasons for this interference to all concerned.

Among the rather rare examples of this kind of conflict at GM may be mentioned the debate over the establishment of assembly plants and acquisition of factory facilities abroad. While obviously it was the executive committee's domain to allocate the funds, the export division felt strongly that the manner of selling cars should be left to its discretion; clearly the establishment of foreign plants would hurt it. But the executive committee felt that since this was a problem of basic policy on which it had to make a decision— quite correctly so, as it turned out from a long-range view—the establishment of a new policy was essential.

In another instance, however, the internal management won out over the executive committee of the board. Several GM executives advocated the promotion of diesel engines to the railroads during the Great Depression. But one of the members of the executive committee objected strongly on the ground that the bankruptcy of so many of the railroads made this fruitless. The executives brought proof that the director was wrong and carried the day without any further interference.

Fourth, the president as chief executive officer was to be the connecting link between policy and administrative control. He made the distinction from the viewpoint that there should be no undue interference with the prerogatives of individuals in the organization and that they had full latitude and responsibility for their tasks. And in case of doubt he would obtain a statement of policy from the executive committee or the board.

That a finance committee, which the partial proprietors dominated, should supervise the financial and accounting departments instead of giving the president jurisdiction in this area was a plan taken over from Du Pont, which had probably learned it from J. P. Morgan at U.S. Steel and a number of New England companies. Many Du Pont ideas relating to staff services and the concept of general management were taken over also. Even management procedures were adopted in their entirety.

The organizational problem arising from the fast growth of units not well consolidated when they were originally put together subjected the company to some strain. As far back as 1925 Sloan emphasized at a GM sales committee meeting the difficulty of pushing ideas through to achievement in a large organization such as GM. "So many people must be sold on an idea, such a tremendous effort is needed to put ideas across, that it appears overwhelming as opposed to the benefit of the idea ... action is not taken upon many such ideas until competition forces it." Over the years Sloan felt that the finance and executive committees of GM tended to take up somewhat the same matters of policy, whereas the line between policy and operations was fairly clear. Hence he thought that a combination of the two committees into a policy committee would reduce overlapping and confine it to its proper field, while the administration committee could devote itself to carrying out policy. This proposal was objected to by Lammot du Pont and Walter

Carpenter, who had long been accustomed to the two principal committees of the board and felt that the separation was not too important since both were located in Wilmington.

This reorganization was finally, and reluctantly, agreed to by the Du Pont directors, though they continued to bring up the subject. It was apparently one of the few occasions when they were not entirely "sold" by GM and Sloan failed to follow his own philosophy. In a lengthy correspondence with Donaldson Brown at the beginning of 1941, Walter Carpenter spoke with approval of the old division in the Du Pont and General Motors management between financial and operating responsibilities. He pointed out that the financial side was at least equal to, and often dominating in, the consideration of major policy, remembering the tremendous influence on Du Pont policy when P. S. du Pont, Raskob, and Brown were in charge of Du Pont financial management (P. S. du Pont was treasurer *and* chief executive officer). Carpenter was concerned that with Brown assuming a more general executive position at GM and Bradley on the operating side, there would be no one serving as general financial executive. This was especially serious since Brown had pointed out that Donner would need operating experience and Wilson "never had the job of meeting the payroll at the end of the week."

All this really portended the eclipse of outside financial influence at GM and meant that important decisions were more and more influenced from the operating standpoint. With the absence of specifically assigned financial responsibility, the great financial moves made in the past by Pierre, Brown, and Raskob might not be continued, that is, the continuation of the acceptance business, the questioning of the corporation's credit, attention to the standing of its securities, the provision of adequate cash balances, the Managers' Securities Plan. "We are not a static organization. I believe we should organize accordingly," wrote Walter Carpenter.

Again, in 1942, Carpenter brought out his dissatisfaction and that of other Du Pont directors over the increasing strength of the policy committee in setting up major policies and the weakening of the administration committee in carrying them out. He felt that it was very difficult to distinguish between policy and operations, and hence that there was a great deal of overlap. He believed, from past experience, that the division on the basis of subject matter was not satisfactory, and therefore he proposed a reversal to a division by function—that is, finance on the one hand, administration and operations on the other. Carpenter then proceeded to make very detailed recommendations for membership on the committees. He urged especially the separation of committee members from operating responsibilities so that their contributions to broad policy should not suffer. He specifically recommended that new Du Pont directors should become acquainted with GM operations and its people (though not too closely involved) whereas the GM operating people should broaden themselves by dealing with both finance and policy.

Lammot du Pont joined in these discussions and frankly advocated not only a revival of the finance committee as it used to be in the twenties but that it should be so constituted that "it could appropriately be considered as an informal representation of large stockholding interests, that the personnel of the Finance Committee should be confined to representatives of large stockholders and that the Du Pont influence should be represented here and reduced elsewhere."

In his reply Sloan stressed that the fundamental principles would have to be determined first and that these would relate to the two principal committees. He was against the separation of the two committees on a functional basis and in favor of informal representation of large stockholders, but thought that this should go beyond finance into operations "because if the operations of the Corporation are not intelligently and agressively conducted, then the financial departments can do very little about it."

Sloan therefore continued to advocate one top committee representing large stockholder interests and financial and operating skills properly balanced. He felt strongly that the Wilmington setup was not only different, but not as effective as it might be, that the creative functions of Du Pont's executive committee members were being taken over to some extent by GM's staff and the functional policy committee. Sloan felt there should be one, not two, top committees; that it should deal with broad questions of operating policy as well as with financial policies; and that "we should always recognize the importance of having on that committee a cross-section of interests." In the 1958 reorganization the old separation between finance "to coordinate control" and to act as a check or counselor to operations was reestablished. The former was re-activated in "New York" as the finance committee and a board chairman drawn from finance (Fred Donner) and in "Detroit" headed by an operating man in president John Gordon. Thus the potentiality of rebuttal power was retained at GM. It may continue to function even without the Du Ponts, though it remains to be seen whether the results will be as effective as before.

Board Membership

A considerable contribution can be made by partial proprietors through suggestions of new candidates for the board of directors who will enable it to continue to serve as a check and a sounding board for the internal management. Certainly this was a major contribution made by the large General Motors stockholders. P. S. du Pont brought with him outstanding and experienced associates from Du Pont. It would be impossible within the scope of this chapter to indicate the whole range of suggestions made over the years at General Motors. Some of the discussions from the war and immediate postwar period must suffice.

In 1945 Alfred Sloan proposed to Lammot du Pont that the membership of the GM policy committee be increased by including Kettering (Lammot noted a heavy "No" on the margin of Sloan's letter). Sloan explained that while in the past Kettering had not been asked to serve because he is "so engrossed with technical matters" (Lammot noted, "Good reason"), so "the meetings become one of listening . . . but business must be carried on." "Mr. Kettering indicates a broadened interest in matters outside the technical area. Altho I know he was always critical of my tirades against the New Deal, yet, in a different way, he now finds himself in about the same position. As Kettering might be easing off from his intensive work and being a large stockholder, he might be a contributor to the policy plan of the Corporation's activities." (Lammot noted, "No, for lack of experience.")

A short time later Sloan submitted to Walter Carpenter his formula for choosing outside directors:

1. He was opposed to bankers except George Whitney. "I am against Bankers on Boards of industrial companies because they are accused (wrongly of course) of dominating the financial policies." (Sloan had not forgotten Judge Leibell's remark during the GM

bonus suit that the president of GM could not adopt any policy without the approval of Mr. Morgan, a point with which Sloan sharply disagreed.)

2. There should be geographical representation.

3. Interests related to GM, especially in the buying and selling area, should be represented.

4. There should be no more than one person from the same industry.

5. Du Pont representatives should be selected by that company.

6. Directors should have some knowledge of the company's personnel background and of the business and its problems.

7. The smaller the company and the smaller the board of directors, the greater the opportunity to contribute.

Lammot du Pont in writing to Sloan added to this formula by stressing the need for broadest possible business experience on GM's policy committee, but noted that Du Pont lacked such men except for those about fifty-five years of age and that it would possibly take such a man five years to become thoroughly familiar with GM problems, organization, personnel, and business. Hence he suggested consideration of H. B. du Pont for the GM policy committee, saying that he was well qualified because he was familiar with Du Pont operations, having been an assistant to the president and vice president at Du Pont.

Later discussion between GM management and the Du Pont stockholder-directors revolved increasingly about the desirability of adding outside directors who could represent a public point of view as well as influence it. For example, soon after World War II, John Lee Pratt urged Sloan to consider adding General Marshall to the GM board of directors. (Later General Eisenhower was proposed.) Pratt was impressed with the fact that General Marshall selected younger men and promoted them over older men. But Sloan felt, "he is talking about broad generalities without specific knowledge." In any case a director could make a comment once or twice about a point he has in mind, but "the only way to make a point effective is to hammer it continuously day in and day out and maybe after four or five years, you begin to get somewhere." Sloan thought that Marshall might offset criticism growing out of the prevailing negative attitude toward big business. Lammot du Pont agreed with Sloan: "My reasons for not favoring his [General Marshall's] membership on the Board are: First, his age; second, his lack of stock-holdings; and, third, his lack of experience in industrial business affairs." But Pratt won his point later when General Clay was made a member of GM's board. Later still, the former governor of the Bank of Canada also joined the GM board.

Thus the GM board continued strongly representative of major stockholders, but added the views of men with a broader outlook.

Controls

A distinguishing characteristic of partial proprietary directors has been their emphasis on objective and measurable goals against which performance can be measured. In part, this may be a carryover from the old New England tradition under which the treasurer was in fact the chief executive interested in the best utilization of the investment.

Stress on financial objectives certainly was paramount in board considerations at GM. As Donaldson Brown described it:

In gauging the effectiveness of management the first approach always is to examine the over-all result, which is the rate of return on capital employed. If this be subnormal, having due regard to the character of the business and the competitive situation, it is self-evident that something is wrong with the management. The second step is to identify the cause—and correct it ... the task in these early years was to find some means whereby the significant accounting facts and financial considerations affecting the business would be revealed. Then it would be necessary to get them understood and appreciated by those who were responsible for the various operations; management at all levels must be made more aware of the constructive opportunities which existed for planning better the long-term interests of the stockholders.

This of course has been the practice of outstanding partial proprietors. In a number of the companies interviewed in this study the principal shareholder set the financial objectives; the company must be comparable with the principal competitors over a long period, say, five years, in terms of rate of return on investment, sales, production, stock price. Then it is up to operating management to state the tools it requires to produce the results. There is no quibbling over details. There is no quizzing over the soundness of every move. Apart from checking on the execution of objectives, only change in top personnel and its remuneration and change in basic objectives concern the principal stockholders.

Thus the combination of business acumen, catalytic effort, organization, controls, and provision of an opportunity for discussion are among the chief contributions of the partial proprietors to the corporations with which they are associated.

If, then, rebuttal power was a genuine organizational means of profound significance in the rise of General Motors and if its present arrangement is to be terminated, how will it be replaced? On the answer the future of GM will depend in part at least, and that of many other corporations as well.

B. Relationship between Degree of Concentrated Ownership and Corporate Performance

In order to determine whether any relationship exists between corporate performance and the degree of concentrated ownership, data from *Fortune's* 1956 and 1957 lists of 500 leading companies were matched against a list showing the percentages of common stock held by institutions, officers, directors, associates, and large stockholders.[1] The latter list, probably the most up to date available, was prepared by Harold Clayton of Hemphill-Noyes, in 1954, and includes all companies listed on the New York Stock Exchange in that year.

For the purposes of the present study, a company in which institutions, officers, directors, associates, and large stockholders held less than 10 per cent of the shares was assumed to have a highly diffused ownership, or a low "concentration ratio." It was further assumed that because of this diffused ownership, no one stockholder or group of stockholders was in a position to offer a serious challenge to management and that the company was therefore an "inside company," or one in which management had complete control. Conversely, a concern in which the concentration ratio was 50 per cent or more was classified as under complete proprietary control, and one with a ratio between 10 and 50 per cent as under partial proprietary control.

Admittedly, these classifications are somewhat arbitrary and open to criticism since the concentration ratios may give a misleading

[1] *Fortune*, July, 1958, pp. 131–150.

impression of the actual extent of proprietary control. A concern may have a high concentration ratio because it is a favorite of institutional investors who do not participate in the decision-making bodies. Or it may have a low concentration only because substantial holdings are divided among members of the same family. Such an understatement of concentration is made possible by the requirement that proxy statements list only those who own 10 per cent or more of the voting stock, except in the case of officers and directors. Since the Hemphill-Noyes data are based on proxy statements, the holdings of family groups in many firms may not be evident.

The justification for the classification, despite these possibilities, is that errors will tend to cancel themselves out in a large sample, and in any case a rough approximation of the truth will be sufficient to indicate trends.

The sample originally consisted of the 200 companies with the largest sales in 1954, 1955, 1956, and 1957, the years for which *Fortune* data were available. These, it should be noted, were not necessarily the same concerns each year since ranking varied from year to year.

Among the first 200, however, were several for which Hemphill-Noyes data were not available. Some of these (for example, Western Electric) were known to have a highly concentrated ownership and were placed in the 50 per cent and over category. Others were omitted from the analysis and replaced with concerns with lower sales ranking to keep the sample at 200. About 32 companies on the 1956 and 1957 lists were passed over in this way, and a list of them is shown at the end of this section.

It was not possible to make an analysis for the years 1954 and 1955 because the data furnished by *Fortune* for those years included neither figures showing profits as a percentage of sales nor profits as a percentage of investment. Although the data supplied made it possible to compute profits of a percentage of sales, this was not done because of the reservation, later explained, about the validity of this figure as a satisfactory measure of performance.

Accordingly, the study was confined to the years 1956 and 1957, and profits as a percentage of sales and a percentage of investment were tabulated for 200 companies in each of those years. Results indicated that concerns under partial proprietary control have had better records of performance generally than those under complete management control or complete proprietary control. (The evidence is not conclusive enough to warrant any sweeping conclusions, except that our thesis is not disproved.) The 200 companies whose 1956 records were studied were divided as follows:

Concentration ratio, per cent	No. of companies
Less than 10	61
10–19	71
20–29	29
30–39	12
40–49	3
50 and over	24

The average of profits as a percentage of sales for each of the four intermediate categories (concentration ratios from 10 to 49 per cent) was, with one exception, higher than the average for the extreme categories (under 10 and over 50 per cent). The average profit as a percentage of investment was higher in every one of the intermediate categories than in the extreme.

Medians of profits as a percentage of sales presented a different pattern. Here the extremes were higher, with one exception, than the intermediates. But the medians of profits as percentages of investment, probably the best test of group performance, were higher, without exception, for the intermediate groups. This is shown in Table 6-1.

TABLE 6-1. A COMPARISON OF CONCENTRATION RATIOS AND MEASURES OF CORPORATE PERFORMANCE, 200 FIRMS, 1956

Concentration ratio, %	Average, profits as a per cent of:		Median, profits as a per cent of:	
	Sales	Investment	Sales	Investment
Less than 10	6.2	11.9	5.6	11.2
10–19	7.1	13.9	5.4	12.8
20–29	5.6	12.2	5.1	12.3
30–39	6.5	14.4	4.3	14.9
40–49	9.4	16.3	11.2	14.8
50 and over	5.9	11.6	5.7	11.6

In inter-industry comparisons, as in this study, the usefulness of profits as a percentage of sales as a measure of corporate performance is limited. By the very nature of the productive processes, this percentage should vary from industry to industry. Therefore a firm in one industry with a low profit as a percentage of sales figure may actually operate more efficiently than a concern in another industry with a high figure, provided the former has a correspondingly larger turnover of investment. The chief usefulness of this measure lies in intra-industry comparisons. Different industries require different combinations of capital and labor. This is a technical fact. But the economic fact of the market tends to force, over the long run, an equal return on capital ("tends to" rather than "does" because of certain institutional impediments). Capital will flow from low-profit industries to high-profit industries. This implies a higher return on sales in the capital-intensive industries and a lower return in the labor-intensive industries.

In the period 1947 to 1950, the average profit (after taxes) as a percentage of sales of all private manufacturing corporations was 6.7. The industry figures ranged from 3.1 per cent in apparel and related products (a low-capital-intensity industry) to 11.0 per cent for petroleum refining (a high-capital-intensity industry). These discrepancies are bound to exist as long as (1) capital intensities vary and (2) there is a tendency for the rate of profit to be equalized.

Profit as a percentage of investment is a better measure for inter-industry comparisons. It enables one to see how effectively a company turns an investment into an income-producing asset. Since the anticipated return is probably the most significant factor in an investment decision, the actual return is the criterion by which the wisdom of the decision is judged. It can be assumed that firms with consistently higher returns on investment utilize their assets in a more efficient manner. This should hold true regardless of industry.

For groups, the median is a better measure of performance than the mean. The presence in a group of one or a few firms with very high rates of return, for instance, could raise the mean of the group considerably and distort the picture of the group's performance as a whole. The median, on the other hand, is not affected by the presence of a few firms with larger rates of return. Since it merely indicates the rate of return which divides the firms equally, it gives a more accurate picture of group performance. By comparing the medians of two groups, one can determine in which group the majority of firms fared better. If, for instance, one group has a higher median than the other, then a higher percentage of firms in the former group are more efficient than in the latter.

In Table 6-1 the median of the rate of return on investment of the group with a concentration ratio of less than 10 per cent is 11.5 per cent. Thus one-half the firms in this group have rates of return of less than 11.5 per cent and one-half have rates of more than 11.5 per cent. The median for the group with a concentration ratio of 10 to 19 is 12.8 per cent. This means that more than half the firms in this group had a higher rate of return than 11.5 per cent (the rate of return in the less than 10 per cent group). Thus a higher percentage of firms in the 10 to 19 per cent concentration group turned in a better performance than in the less than 10 per cent group.

In 1957 the pattern for the 200 companies was similar to that in 1956:

Concentration ratio, per cent	No. of companies
Less than 10	61
10–19	71
20–29	31
30–39	12
40–49	4
50 and over	20

The averages of profits both as a percentage of sales and as a percentage of investment in intermediate groups were, with one exception, higher than for the extreme groups. The picture was similar for the medians of profits as a percentage of sales. The medians of profits as a percentage of investment followed the 1956 pattern. It was higher, without exception, in each one of the intermediate groups. This mix is shown in Table 6-2.

In addition to the comparison of the medians and averages, a study was made of the relationship between performance rank and concentration ratios. The firms were ranked for each of the two years according to their profits as percentages of sales and investment. The firm with the highest profit as a percentage of sales or investment was given a rank of 1; the lowest, a rank of 200. These

TABLE 6-2. A COMPARISON OF CONCENTRATION RATIOS AND MEASURES
OF CORPORATE PERFORMANCE, 200 FIRMS, 1957

Concentration ratio, %	Average, profits as a per cent of:		Median, profits as a per cent of:	
	Sales	Investment	Sales	Investment
Less than 10	5.8	11.3	5.0	10.3
10–19	6.3	12.5	5.0	11.3
20–29	5.3	10.0	5.1	11.3
30–39	6.1	12.1	4.6	13.3
40–49	8.3	11.4	6.3	11.3
50 and over	5.6	11.0	4.7	10.8

firms were then divided by rank into five groups of forty each. The forty firms with the highest profits as percentages of sales or investment were placed in the first quintile; the forty firms with the next highest in the second quintile; and so on. Again the results bore out the general pattern. A higher percentage of intermediate firms were in the top quintile. Table 6-3 shows the 1956 data for profits as percentages of sales, and Table 6-4 shows the same data for profits as percentages of investment.

The 1957 results were similar to those of 1956. Concerns with intermediate concentration ratios generally had a greater percentage in the top quintile than those with extreme ratios. This is shown in Tables 6-5 and 6-6.

Perhaps we can at least conclude from this detailed statistical report that it does not *disprove* the thesis that the companies with partial proprietary control may be more successful financially than those without it.

TABLE 6-3. RELATIONSHIP BETWEEN CONCENTRATION RATIOS AND PROFITS
AS A PER CENT OF SALES, 200 FIRMS, 1956

Concentration ratio, %	Ranking, quintile					
	1	2	3	4	5	Total
Less than 10	11	13	13	8	16	61
10–19	15	14	15	19	8	71
20–29	5	7	4	4	9	29
30–39	3	1	1	5	2	12
40–49	2	0	1	0	0	3
59 and over	4	5	6	4	5	24
Total	40	40	40	40	40	200
	Percentage (vertical)					
Less than 10	27.5	32.5	32.5	20.0	40.0	30.5
10–19	37.5	35.0	37.5	47.5	20.0	35.5
20–29	12.5	17.5	10.0	10.0	22.5	14.5
30–39	7.5	2.5	2.5	12.5	5.0	6.0
40–49	5.0	0.0	2.5	0.0	0.0	1.5
50 and over	10.0	12.5	15.0	10.0	12.5	12.0
Total	100.0	100.0	100.0	100.0	100.0	100.0
	Percentage (horizontal)					
Less than 10	18.0	21.3	21.3	13.2	26.2	100.0
10–19	21.1	19.7	21.1	26.8	11.3	100.0
20–29	17.2	24.1	13.8	13.8	31.1	100.0
30–39	25.0	8.3	8.3	41.7	16.7	100.0
40–49	66.7	0.0	33.3	0.0	0.0	100.0
50 and over	16.7	20.8	25.0	16.7	20.8	100.0
Total	20.0	20.0	20.0	20.0	20.0	100.0

TABLE 6-4. RELATIONSHIP BETWEEN CONCENTRATION RATIOS AND PROFITS AS A PER CENT. OF INVESTMENT, 200 FIRMS, 1956

Concentration ratio, %	Ranking, quintile					
	1	2	3	4	5	Total
Less than 10	9	9	13	14	16	61
10–19	17	16	12	16	10	71
20–29	7	6	4	3	9	29
30–39	3	4	4	0	1	12
40–49	1	1	1	0	0	3
50 and over	3	4	6	7	4	24
Total	40	40	40	40	40	200
	Percentage (vertical)					
Less than 10	22.5	22.5	32.5	35.0	40.0	30.5
10–19	42.5	40.0	30.0	40.0	25.0	36.0
20–29	17.5	15.0	10.0	7.5	22.5	15.5
30–39	7.5	10.0	10.0	0.0	2.5	6.0
40–49	2.5	2.5	2.5	0.0	0.0	2.0
50 and over	7.5	10.0	15.0	17.5	10.0	10.0
Total	100.0	100.0	100.0	100.0	100.0	100.0
	Percentage (horizontal)					
Less than 10	14.8	14.8	21.3	22.9	26.2	100.0
10–19	23.9	22.5	16.9	22.5	14.2	100.0
20–29	24.2	20.7	13.8	10.3	31.0	100.0
30–39	25.0	33.3	33.3	0.0	8.4	100.0
40–49	33.3	33.3	33.4	0.0	0.0	100.0
50 and over	12.4	16.7	25.0	29.2	16.7	100.0
Total	20.0	20.0	20.0	20.0	20.0	100.0

TABLE 6-5. RELATIONSHIP BETWEEN CONCENTRATION RATIOS AND PROFITS
AS A PER CENT OF SALES, 200 FIRMS, 1957

Concentration ratio, %	Ranking, quintile					
	1	2	3	4	5	Total
Less than 10	12	12	10	14	13	61
10–19	16	12	18	17	9	72
20–29	5	9	4	1	12	31
30–39	3	1	3	3	2	12
40–49	1	1	1	0	1	4
50 and over	3	5	4	5	3	20
Total	40	40	40	40	40	200
	Percentage (vertical)					
Less than 10	30.0	30.0	25.0	35.0	32.5	30.5
10–19	40.0	30.0	45.0	42.5	22.5	36.0
20–29	12.5	22.5	10.0	2.5	30.0	15.5
30–39	7.5	2.5	7.5	7.5	5.0	6.0
40–49	2.5	2.5	2.5	0.0	2.5	2.0
50 and over	7.5	12.5	10.0	12.5	7.5	10.0
Total	100.0	100.0	100.0	100.0	100.0	100.0
	Percentage (horizontal)					
Less than 10	19.7	19.7	16.4	22.9	21.3	100.0
10–19	22.2	16.7	25.0	23.6	12.5	100.0
20–29	16.2	29.0	12.9	3.2	38.7	100.0
30–39	25.0	8.3	25.0	25.0	16.7	100.0
40–49	25.0	25.0	25.0	0.0	25.0	100.0
Total	20.0	20.0	20.0	20.0	20.0	100.0

TABLE 6-6. RELATIONSHIP BETWEEN CONCENTRATION RATIOS AND PROFITS AS A PER CENT OF INVESTMENT, 200 FIRMS, 1957

Concentration ratio, %	Ranking, quintile					
	1	2	3	4	5	Total
Less than 10	12	11	9	13	16	61
10–19	16	13	14	18	11	72
20–29	6	6	8	3	8	31
30–39	4	3	2	2	1	12
40–49	1	1	0	1	1	4
50 and over	1	6	7	3	3	20
Total	40	40	40	40	40	200
	Percentage (vertical)					
Less than 10	30.0	27.5	22.5	32.5	40.0	30.5
10–19	40.0	32.5	35.0	45.0	27.5	36.0
20–29	15.0	15.0	20.0	7.5	20.0	15.5
30–39	10.0	7.5	5.0	5.0	2.5	6.0
40–49	2.5	2.5	0.0	2.5	2.5	2.0
50 and over	2.5	15.0	17.5	7.5	7.5	10.0
Total	100.0	100.0	100.0	100.0	100.0	100.0
	Percentage (horizontal)					
Less than 10	19.7	18.0	14.8	21.3	26.2	100.0
10–19	22.2	18.0	19.4	25.0	15.3	100.0
20–29	19.4	19.4	25.8	9.6	25.8	100.0
30–39	33.3	25.0	16.7	16.7	8.3	100.0
40–49	25.0	25.0	0.0	25.0	25.0	100.0
50 and over	5.0	30.0	35.0	15.0	15.0	100.0
Total	20.0	20.0	20.0	20.0	20.0	100.0

TABLE 6-7. FIRMS NOT INCLUDED IN SAMPLE OF 200

Firms	Fortune's sales rank	
	1957	1956
1. Ogden	77	60
2. Ralston-Purina	87	91
3. Weyerhaeuser Timber	93	119
4. Foremost Dairies	96	94
5. Whirlpool	97	98
6. Hygrade Food	103	102
7. Kaiser Industries	105	150
8. Carnation	108	108
9. American Motors	112 *	87 *
10. Singer Manufacturing	114	101
11. Lever Brothers	119	not given
12. McDonnell Aircraft	124	211
13. Hormel	125	121
14. Rath Packing	144	151
15. Seagram and Sons	165	179
16. Sherwin-Williams	168	not given
17. McGraw-Edison	171	191
18. Arden Farms	172	162
19. Time, Inc.	176	177
20. Mayer (Oscar)	179	183
21. American Marietta	188	195
22. Anheuser-Busch	191	186
23. Kellogg	200	196
24. Studebaker-Packard	201 *	130 *
25. Kaiser Steel	202	197
26. Lilly (Eli)	212	214
27. Grinnell	216	206
28. Central Soya	217	235 ‡
29. Hearst	218	189
30. Eastern Gas and Fuel	226	221
31. Avco Manufacturing	†	121
32. Rheem Manufacturing	†	224 *
33. Pittsburgh Steel	234 ‡	219
34. Norton	239 ‡	228
35. Alco Products	258 ‡	229

* Profits not given for year.
† Included in sample for year.
‡ Too low a rank to be included in sample for year.

Index

Acton, Lord, 186
Administrative Science Quarterly, x
American Iron and Steel Institute, 120
American Railroad Journal, 19
American Telephone and Telegraph
Company, 211
American Tin Plate Company, 122
Argyris, Chris, 23
Armour & Company, 56
Armstrong, J. Sinclair, 205*n*.
Atlantic Dynamite Company, 40
Atlas Powder Company, 54
Attlee, Lord, 140
Avery, Sewell, 10, 184

Baker, George F., 78*n*.
Baltimore and Ohio Railroad, 40
Bank of Canada, 260
Bank of Pittsburgh, 124
Barksdale, Hamilton M., ix, 39–48, 52–
53, 58, 64, 66, 253
Barnard, Chester I., 12, 23
Barnes, Irston R., 180*n*.
Beardslee, L. R., 31*n*.
Beck, Dave, 184
Benrus Watch Company, 179
Berlin, Isaiah, 31*n*.
Bethlehem Steel Company, 180
Billion Dollar Club, 100
Black, Hugo L., 176*n*.
Bonus system, Du Pont, 41, 45; General Motors, 96–97
Boulding, Kenneth E., 23
Braddock Wire Company, 122
Bradley, Albert, 86, 90, 256
Brennan, William J., Jr., 176*n*.
British Munitions Board, 62
Brooklyn Edison Company, 159
Brown, Alvin, 5
Brown, Donaldson, vii–ix, 31*n*., 50, 56,
62, 71*n*., 86, 93–94, 241, 253, 256, 260
Brown, J. A. C., 197*n*.
Brown, Lewis, 208
Bruehl, W. G., 205*n*.
Budgeting, flexible, 151
Burck, Gilbert, 210*n*.
Burton, Harold H., 176*n*.
Business Week, 107, 205, 212
Butler, Nicholas Murray, 8

Caesar management, 11, 146; Du Pont
Company, 32, 63

California, University of, x
California Management Review, x
Carlson, Sune, 12
Carnegie, Andrew, 125
Carpenter, R. R. M., 53
Carpenter, Walter S., Jr., viii, 31*n*.,
50, 53, 71*n*., 241–242, 246, 255–258
Carter Car Company, 75
Census Bureau, 225*n*.
Census of Manufactures, 224, 225*n*.
Chandler, A. D., 18
Chase Manhattan Bank, 213
China, 4
Chrysler, Walter P., 72, 74*n*., 76–78
Chrysler Corporation, 194, 250
CIO unions, 140
Civil War, 33
Clark, Tom C., 176*n*.
Clay, Lucius, 260
Clayton, Harold, 261
Clayton Act, 180, 193
Clements, R. V., 25
Coffin, Charles A., 145
Columbia University, 8
Commercial Solvents Company, 177
Communist Party, 194
Congress, 184
Constitution, 186
Control, span of, 6
Copeland, Lammot du Pont, 31*n*., 241
Cornell University, x, xi
Cravath, Swain and Moore, 143*n*.
Cresap, M. W., Jr., 143*n*.
Crossman, Richard, 4
Crowther, Samuel, 98*n*.
Culture, science of, 17
Curtice, Harlow C., 107, 197

Dale, Ernest, 8*n*.
Daley, J. F., 31*n*.
Davis, John W., 125
Decentralization theory, 101
Demmler, Ralph H., 205*n*.
Department of Justice, 180, 239; Antitrust Division, 181
Department of Labor, 44
Dickens, Charles, 137
Directors, Block, 176; Mellon, 176;
public, 207–209
Donner, Frederick C., 10, 198, 256, 258
Douglas, William O., 176*n*.